The Insider's GUIDE to Demographic KNOW-HOW

REVISED EDITION

The Insider's GUIDE to Demographic KNOW-HOW

Everything You Need to Find, Analyze, and Use Information About Your Customers

DIANE CRISPELL

PROBUS PUBLISHING COMPANY
Chicago, Illinois
Cambridge, England

American Demographics Press
A Division of American Demographics, Inc.
108 N. Cayuga Street, Ithaca, NY 14850

ISBN 1-55738-472-X

Printed in the United States of America

IPC

1 2 3 4 5 6 7 8 9 0

Compositor: James Madden

This book is dedicated to Lisa, Karin, and Amy J.
— my sisters and my best friends

Acknowledgments

I would like to acknowledge the assistance of many people at American Demographics: Marty Riche, my mentor and friend; Pat Driscoll, for her assistance in compiling the information; the staff of American Demographics Books for producing this book; and last, but not least, Cheryl Russell, who introduced me to the wonderful world of demographics.

Preface

In the original version of *The Insider's Guide,* we introduced you to the world of demographic data sources—including federal agencies, state and local sources, private companies, and nonprofit organizations. But this is an ever-expanding universe, and the number of sources grows each year. This update includes dozens of new sources for consumer information.

This edition also includes several new chapters dealing with emerging issues in consumer research. One new chapter tells you what to expect from and what to do with the 1990 census. In the face of a commercially united Europe in 1992 and a global economy, it is becoming increasingly important for American business to be up on international trends. Hence a new chapter on international data sources. Yet another new chapter lists academic, non-profit, and trade sources for consumer and industry segments such as women, the affluent, and food. To learn more about what's where, read the introductions that head each chapter.

This book is organized by type of source—federal agencies, state and local sources, private companies, and so on. Read Chapter 1 for an overview of who provides what. But be aware that information on a given subject may be available from a number of sources. To find out who produces data for the mature market, or what's available on media behavior, look in the subject index. It will point you to all of the government, private, and other sources that cover your topic of interest.

TABLE OF CONTENTS

CHAPTER

Introduction

How to Hunt For the Best Source

How to Hunt for the Best Source

Ask the right questions and you, too, can negotiate the data jungle.

Once upon a time, demographic data were as scarce as polar bears in Miami. But times have changed—now you're likely to get swamped by data. So how do you track down the information you need? As with any quarry, knowing what you're after provides clues to its whereabouts.

Keep these rules of thumb in mind when you begin any data hunt:

1. ***Be as specific as possible.***
   Instead of looking for income, look for median household income.

2. ***Adapt when necessary.***
   If you can't get the exact data you need, work with what's available.

3. ***Ask yourself, "Who would need these data?"***
   The answer can shed light on where to look.

There are so many kinds of demographic data that it is helpful to categorize them. You should do this before you begin your search.

IDENTIFY THE SPECIES

Consumer information ranges from simple population counts to socioeconomic characteristics, media and purchasing behavior, and attitudinal and lifestyle classifications (psychographics). Pinpoint the type of data you need, and the source becomes apparent.

The government specializes in demographic and other socioeconomic characteristics of the population—including age, race, sex, educational attainment, labor-force status, household composition, marital status, occupation, income, immigrant status, and more.

The agencies that compile these data are often obvious. The Bureau of Labor Statistics follows employment trends. The Department of Education surveys students, teachers, and schools. The Department of Health and Human Services studies health knowledge and practices, illnesses and injuries, and use of health-care providers and facilities. The Census Bureau covers just about everything.

Chapter 4 lists in detail the federal agencies that provide demographic and consumer data. Just take a look at the Census Bureau's extensive offerings.

Demographic data are a good start, but retailers, nonprofits, and other organizations also need to know how Americans use media, what they buy, and why they buy what they do. The place to go for most media preference, buying behavior, and psychographic data is the private sector. Who else has such a stake in understanding consumer behavior?

An information industry has grown up around the need for consumer data. Hundreds of companies specialize in collecting and selling data in the form of syndicated surveys, media-measurement research, market studies, lifestyle analyses, and so on. An increasing number of firms link demographics, psychographics, media use, and purchase behavior to offer a complete market research system. See ***Chapter 5*** to find out which vendors provide what.

There are sources beyond the consumer information industry. Remember the rule of thumb: Who needs these data? Trade associations usually do. It's a good bet that the National Association of Realtors is interested in homebuying trends, and indeed, it publishes regular studies of homebuyers. ***Chapter 6*** will point you towards industry groups, nonprofit organizations, and academic research centers that collect the information that no one else does.

MARK OFF THE TERRITORY

Do you want data for the U.S. as a whole, or for smaller areas like states, cities, or ZIP Codes? Do you want standard census geography—counties, metropolitan statistical areas, places, minor civil divisions, blocks, and census tracts? Or do you need other kinds of standard areas, like telephone area codes? Do you need customized geography like sales territories or a radius around a store?

Before you hunt for data, know the level of geography that you need.

All data are not available for all geographies. Except for the decennial census, most government data are limited to the national, regional, and sometimes state level. So are much of the data available from nonprofit organizations and private data companies. A number of demographic data companies, however, produce population estimates and projections for any geographic area. Many even link their consumer databases to local population information.

The most useful data about a local area most often come from the place itself. There are many state and local government agencies with the intimate knowledge crucial to understanding a specific geographic area. ***Chapter 7*** gives you contacts in each state for local demographic, economic, and employment data.

With the approach of a united Europe in 1992, it's more crucial than ever to be aware of the global market. ***Chapter 8*** lists organizations that will help you in the quest for knowledge about foreign territories.

SELECT THE SEASON

Do you need 1990 data? Or can you live with 1987 numbers? All data are not available for all time periods. Trend data and projections can be hard to find.

Government surveys are a valuable resource for tracking trends over time, because they are conducted in a consistent way year after year. A few private companies conduct ongoing surveys, especially the public opinion pollsters. The Gallup Organization, for example, has been studying Americans' religious beliefs for over 50 years.

Simple population projections—by age, race, and sex—are easy to find, in both the public and private sectors. Socioeconomic projections are rare beasts, limited in most cases to private-sector forecasts of household income.

You may have to make a trade-off between length of forecast and level of geographic detail. Most demographic data companies project basic population and a few socioeconomic characteristics only five years ahead, but for all geographic areas. Econometric forecasting firms take a longer-term view, often going 20 years into the future, but their geography is limited to counties, metropolitan areas, and states. The Census Bureau projects population by age, sex, and race to 2080, but only for the U.S. as a whole. Its state projections go to the year 2010.

If it's vital that the data be fresh, go to the private sector. Private companies offer up-to-date numbers and quick service. Government agencies sometimes accept requests for custom tabulations of data, but their turnaround time is slow. Government reports are notorious for being out of date—analysis and publication can take years.

DO YOU WANT RAW OR PACKAGED DATA?

People tend to think of government data as unfriendly, arriving as masses of printed tables or hefty computer tapes. The government produces no-frills data to avoid competing with the private sector. This makes the government data relatively inexpensive. And some government publications are easy reads, such as the Census Bureau's *Current Population Reports* series and the Bureau of Labor Statistics' *Monthly Labor Review*.

If you want CD-ROMs with crackerjack software, go to the private sector. But be aware that some of the data you get from private suppliers can be as unwieldy and inaccessible as government reports. Find out ahead of time what kind of analytic support you can expect from a vendor.

CONSIDER COST

Will you spring for the luxury two-week safari, or are you limited to the local fishing hole? If you're a do-it-yourselfer, you can buy data inexpensively from the government and do your own manipulations. But if you need a powerhouse computer system loaded with current data for every place in the country—yet simple enough for the beginner to use—expect to pay more in the private sector.

The challenge to people seeking consumer information used to be to find any data. Marketers were limited to the decennial census, and those brave enough to face it ploughed through shelves of heavy volumes, deciphering tables of microscopic numbers. Today the challenge is to find the best data for your specific needs among the many bewildering choices. If you get prepared for the hunt and keep your goal in mind, the odds are that you'll bag your data.

CHAPTER 2

How, When, & Why to Use Demographics

Before you plunge into the potentially murky depths of demographic data, it's wise to know what to do with them. The following sections, which originally appeared in American Demographics *magazine, shed light on the whys and wherefores of managing and evaluating demographic and consumer information.*

How to Manage Consumer Information

Here's the step-by-step way to knowing exactly who your customers are, what they want, and how to wrap it all up into a spectacular target marketing program.

by Peter Francese

The sea of consumer information is now at high tide. There are at least 70 firms that make it their business to provide researchers with information about consumer markets. With so many demographic, psychographic, media use, and purchasing behavior statistics around, planners and researchers need to know how to manage them, just like lottery winners need to know how to manage their money. Such newly rich must research the many investment alternatives and then match their investments with their need for financial security, additional income, and asset growth.

In the same way, business people should manage consumer information by researching alternative sources of data and matching what is available with their firm's need for securing market share through effective advertising, for creating additional income by increasing the market penetration of their products, and for generating corporate growth through the development of successful new products and services.

The volume of consumer information has grown enormously in the past 15 years partly because the mass market has splintered into many market segments, each of which must be tracked by businesses selling to those segments. At the same time, the cost of buying and processing consumer data has fallen. It is now far cheaper to buy data about the characteristics of a market segment or a potential store site than to have a new product or a new store fail.

There are many reasons why consumer product and service companies buy information, but they fall into four main categories: 1) market management, 2) product analysis, 3) advertising strategy, and 4) strategic planning.

Market management involves the assessment of market potential in each geographic area, the allocation of sales territories by market potential, and the choosing of sites for sales outlets or distribution points.

Product or service analysis involves calculating a product's market potential as well as the manufacturer's market share, determining the characteristics of the people who most often buy the product or service (the prime market segments), and assessing the amount of the product or service, in units or dollars, that is purchased by each market segment.

Advertising strategy involves selecting the most cost-effective media (TV, radio, print, or direct mail), allocating an advertising budget among competing broadcasters or publishers, and developing a message that will be most effective at getting the consumer's attention and selling the goods.

Strategic planning involves tracking the growth or decline of existing markets, finding new growth markets, and determining what new or existing products are most likely to be successful in those markets.

Each of these activities requires the analysis of consumer information. Most consumer product companies have large budgets for buying data. But after several years of data gathering, a business can end up with a chaotic collection of data files, each purchased to solve an immediate problem. With an understanding of how to manage consumer information, however, businesses can create an integrated consumer information system that matches assorted data files with an array of research needs.

VISUALIZING THE FLOW

Where does all this information come from? People do four things that generate information *(see figure 1)*. First, people answer the census every ten years. In addition, each March a random sample of about 50,000 householders answers the demographic questionnaire included in the Current Population Survey. These two sources provide the basic demographic information about consumers—their age, sex, race, income, education, occupation, and household structure. Demographic information is essential to businesses as they attempt to project the demand for products such as toys, lawn care supplies, and retirement homes, a demand that is determined by the age, household structure, and income distribution of the population.

As essential as they are, however, demographics are not enough. Two people, both aged 40, both with incomes of $50,000 a year, will want different products depending on their lifestyle. That's why one of them will buy a Mercedes and the other a Winnebago. Both products meet the need for transportation, but each product satisfies a different want—the one a desire for status, the other a desire for recreation.

By responding to surveys, consumers provide researchers with this second type of information: a psychographic profile. A business must know how con-

THE FOUR TYPES OF CONSUMER INFORMATION

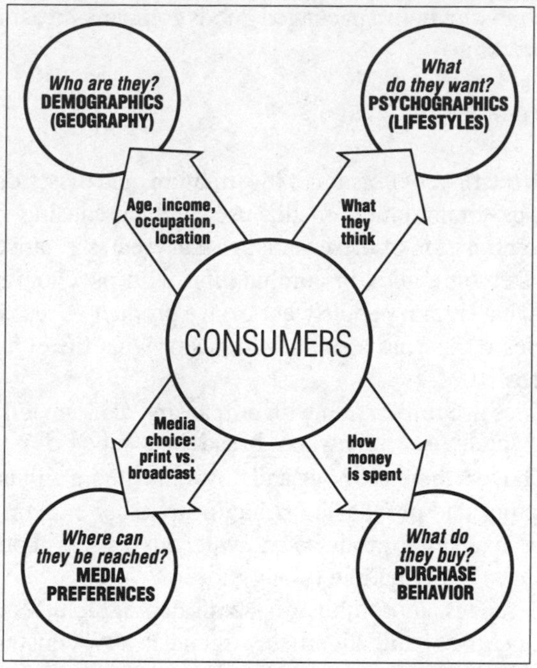

Figure 1. **Consumers generate four types of information of importance to businesses. By linking this information together, companies can build a complete picture of the consumer.**

sumers feel about themselves and the world around them to effectively communicate their product's ability to satisfy consumers' wants and needs.

The third way that consumers generate information is by revealing through monitoring devices and surveys what they watch on TV, what they listen to on the radio, and what newspapers and magazines they read. Nielsen and Arbitron, for example, find out who watches what TV shows and who listens to what radio stations, while Simmons Market Research Bureau and Mediamark Research determine who reads what magazines or newspapers.

Fourth, consumers, by definition, spend money. This also generates information. Every time people use a credit card, the slip of paper that they sign becomes a statistic about a purchase. Every time someone in a test market panel buys groceries in a scanner-equipped store, he or she generates another purchase statistic. Panel diary firms and the Census Bureau through the Consumer Expenditure Survey also collect data on purchasing by asking householders to keep track of everything they buy for several weeks. All of these purchase statistics help a packaged goods company measure how well its advertising is working.

THE UNBROKEN CIRCLE

There is more to the flow of consumer information than these four segments—demographics, psychographics, media use, and purchasing behavior—because it is the combination of these statistics that creates a statistical picture of the consumer. Demographics in combination with psychographics, for example, can tell what certain people want from a product. A researcher can find out what Yuppies want from a suit of clothes or what the elderly want from financial services.

Demographics in combination with purchasing data can tell a food retailer or bakery firm who buys whole wheat bread, how much of it they buy, how many potential buyers there are now, and how many there will be in the future.

Psychographics and purchasing behavior together explain, for example, why people buy mail-order products and what advertisers should say in their promotional efforts to get people to buy more.

Media preferences, in combination with demographics and purchasing behavior, tell advertisers and advertising agencies how consumers get information, with what media consumers can be most efficiently reached, and how much it will cost to reach consumers who play golf or gamble in the futures market.

A growing number of companies are now offering hybrids of consumer information based on these four types of data. SRI International and Yankelovich Clancy Shulman, for example, provide psychographic profiles of consumers in combination with demographic statistics. They offer age and income profiles of attitudes and lifestyle groups. By asking consumers about purchasing behavior and media use, both SRI and Yankelovich Clancy Shulman also offer psychographic profiles of, for example, people who watch a lot of daytime television or who eat white bread.

Mediamark Research, Inc. and Simmons Market Research Bureau ask about 20,000 adults each year detailed questions about what magazines and newspapers they read, what TV shows they watch, and which radio stations they listen to. But MRI and SMRB also ask, and then cross-tabulate, demographic questions such as age, income, occupation, education, residence, and household type, as well as questions about the products and services that consumers recently purchased. These firms then combine their media use data with psychographic profiles to provide a more complete picture of, for example, who reads *Money* magazine.

PUTTING CONSUMER INFORMATION TO WORK

	DEMOGRAPHICS	PSYCHOGRAPHICS	MEDIA PREFERENCES	PURCHASING BEHAVIOR
MARKET ANALYSIS	●			●
PRODUCT ANALYSIS	●			●
ADVERTISING	●	●	●	●
STRATEGIC PLANNING	●			●

Figure 2. **Companies use consumer information for four purposes. Demographics and purchasing behavior are important to all four, while psychographics and media preferences are important for advertising.**

Nielsen and Arbitron monitor the broadcast industry to see which stations reach the largest proportion of households. But Nielsen also collects data from store audits to track consumer purchasing behavior. And Arbitron recently introduced an in-home scanning device which combines purchasing behavior with exposure to broadcast advertising.

Finally, the Consumer Expenditure Survey and syndicated panel diaries (National Family Opinion, NPD Research) link information on purchasing directly with demographics.

PIECES OF THE PUZZLE

A complete consumer information system should contain the four types of consumer-generated data along with some way of linking the demographic, psychographic, media use, and purchasing statistics, as shown in figure 1. Every business may not need every piece of the puzzle; it depends on the kind of business it is and what research activities—market analysis, product analysis, advertising, or strategic planning—it is involved in *(see figure 2)*. For each purpose, some pieces of data are more important than others.

For market management, the most important piece is demographic, because it is the most readily available data for small geographic areas. Purchasing behavior is also important to market managers so that they can determine the amount of potential business by ZIP Code or census tract. Psychographic and media data are less important to market analysis, partly because they do not describe the volume of consumption and because they are not available for small areas.

For product analysis, both demographic and purchasing behavior are important. These two pieces of information identify important market segments and determine how well they are being served.

Reaching consumers efficiently with a convincing message about a product or service requires the greatest amount of information. Designing an ad message involves psychographics and demographics; choosing between broadcast and print media requires statistics on media use and demographics, as does choosing particular stations or newspapers or magazines in which to run an ad. Perhaps this is why cluster analysis, which is a statistical way to combine data, is so popular in advertising agencies.

For strategic planning, a business needs demographic projections combined with statistics on purchasing behavior. Strategic planners use this information to predict such things as the future market for four-wheel drive vehicles. Data on lifestyles and media preferences are less useful to strategic planners because lifestyles and the media can change unpredictably.

There are other issues of importance in gauging what information a business needs, such as the accuracy and timeliness of data, but these factors are secondary to the main question: How does it all fit together? Consider this model of consumer information as data processing software for the mind.

How to Size Up Your Customers

To survive in today's competitive environment, you must find and exploit your niche by systematically identifying the distinct market segments into which your customers fall.

by Marvin Nesbit and Arthur Weinstein

Retailers have long depended on their ability to size up their customers when they walk in the door. Customers give themselves away by their clothing, speech, mannerisms, and body language. While gut instinct still works for some retailers, the era of successful scrutiny has passed. You can no longer pigeonhole at a glance because the increasing diversity of consumers has made such stereotyping futile. Today you need a more systematic way to understand your customers.

Some managers are skeptical about the effectiveness of demographics in defining distinct markets because no single demographic variable explains buyer behavior. There are exceptions, of course—new parents buy diapers; Minnesotans buy winter coats. While it usually takes more than demographic knowledge to understand a market, the demographics should not be ignored for several reasons.

First, demographic information is the most accessible and cost-effective way to identify a target market, and it is within practically everyone's budget. Even if demographic statistics are a less than perfect marketing tool, they frequently can provide you with a competitive edge.

Second, demographic variables are good indicators of purchasing behavior for many broad product and service categories. While they cannot predict brand choice, most businesses are more concerned with product choice than brand choice.

Third, demographic variables reveal ongoing trends—such as shifts in age distribution and household types. These trends can create new market segments and provide a business with opportunities that could be profitable.

Fourth, businesses can use demographics to evaluate their marketing efforts. A business can compare internal sales records with the demographics of its target markets—for example, readjusting its marketing strategies to reflect changing market demographics.

THE FOUR Rs

Is it worthwhile to segment your market? To decide, you should ask yourself four key questions. If you answer "yes" to these questions, then segmenting your market is worth pursuing. We call these criteria the Four Rs.

- ***Can you rank your target markets by their importance to your overall market?***
- ***Are your target markets of realistic size, large enough to profitably pursue?***
- ***Can you reach your targeted customers easily?***
- ***Will your targeted customers respond to marketing strategies?***

CAN YOU RANK YOUR TARGET MARKETS?

You must evaluate, both objectively and subjectively, the potential of one target market relative to another in order to decide which one is worth pursuing. To do this, you need to quantify your total market and each of its segments.

Demographics can be an effective tool for measuring markets. One client of Florida University's Small Business Development Center—a dentist—wanted to specialize in cosmetic dentistry, including bonding, implants, and related aesthetic services. But he didn't know whether the market for cosmetic dentistry in his service area was large enough to be worth pursuing as a specialization. We knew that potential cosmetic dentistry patients were professionals, managers, and administrators near their earnings peak. Most prime candidates for cosmetic dentistry have discretionary income.

Using cluster analysis, we determined the size of the overall dentistry market in his area, then zeroed in on the potential market for cosmetic dentistry. The cluster analysis included such variables as household income, age distribution, homeownership, and education.

We found six potential dental market segments in the area. We ranked as potentially profitable for cosmetic dentistry three segments, the Up and Comers, American Dream, and Home Base, primarily because of their size and income level. A fourth segment, The Condo Dwellers, could have been profitable, but its small size made the cost of reaching this market too expensive to pursue. We considered unprofitable for cosmetic dentistry the remaining two segments, Opa-Locka (a low-income area), and the Squeezed Seniors, in part because of their income levels but also because of their distance from the dental office.

Our research indicated that only 10 percent of this dentist's service-area population were prime candidates for cosmetic dentistry. Even if cosmetic dentistry were a well-known specialization, the potential market, according to the cluster analysis, was small. Two other dental markets were larger than cosmetic dentistry—preventive and preventive-remedial dentistry, accounting for more than 44 percent of the dentist's market potential.

IS THE TARGETED MARKET REALISTIC IN SIZE?

Each market that you target must be large enough to support the cost of the marketing effort. You should consider both the number of potential customers and their incomes in order to estimate the purchasing power of the segment.

Another client of the Center wanted to open a day-care center; she needed to find the best site for it. We identified three potential sites for the center using demographic information from the Census Bureau, looking for census tracts in which a large number of working mothers with children under age six lived. We also plotted the existing day-care centers in a map, together with the population density of working mothers. This competitive analysis supplemented the demographic data and helped assess the feasibility of the venture.

The map pinpointed the areas that had at least 2,500 mothers in the labor force with children under six and no existing day-care center. The final site selection was done by the client, choosing only among the best locations.

CAN YOU REACH THE TARGETED CUSTOMERS?

Your targeted customers should be readily accessible. For market segmentation to work effectively, you have to be able to reach distinct markets through select media and targeted messages. The higher cost of reaching a distinct market must be justified by higher sales to that market.

You can use demographics to identify the media that reach your target markets most efficiently. Once you have a demographic profile of your customers, you can compare it with the readership profile of a newspaper, the listenership profile of a radio station, or the ZIP Code demographics that you will reach through direct mail. Even if a perfect match is impossible, your business can gain a competitive edge by knowing how your targeted customers' demographics match with the media you are using to reach them.

You can also use the demographic profile of your targeted customers to design your promotional campaigns and advertising. We developed a cost-effective promotional plan, based on demographic information, for a minority-owned Goodyear automotive franchise owner. First we examined the franchise owner's market, finding that it was a relatively poor, black neighborhood with a youthful population and rapid population turnover. Based on these demographics and the experiences of similar businesses, we recommended that the company use coupons, special offers, premiums, and contests in its promotions to stimulate new business. We also suggested that these promotions be directed at the black population through local radio stations and newspapers. We encouraged the franchise to sponsor special promotional events. One such event, a car-care clinic especially for women, proved successful.

WILL YOUR TARGETED CUSTOMERS RESPOND TO MARKETING STRATEGIES?

If the targeted customers don't respond to your marketing efforts, you shouldn't be marketing to them. Thorough market research, including surveys of noncustomers as well as customers, can help you identify whether potential customers need your particular product or service before you spend money trying to sell to them.

Demographics, combined with market survey research, can identify potentially responsive market segments. One Small Business Development Center client had a retail office supply business that was declining in a changing neighborhood. At first he thought he needed to relocate in order to make his business grow. But after relocating, his sales continued to lag.

We analyzed his new trading area, using data from the local county planning department. The analysis revealed a large concentration of school-aged children in his trade area. Further research indicated that sales of school supplies, which peaked in September, represented a significant business opportunity for him. Sales to small businesses located in his new market area represented another opportunity.

The retailer changed his merchandising mix, store hours, and promotional strategies to better meet the needs of the area. The small businesses needed custom office products and computer-related supplies. The school age population needed economical and attractive school supplies. After implementing the changes, his sales jumped 300 percent in the first year. In September alone the store increased its sales of school supplies 16-fold.

Smart managers know that when they size up their customers, appearances can be deceiving. Demographics are also sometimes deceiving, but at least you can go back for a second look.

FOUR TIPS

If, after analyzing the Four Rs, you decide that it might be profitable to segment your market, here are a few tips that should help you.

1. ***Get the demographic information you need for decision making.***
   The first step in demographic analysis is planning. You need actionable information, not just numbers. Any information you collect should help you solve specific marketing problems. First determine what you already know about your customers. Then determine what else you need to know, isolating the demographic component of your information needs. Sources of demographic data include local planning departments, state data centers, private data firms, and federal statistical offices. The local public library might be the best place to begin.

2. ***Use relevant demographic variables.***
   One or two demographic variables, such as age and income, may not be enough. Demographic data include education levels, household types, marital status, occupation, and so on. Cluster analysis, a technique that classifies neighborhoods by statistically grouping demographic variables that are linked to one another, may be useful for some businesses.

3. ***Use demographics to enhance—not replace—intuition.***
   Despite the value of research, you shouldn't ignore your gut instincts about your customers. Demographic information can add insight to your instincts, stimulating you to market more creatively. Demographic change is the result of many social, economic, and cultural trends, and demographic information can give you a context for understanding how your customers are changing.

4. ***Use census information, current estimates, and projections.***
   A market changes as the people who live there change. The 1980 census will give you the historical information about your area that will help you understand the ongoing change. You also need up-to-date information on the local area, available from your state data center, your county planning department, or from private data companies. In addition, local area projections—available from state data centers or from private data companies—can give you a look into the future, aiding you in long-range business planning.

Psychographic Glitter and Gold

There's gold in lifestyle research, but it's not a get-rich-quick proposition. You still have to mine it, and that takes staying attuned to changes in the consumer marketplace.

by Bickley Townsend

Anheuser-Busch decided to develop a new kind of beer, one that would capitalize on the shift in consumer values toward natural products and healthy lifestyles. Given Americans' interest in diet, health, and nutrition, what could be more logical than a beer called Natural Light? But Natural Light bombed. So did Real cigarettes, positioned on a similar premise: that there are smokers who are seeking a natural, unadulterated cigarette. Anheuser-Busch eventually came up with a winner, Bud Light, but only after relinquishing the brand name and the positioning that assumed naturalness was meaningful to beer drinkers.

Psychographic segmentation promises a lot, but doesn't always deliver. Anheuser-Busch and the makers of Real cigarettes found out the hard way the danger in taking lifestyle research too far or too literally. "In both instances, the lifestyle assumptions were wrong," says Tony Adams, marketing director of Campbell Soup Company. "Attitudinal segments that may have worked in other product categories could not translate to beer and cigarettes."

But General Foods made psychographic analysis work for Sanka, which suffered from a staid, older image; after all, wasn't it only elderly people who needed decaffeinated coffee? Yet the same trend that set Anheuser-Busch off in the wrong direction—consumers' growing health-consciousness—gave General Foods the opening it needed to shift Sanka's positioning. The new campaign targeted active achievers of all ages, picturing them in pursuit of adventurous lifestyles—such as running the rapids in a kayak—with the tag line that Sanka "Lets you be your best"—a classic achiever appeal.

DISSECTING PSYCHOGRAPHICS

Psychographics describes "the entire constellation of a person's attitudes, beliefs, opinions, hopes, fears, prejudices, needs, desires, and aspirations that, taken together, govern how one behaves," and that in turn, "finds holistic expression in a lifestyle" (Arnold Mitchell, *The Nine American Lifestyles*, New York: Macmillan, 1983, p. vii).

The idea is to go beyond standard demographics to learn your best customers' dreams, hopes, fears, and beliefs. By grouping people into homogeneous segments based on their lifestyles, many marketers believe they have a new tool for understanding the consumer and increasing their bottom-line results.

"It's not to say that demographics don't matter. Of course they do," says Gene Cooper, manager of primary research at ABC News and Sports. "But it is psychological motivation which is the driving force behind behavior."

Interest in psychographics has been on the rise since marketers first began to see the mass defection of the baby-boom generation from expected patterns of behavior and consumption, as the children of Buick-driving Republicans registered Democratic and bought Volkswagens. Even pizza caught on big, according to some observers, because it was the perfect protest food: not only did parents not like it at first, but eating it violated one of the basic rules the boomers had grown up with—never eat with your fingers.

DO-IT-YOURSELF PSYCHOGRAPHICS

Researchers who want information on values and lifestyles can buy Yankelovich Clancy Shulman's *Monitor*, subscribe to VALS *(see pages 149-150 for more details about the* Monitor *and VALS)*, or they can develop their own psychographic segmentation system. Sometimes the choice is determined by cost or convenience. How appropriate an "off-the-shelf" system may be, compared with a tailored segmentation study, also affects the choice.

When ABC wanted to segment the television-viewing audience, it considered using VALS, but rejected it as not applicable enough to its needs. Moreover, says ABC's Cooper, "We believe that many of the VALS groups are demographically driven." So ABC developed its own system for classifying viewers into clusters relevant to television viewing. ABC interviewed a national probability sample of 1,000 respondents by telephone, using an 81-item questionnaire designed to measure self-esteem, opinion leadership, need for group inclusion, cosmopolitanism, and other psychological attributes. Cooper emphasizes that, "First, we did not use demographics to form the groups. Second, we did not use any television viewing or program-preference items in the cluster instrument. Our approach was to use fundamental psychological attributes which we felt would be far more stable and more powerful than transient items related to television."

A factor analysis resulted in eight cluster groups in three broad categories:

a "mainstream middle-America" group, a group that is out of the mainstream in various ways, and a "counter-mainstream" group. Individual clusters were given names like Organized Participants, Family Oriented, Liberal Cosmopolitan, and Rigid and Resistant.*

ABC continues to expand the role of psychographics in its research efforts—for program diagnostics, scheduling, and promotion, and in examining potential markets for new technologies such as pay-cable services.

PROMISE OR PERFORMANCE

Has the performance of psychographic segmentation met its promise? It depends on who you talk to. Some researchers question the methodology. "VALS is the *Reader's Digest* of marketing research," says Edward Spar, president of Market Statistics. "With these predigested, prepackaged systems, someone else gives you the answers and as a statistician, that makes me a little nervous. They won't tell you the factor loadings or rotations or the explained variance."

John Mather, senior vice president and director of marketing research in Ketchum Advertising's Pittsburgh office, doesn't have any problem with VALS' proprietary secrets. "That's the little black box—it's how they keep us. I know from my own graduate work that a discriminant-function model takes a lot of time to build and refine to be sure it's valid and reliable." Adds Francois Christen, a VALS manager, "The proof is in the pudding—whether VALS predicts how people will differ in terms of product consumption and use. Clearly, it does."

Other critics question how useful psychographic research is, arguing that too often it tells you what you already know. "One of the most frustrating aftermaths of any research is a result that is so obvious everyone is thinking 'So what's new?'" says Tony Adams of Campbell Soup.

Think about a bag lady living in a low-rent hotel room, Adams asks. "Do we need a battery of lifestyle questions to label this consumer as a light user of Gucci shoes, Jordache jeans, Chivas Regal, and Godiva chocolates?" It doesn't help, he adds, when researchers attempt to dress up the obvious: "Men and women who like to cook become Culinary Artisans; people involved in

**Cluster analysis is often described as lifestyle analysis, but this is a misconception reinforced by cluster names like "Porch Swings & Apple Pie," "Blue Blood Estates," and "Tough Times." Cluster systems are based not on attitudes or values, but on demographic data. They can complement psychograophics by helping to locate the target segments "on the ground," while psychographics tell you how to shape the message.*

church and community become the Societally Conscious." Why not use plain English instead of jargon, asks Adams.

Psychographic researchers acknowledge that most people don't fit a pure type. In the VALS system, all respondents are assigned a score not only for their primary lifestyle type, but also for each of the other VALS types, based on how closely their questionnaire responses conform to the profile of each type. The VALS researchers have gone further by specifying important subgroups within lifestyle segments. For example, if your customers are primarily Achievers, they might be Achiever/Belongers, Achiever/Societally Conscious, or Super Achievers. Although each group scores highest in the Achiever segment, there are important differences. While Achiever/Belongers are relatively conservative, older, female, and less well-educated, Achiever/Societally Conscious people are more apt to be younger professionals, socially liberal, and able to say "I've got all I need; now I'm ready to start contributing to causes and getting involved in the community," as Ketchum Advertising's John Mather explains it. Super Achievers, by contrast, are "win at all costs" workaholics, totally committed to success in their fields, the most male, most managerial, most affluent, and most Republican of any Achiever subgroup.

Where your customers cluster among these Achiever subgroups may make a difference in how you pitch your product. Such cross-classification is an attempt to increase the subtlety of the VALS typology, although, says Mather, "a lot of us are still trying to become better users of the primary groupings."

GOLD IN THE GLITTER

There's gold in the psychographic glitter, but it's not a get-rich-quick proposition. You still have to mine it, and that takes staying attuned to changes in the consumer marketplace. America is moving into the "decade of the real thing," according to VALS' Arnold Mitchell, celebrating light food and drink, natural products and processes, having a "love affair with the lemon," as Ann Clurman, formerly of Yankelovich Clancy Shulman's *Monitor,* has quipped. These are useful insights into lifestyle trends—but they didn't work for Real cigarettes or Natural Light beer.

"It's important to remember," cautions Ketchum's John Mather, "that lifestyle analysis is not a panacea, it's not the magic crystal ball we've all been looking for in our file cabinets. But used well, psychographics can give us that critical bit of insight we need for added leverage in the marketplace."

Back to the Source

Single-source data can be a powerful weapon in your battle with the competition. To win the war, however, you still need to know the trends.

by Joe Schwartz

Even after World War II, many engineers believed that the sound barrier would never be broken. Technological advances and some daring test pilots proved them wrong.

Today, many believe that it is impossible to measure marketing performance precisely. Technological advances and some innovative researchers could prove these skeptics wrong as well. Single-source systems that directly link consumers' exposure to advertising and promotions with what they buy could provide the elusive link between marketing efforts and consumer activity. The potential of single source to measure market performance is so great that it exposes many marketers and their companies to a grave danger: they could become overwhelmed with single-source detail, losing sight of their company's long-range goals.

The single-source concept is like a new invention—nobody quite knows what its effect will be. "The information age is coming to marketing. It is going to bring us better market information, just as worldwide communication and fax machines brought better communication to businesses," says Michael J. Naples, president of the Advertising Research Foundation in New York City. "The future is difficult to predict, but there will be new jobs, new opportunities, and new businesses."

This information revolution is changing the rules of marketing. Retailers are assuming promotional duties once performed by packaged-goods manufacturers. Manufacturers are facing the dual tasks of producing products for consumers and selling them to market-wise retailers. Networks are scrambling as new audience-measurement schemes expose their weaknesses, while cable television executives are expecting their audience share to grow as more accurate data are produced.

The central idea of the information revolution is the use of electronic monitoring in consumer research. Laser scanners, television meters, and other innovations are the vehicles for this change.

Demand for the revolution comes from the business community's need to reach consumers more effectively. American businesses spent $110 billion on advertising in 1987, according to Robert Coen, director of forecasting at McCann-Erickson Advertising in New York City. "Obviously, there is tremendous leverage for advertisers to better manage that spending, and to channel that spending where it is going to be most efficient and most productive," says Andrew Tarshis, president of NPD/Nielsen, Inc., a consumer research firm in Port Washington, New York.

THE ELECTRONIC EDGE

Electronic monitoring has several advantages over the old diary and interview methods of gathering information. Researchers can now gather more information about consumers with far less effort. The information is generated quickly, in staggering quantities, and in unprecedented detail. As a result, consumer product manufacturers have a far more accurate basis upon which to make marketing decisions.

"Detail is the catalyst of this entire revolution. We were doing consumer research the same way for 50 years until scanner data came along," says J. Walker Smith, director of marketing research at DowBrands (formerly Dow Consumer Products). "The opportunity lies in monitoring this incredible amount of data and making it meaningful for business."

Two electronic monitoring tools create the modern single-source system: television meters, which produce more accurate descriptions of who watches TV and what advertising they see; and laser scanners, which "read" the UPC codes on products and produce instantaneous information on sales. Separately, each monitoring device provides marketers with current information on the advertising audience and on sales and inventories of products. Together, television meters and scanners measure the impact of marketing.

Before scanners, sales information was available to grocers and manufacturers monthly or quarterly. With scanners, both parties can monitor sales on a weekly or even daily basis, for a single store or chain of stores. "Weekly store scanner data is a revolution because people had never before been able to look at store performance with the speed and accuracy that scanner data provides," says DowBrand's J. Walker Smith.

The volume of scanner data requires national firms to decentralize their marketing efforts. "We, and other corporations, are changing our local sales offices," says Douglas Haley, director of market information at Nestlé Foods in Purchase, New York. "We are putting in analytical people at the zone office level to provide the local sales guys with better information based on single-source data." Scanners make grocers more sophisticated because they, too, know what sells and what doesn't.

"It's an 'arms race' between retailers on one side and manufacturers on the other. Whoever has the better information determines which programs are accepted and which ones are rejected," says Haley. "Brand managers can see much more response from promotion investments. You base advertising spending decisions on faith, and you make promotion decisions on a direct financial analysis of payback from your scanner data."

Better-informed grocers force packaged-goods manufacturers to persuade them to buy, just as the grocers must persuade consumers to buy. "Our emphasis is providing an effective selling message to the retailer as well as the end consumer," says Smith. "The retailers, in turn, are taking on more of the task of marketing to consumers."

Scanner data are fueling an interest in coupons and other short-term promotions. "So much money is going to promotions these days," says Tarshis of NPD/Nielsen. "About two-thirds of packaged-goods marketing funds go to promotion. Fifteen years ago, advertising was two-thirds of that budget."

METER READERS

Scanners have revolutionized the packaged-goods business. Television meters have not yet revolutionized the television-advertising business, but they probably will.

"Television meters caused a shift in the audience estimates," says Barry Cook, vice president for media research at NBC. "Nevertheless, business is pretty good."

"Up-front" business—or total network-television advertising paid for in advance—increased by 28 percent industry-wide from the 1986–87 television season to the 1988–89 season, Cook says. Increases in up-front business are an indicator of confidence in TV advertising. "As long as there is fundamental credibility in the measurement system, the law of supply and demand is most important," says Cook.

As the switch from diaries to television meters continues, the precision of national television audience measurement increases. So far, the results don't make much difference to the networks. The initial people-meter data showed ABC's network news in first place, for example, while the former diary system showed NBC news in first place. "That means more to salespeople because they have to show who's in first, second, and third place," Cook says. "But statistically, the differences are insignificant. During the summer of 1988, one-fifth of a rating point has separated first and third place in network news."

Other television executives say that TV meters will have a greater impact. "Independent (stations) always gain share when markets go from diaries to meters," observes Howard Shimmel, vice president for research and advertising sales at MTV Networks. "I think the whole move to television meters and single-source data has helped cable stations. Our audiences were never measured well by diaries. Teenagers and young adults are impatient, especially when you have programming vehicles such as MTV or CNN where you can zip in for three minutes and catch a video or a newscast, and zip back to a network program." Television meters, unlike diaries, measure viewership in seconds. They will catch "zip ins." Diaries, which rely on viewers recalling their viewing habits, often miss them.

Television meters improve the definition of cable-TV audiences, says Shimmel: "MTV and other cable stations offer an advertiser a highly targeted audience. Just being able to prove that, with meters, is going to benefit all of cable TV."

One of the major obstacles in the way of television meters is their cost, especially in local markets. Monitoring a single home with a television meter costs much more than a diary, although industry officials refuse to reveal the cost of buying and installing the meters. "Even if you had a national sample of 100,000 homes, you probably still wouldn't have enough meters in the smaller markets," Cook says. Diaries still are a cost-effective method of reaching the local markets, and reaching the local markets is the key to the quarterly network "sweeps," when audiences are polled. The sweeps take place in November, February, May, and July, when the diaries go out. The cost of saturating local markets with meters would be prohibitive, Cook says.

This disadvantage is not permanent. As technology improves, the cost of a high-tech product usually drops. And once meters supplant diaries in both national and local markets, the television-advertising business will play by a new set of rules, says Ken Wollenberg, vice president for advertiser/agency sales and marketing at Arbitron Ratings Company. "Television meters could spell the end of sweeps," Wollenberg predicts.

TAPPING THE SOURCE

By definition, a single-source system gathers its information from a single panel of respondents by continuously monitoring the advertising and promotion the panel is exposed to and what it subsequently buys.

The term "single source" was first mentioned about 1966 by the J. Walter Thompson advertising agency in England to describe a research-interview operation that recorded the demographics, reading, viewing, and purchasing behavior of panelists, says the Advertising Research Foundation's Michael J.

Naples. Today, the annual surveys of the media habits and buying behavior of thousands of consumers done by Simmons Market Research Bureau and Mediamark Research have taken the panel-diary-and-interview technique to its limit. With the new electronic tools, that limit has been shattered.

Single source was not a practical idea until scanners and television meters were introduced in the 1980s. "You can look back 20 years and see examples of attempts to get single source," says Tarshis of NPD/Nielsen. "But there was no way to get continuous purchasing behavior tied in with continuous viewing—commercial and promotional exposure—other than asking people, and recall is far less accurate than continuous measurement systems."

A significant weak point of today's single-source systems is that they don't record the thousands of marketing messages that consumers are exposed to. "We do not have a fully integrated single-source system, because key parts of the puzzle are missing," says Joseph R. Russo, manager of market research and new products at Thomas J. Lipton in Englewood Cliffs, New Jersey. "Print ads, outdoor advertising, shelf position, and radio ads are missing. Single source, as we have it now, is not the ultimate product. I think what we have is in its embryonic stages."

THE SOURCES

Dozens of companies ask panels of respondents about their demographics, their buying habits, and their media use, but three companies are building national electronically monitored single-source panels: Arbitron Ratings Company of New York City; Information Resources, Inc. (IRI) of Chicago; and NPD/Nielsen of Port Washington, New York.

Arbitron's single-source system, ScanAmerica, began operating in May 1987 with 600 households in Denver, Colorado. The households have meters attached to their television sets, and they have scanning "wands" that panelists use at home to record the UPC codes of the products they buy. ScanAmerica panelists also list which newspapers, magazines, and other print media they read.

ScanAmerica is building a national database, according to Arbitron's Ken Wollenberg. In the fall of 1989, the company will have a total of 1,000 panel households from the New York City, Los Angeles, Chicago, Atlanta, and Dallas markets. By 1992, the company plans to have a national panel of 5,000 households.

IRI pioneered electronically monitored single source with the introduction of Behaviorscan in 1979. Today, IRI has a total of 70,000 panel households in 27 markets, according to Magid Abraham, executive vice president for product management at IRI. Each panel householder has an identification card with a bar code. When panelists shop at participating stores, the cashier scans their identification cards along with their purchases. Of the 70,000 panel households, 10,000 households also have television meters. IRI also keeps track of panelists' print subscriptions.

NPD/Nielsen has 15,000 panelist households with home product scanners, 2,500 of which have television meters. Another 8,000 households will have identification cards as well. By 1990, 7,500 of the panel households will have television meters. The company will use the information generated by identification cards to make market-by-market analysis of promotions; it will use the information generated by the in-home scanners to analyze advertising effectiveness.

Those who are most confident of single source say it will be welcomed by advertising agencies, product manufacturers, and the media.

"It will help everybody in this business, because we are going to make more knowledgeable decisions on where to place advertising," says MTV Network's Shimmel. "The advertisers and their agencies especially are going to love this system, because they are no longer buying shows with the best demographic composition. They will be basing their decisions on buying behavior."

Basing media decisions on buying behavior is extremely attractive to businesses, but it is important to keep single source in perspective.

Single source gauges marketing performance. It reveals how consumer behavior is changing, and which consumer groups respond to marketing efforts. But single source cannot predict how consumer groups will change or explain why they are changing. For that, you need to know the trends.

"Single source shows only the present and the past. What you need is a broader view of testing and strategies offline," says NBC's Barry Cook. "You must also understand changes in the products, in competitors, and in demography. Single source is simply the measurement portion of the experiment. It measures performance. It does not explain changing conditions."

How To Evaluate Population Estimates

If the data you need to gauge an estimate's accuracy are available, then you don't need the estimate. Here are a few rules of thumb that can help you judge the accuracy of population estimates.

by William P. O'Hare

Each year, the Census Bureau produces estimates of the total population of states and counties through its Federal-State Cooperative Program for Local Population Estimates. In this program, the bureau publishes estimates that it and the states have agreed upon. The bureau uses its county numbers to produce estimates of the population of metropolitan areas. Every two years, the bureau also produces estimates for 39,000 government units that once received General Revenue Sharing funds, including all cities, towns, villages, and subcounty jurisdictions. The revenue-sharing program has ended, but the estimates will continue.

The Census Bureau tests its estimates extensively, and the patterns observed in these tests provide a set of guidelines about the likely accuracy of population estimates in general. The most recent evaluations are published in the Census Bureau's Current Population Reports series: state estimates are evaluated in Series P-25, No. 957; county estimates are evaluated in Series P-25, No. 984; and subcounty units in Series P-25, No. 963.

Generally, these rules of thumb can also be applied to the population estimates and projections for census tracts, ZIP Code areas, block groups, and other pieces of geography produced by private data companies.

RULE 1. *Large populations can be estimated more accurately than small populations.*

It is easier to estimate the population of New York City than a small village in upstate New York because random fluctuations have a much bigger impact on small populations than on large ones. Also, large cities often have better administrative records on which to base estimates.

As the size of a population increases, there is a steady decline in an estimate's error *(see chart on next page)*. Fifty-nine percent of places with populations of less than 100 have estimation errors in excess of 20 percent, and the average error for these places is 35 percent. But for places with populations of 100,000 or more, the average error is only 3.9 percent, and none are off by 20 percent or more. Average error for all places is 15 percent.

RULE 2. Moderately growing populations can be estimated more accurately than rapidly growing or declining populations.

The 1980 estimates for populations that had fallen by 15 percent during the 1970s had an average error of 36 percent when compared with the 1980 census results. The average error for populations that grew by 50 percent or more was 22 percent. Yet the average error for populations that grew less than 10 percent was only 10 percent.

RULE 3. Averaging several estimates of the population of an area is usually more accurate than relying on only one estimate.

The exception to this rule is when one estimation technique is far superior to others.

RULE 4. Adjusting estimates to match an independently derived control total reduces error.

Estimates of counties within a state, for example, or states within the country as a whole, improve when they are forced to sum to an independent estimate of the total area. The bureau uses this technique to produce its subcounty estimates.

RULE 5. It is easier to estimate changes over a short period of time than over a long period of time.

Most estimates begin with the decennial census population and include changes to the population since the census. There will be less error in a population estimate for 1982 than for 1987, since 1982 is closer to the benchmark year.

RULE 6. The populations for smaller places are more likely to be over-estimated than the populations of larger places.

Of the 2,425 places in the U.S. with a population of 100 or less, 55 percent were overestimated, according to the 1980 census results. On the other hand, only 37 percent of the 160 places with populations of 100,000 or more were overestimated.

PERCENT ERROR BY POPULATION SIZE FOR 1980 ESTIMATES
(calculated by comparing the Census Bureau's 1980 estimates with 1980 census results)

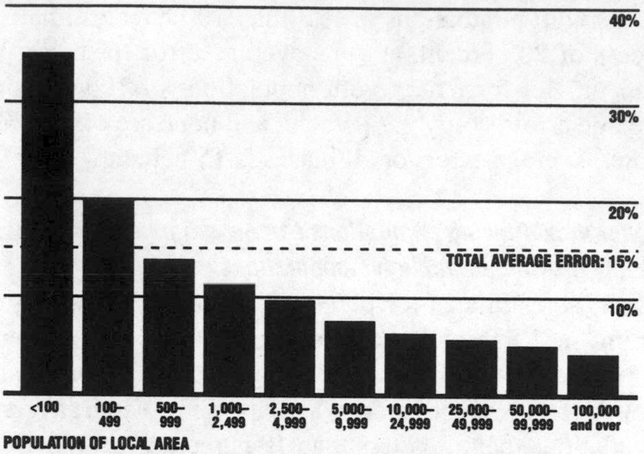

Source: U.S. Bureau of the Census, "Evaluation of 1980 Subcounty Population Estimates," Current Population Reports, *Series P-25, No. 963.*

Expect larger errors when estimating smaller populations.

RULE 7. Places that lost population between 1970 and 1980 were much more likely to be overestimated than those that grew rapidly.

Fully 85 percent of the places that lost more than 15 percent of their population during the 1970s were overestimated according to the 1980 census. Only 23 percent of places that grew by more than 50 percent were overestimated.

Finally, some populations are not worth estimating. For almost half of places with fewer than 500 people, it was just as accurate in 1980 to use the 1970 census figure as the 1980 estimate. For one out of five places with populations of 100,000 or more, the 1970 census figure was a more accurate reflection of the 1980 population than was the 1980 estimate.

As with all rules, there may be some exceptions to these generalizations. Nonetheless, hard evidence about the accuracy of population estimates is seldom available, and these guidelines provide the best basis for evaluating some of the most basic demographic tools.

To paraphrase one prominent demographer, there are three standard requirements for anyone engaged in producing population estimates: 1) a good database; 2) a good set of assumptions; and 3) a good sense of humor.

How to Think Like a Demographer

It's a simple way to look at the world. Populations and markets are the same kind of beast.

by Thomas Exter

Demographers and marketers both view the world in simple terms. One studies populations; the other studies markets. When populations grow too fast, demographers try to slow them down. When markets grow too slowly, marketers try to speed them up. When marketers think like demographers, they gain an understanding of how things work that can help them increase market size, deepen market penetration, and carve out market share.

Births, deaths, and migration are the only things that change a population's size. In marketing, a "birth" occurs when someone wants a product or service. The market for automobiles grows, for example, when more people want a new car. Like the birthrate, the rate at which people need a new car can rise or fall for many reasons, including demographic and economic ones.

Advertising can increase the demand for new cars, especially if the cars have features that drivers want, such as lengthy warranties. Kodak promotes births in its market with advertising that encourages camera buffs to take more pictures—regardless of the brand of film they use. As the dominant company in the field, Kodak gains when it increases the size of the total market.

"Mortality" in the film market occurs when people stop taking pictures. The automobile market loses people when they give up driving. Advertising can postpone mortality and encourage fertility by emphasizing the fun of picture-taking and the features on the latest cars.

When people move to a new city, like Los Angeles, they enter a network of jobs, housing developments, retail establishments, and freeways. When consumers enter the automobile market, they open themselves to sales pitches, advertisements, and to noticing their neighbor's car. Once in the market, their decision-making centers on what brand to buy. Brand selection and brand switching are analogous to migration.

Most demographers agree that the population policies that are hardest to make work are those that try to influence migration. Likewise, brand managers would probably agree that it is hardest to influence brand switching. Advertising can create brand awareness and reinforce brand images, but rarely does it cause brand switching.

MARKET SNAPSHOTS

Since populations are always changing , the only way to measure a population is by stopping the clock. On April 1, 1990 the Census Bureau counted every head in the country and measured our population's size, distribution, and composition.

Market researchers also need to stop the clock to calculate the size, distribution, and composition of their markets. Market researchers rely on consumer surveys to estimate these characteristics. Just as computer technology has revolutionized the decennial population census, technologies like people meters and UPC scanners are changing the collection and analysis of consumer information. But the growing sophistication of data collection should not obscure the common purpose of population censuses and consumer surveys. Both attempt to measure people at one point in time in order to describe their characteristics and calculate how they are changing.

The composition of a population or a market includes people's age, sex, income, educational attainment, occupation, and ethnicity. Population and market composition changes because of births, deaths, and migration. Market composition also changes as people's needs and desires for products shift. Young people may buy more computers at first, but as older people catch on, they also become important to the computer market. High-income innovators may buy microwave ovens initially, but as prices fall a broader spectrum of people buy them. Consumer surveys keep companies on top of the changing composition of their markets.

The distribution of a market depends on consumer geography and technology. Consumers can be part of a market as long as products and services can reach them. New channels of product distribution emerge with new technologies. From walk-in retail outlets to direct marketing by mail, telephone, television, and computer, distribution channels determine the distribution of a market. Marketers in search of an optimal distribution network for their products must consider not only the distribution of the population, but also the efficiency of their market channels.

Brand managers who want to increase the size of their total market need to attract customers to the product category (promote births), retain current customers (prevent deaths), and convert customers of the competition to their brand (encourage migration). A new product will require investing resources in attracting new customers to the product category as well as to the brand. A mature product will require investing resources to increase product use and to point out strategic brand differences.

How to Find Your Next Thousand Customers

Here's a simple way to determine where to put your marketing efforts.

by Thomas Exter

If you knew who your next 1,000 customers were likely to be, you could target your marketing much more precisely. And if you know the ages of your current customers, you can calculate who your next 1,000 customers will be by using population projections and a simple spreadsheet program. To illustrate, let's take a look at the contact-lens market.

The first column of the table shows the Census Bureau's estimates of the U.S. population by age. The second column shows the percent of people in each age group who wear contact lenses, or the penetration rate for contact lenses, based on the 1986 national survey by New York City-based Simmons Market Research Bureau. If you multiply the penetration rate by the population estimate for each age group, you get an estimate of the number of people who wear contacts.

The projections of the population by age for 1991 are the Census Bureau's. To project the number of contact-lens wearers in 1991, you multiply these numbers by the penetration rate for each age group. By assuming penetration rates won't change over the five years, you can see the effects of demographic change on the contact-lens market. You could make some assumptions about how penetration rates might change in order to determine the effects of a market shift on top of demographic change. Right now, penetration rates in the contact-lens market decline with age, because younger people have been more likely to use contacts than older people. Penetration rates should rise among older groups as current users age. Because of this, basing projections on

COUNTING ON CONTACTS

Using a simple spreadsheet, widely available population data, and product usage data from syndicated surveys, you can find your next 1,000 customers.

(estimate and projection of the contact-lens market, 1986-1991; persons in thousands)

						contact lens market	
age	1986 population estimate	percent wearing contacts*	1986 contact lens wearers	1991 population projection	1991 contact lens wearers	change in number of wearers**	the next 1,000 wearers***
All age groups	178,324	13.4%	23,826	186,830	24,764	938	1,000
18 to 19	7,360	15.9	1,170	6,754	1,074	1,074	316
20 to 24	20,613	16.4	3,381	18,583	3,048	1,877	553
25 to 29	22,136	17.4	3,852	20,826	3,624	243	72
30 to 34	20,848	16.8	3,502	22,333	3,752	-100	—
35 to 39	18,775	16.5	3,098	20,399	3,366	–137	—
40 to 44	14,367	13.7	1,968	18,808	2,577	-521	—
45 to 49	11,934	11.2	1,337	14,294	1,601	-367	—
50 to 54	10,889	13.1	1,426	11,724	1,536	199	59
55 to 59	11,268	10.4	1,172	10,390	1,081	-346	—
60 to 64	10,962	8.0	877	10,502	840	-332	—
65 to 69	9,661	6.0	580	9,990	599	-278	—
70 and older	19,511	7.5	1,463	22,227	1,667	-376	—

** Based on Simmons Market Research Bureau's 1986 survey.*
*** These are cohort changes. They show the net increase or decrease over five years between successive age groups.*
**** Formula: (net change / total new wearers) * 1,000; e.g., (1,074 / 3,393) * 1,000 = 316.5; 3,393 is the sum of the positive changes in the number of increases.*

Source: Bureau of the Census, 1986 population estimates and 1991 middle-series projection; Simmons Market Research Bureau, 1986 survey; author's calculations.

current penetration rates, as is done in this article, produces conservative estimates of the size of the contact-lens market in the future.

THE NEXT 1,000

If you assume that no one drops out of the market, then all contact-lens wearers aged 20 to 24 in 1986 would still wear contacts in 1991. By comparing the size of each group of users by age in 1991 with users five years younger in 1986, you can determine the net number of people who will start wearing contact lenses between 1986 and 1991. Our analysis indicates that the 3,381,000 users aged 20 to 24 in 1986 will become 3,624,000 users aged 25 to 29 in 1991, a net gain of 243,000 users, because 25-to-29-year-olds are somewhat more likely to wear contacts than 20-to-24-year-olds. Because the 18- and 19-year-olds in 1991 were only 13 and 14 years old in 1986, they are all new to the market.

Finally, you can calculate a percentage distribution of net new users by age. Then you can convert the percentage to "per 1,000." You can see that of the next 1,000 users, 316 will be aged 18 to 19, 553 will be aged 20 to 24, and 72 will be aged 25 to 29. Only 59 will be aged 50 to 54. The overwhelming share of new contact-lens wearers will be young people.

Because of the decline in the number of young adults in the U.S. population and the aging of the baby-boom generation, the contact-lens aftermarket (the buyers of such things as lens cleaning solution) will be older in 1991 than in 1986. As current customers age, their income, household type, and other demographic characteristics will change. At the same time, their shopping habits, media preferences, and favorite stores probably will change as well. In the contact-lens market, as well as in the cleaning-solution aftermarket, knowing customers means following them through their life stages and adjusting promptly to their changing wants and needs.

CHAPTER 3

The 1990 Census

The 1990 Census was taken on April 1 after years of planning. Data will be slow to emerge, but once they do they will provide the most complete picture of the U.S. population available since 1980. The following sections, which originally appeared in American Demographics *magazine, explain what to expect from the census, scheduled release dates, and how to use the data.*

What the 1990 Census Will Show

Why wait for 1990 census results? The numbers are here.

by Judith Waldrop and Thomas Exter

The results of the 1990 census will show that there are about 250 million Americans—but that won't be the big news. America's changing characteristics will be much more important, especially for the nation's businesses.

Although the number of Americans will have grown 10 percent since the last census, certain groups—Hispanics and Asians, for example—will far outpace this rate. Adapting to cultural and language differences has been a major challenge in the 1980s, but it has also been profitable. Marketers have discovered that the demand for ethnic products and services, from guacamole to acupuncture, reaches far beyond narrow demographic niches.

Apart from race or ethnicity, changes in household composition and employment patterns have altered the way Americans live. Ten years ago, many marketers thought women's labor-force participation had peaked and the time was right for a return to home and family. But women have become increasingly committed to the work force and less likely to marry and have children. Some marketers today still anticipate a return to traditional family life, but the 1990 census will show that it's not in the numbers.

The new demographics have been profitable for some businesses and disastrous for others. As a steady stream of migrants swelled newly emerging population centers in the South and the West, they drained older cities in the North and Midwest. Fortunes were won and lost. As baby boom turned into baby bust, marketers targeting young adults found themselves with a shortage of customers. Those who chased after the mature market were disappointed with its slow growth as the small generation born during the 1930s turned 50. But marketers targeting the "thirty-something" generation have been doubly rewarded. As baby boomers joined these ranks, this group gained in size and purchasing power.

While many population surveys have guided marketers through the past decade, the 1990 census will provide businesses with information to succeed in the decade ahead. Fresh census numbers will help even the most sophisticated forecasters see more clearly into the future. And the degree of detail will dazzle us all.

The 1990 census was the most automated, technically advanced data-collection project ever undertaken. But because of the immense size of the task, its great cost, and its dependence on human labor, don't expect the data to arrive in your next fax transmission. The earliest we can hope to see any numbers will be 1991. And detailed results will take several years to emerge. The complete analysis of census data will take the entire decade of the 1990s. For a look at the wonders to come, American Demographics presents this preview of likely 1990 census revelations.

BEHIND THE NUMBERS

This discussion is based on American Demographics' selection of the best estimates and projections from a variety of sources. All 1980 data are from the 1980 census. All projections are adjusted to April 1, 1990, through interpolation. We used the Census Bureau's middle series population projections for the 1990 population by age and race. The 1990 Hispanic population is based on an average of the bureau's middle and high immigration scenarios. The 1990 populations for states are an average of the bureau's state projections, and projections by Washington, D.C.-based Woods & Poole Economics.

For the 1990 metropolitan-area rankings, we used estimates and projections from state data centers and other local agencies. The geography of metropolitan areas in 1980 and 1990 is based on the June 30, 1988, definition from the Office of Management and Budget.

Households by age and type in 1990 are based on a combination of 1) American Demographics' projections of married couples with children and single-person households, and 2) the Census Bureau's middle series household projections. Labor-force projections are based on unpublished data from the Bureau of Labor Statistics. We based the educational-attainment projections on "Current and Potential Race and Sex Differences in the U.S. Educational Structure," an unpublished paper by Robert Kominski of the Bureau of the Census, and on the latest educational-attainment estimates from the Census Bureau.

THE 1990 CENSUS WILL SHOW THAT THE POPULATION OF THE U.S. HAS REACHED 250 MILLION.

This gain of 23 million is a 10 percent increase over 1980. The median age of the population rose from 30 in 1980 to 33 today. But though the population as

23 MILLION MORE AMERICANS

(population by age, in thousands; percent distribution and percent change, 1980–90)

	1990 population	1990 distribution	1980 population	1980 distribution	percent change
Total	249,870	100.0%	226,546	100.0%	10.3%
Under 5	18,409	7.4	16,348	7.2	12.6
5 to 9	18,333	7.3	16,700	7.4	9.8
10 to 14	17,194	6.9	18,242	8.1	–5.7
15 to 19	17,521	7.0	21,168	9.3	–17.2
20 to 24	18,746	7.5	21,318	9.4	–12.1
25 to 29	21,592	8.6	19,521	8.6	10.6
30 to 34	22,359	8.9	17,561	7.8	27.3
35 to 39	20,080	8.0	13,966	6.2	43.8
40 to 44	17,481	7.0	11,669	5.2	49.8
45 to 49	13,838	5.5	11,090	4.9	24.8
50 to 54	11,496	4.6	11,710	5.2	–1.8
55 to 59	10,644	4.3	11,615	5.1	–8.4
60 to 64	10,765	4.3	10,088	4.5	6.7
65 to 69	10,223	4.1	8,783	3.9	16.4
70 to 74	8,089	3.2	6,799	3.0	19.0
75 to 79	6,079	2.4	4,794	2.1	26.8
80 to 84	3,802	1.5	2,935	1.3	29.5
85 to 89	2,048	0.8	1,520	0.7	34.7
90 to 94	864	0.3	557	0.2	55.2
95 to 99	257	0.1	131	0.1	96.0
100 or older	57	*	32	*	76.6

** less than 0.1%*

a whole is aging, some older age groups have declined since 1980, while some younger age groups have grown.

The number of people aged 50 to 59 dropped as the small generation born during the 1930s entered this age group. And the number of people aged 10 to 24 fell because of the low birthrates of the late 1960s and early 1970s. But the baby-boom generation is now in its childbearing years, and the number of children under age 10 is growing.

The oldest baby boomers turned 40 in 1986, ushering that massive generation into midlife. During the past ten years, the number of people aged 40 to 44 grew by nearly 50 percent. But the 35-to-39 age group saw the largest

ETHNIC SURGE

(population and change in population, by race and Hispanic origin, in millions; percent distribution and percent change, 1980–90)

	1990		1980		1980–90	
	population	percent distribution	population	percent distribution	change	percent change
Total population	249.9	100%	226.5	100%	23.4	10%
White	210.3	84	194.7	86	15.6	8
Black	31.0	12	26.7	12	4.3	16
Asian or other races	8.6	3	5.2	2	3.4	65
Hispanic*	21.0	8	14.6	6	6.4	44

* *Hispanics may be of any race.*

absolute increase. During the 1980s, 11 million people entered their 30s and are now poised to turn 40.

The fastest-growing age groups are the oldest ones. The population aged 95 to 99 has nearly doubled since 1980. And centenarians grew 77 percent. The 1990 census will show that 57,000 Americans have reached that milestone.

THE 1990 CENSUS WILL SHOW INCREASING ETHNIC AND RACIAL DIVERSITY.

During the 1980s, 500,000 legal migrants a year accounted for one-fifth of our population growth. And about 200,000 illegals also joined our population each year. Mexicans, Filipinos, Chinese, Koreans, and Vietnamese are the most common new arrivals. These immigrants are the driving force behind the changing racial and ethnic composition of the U.S.

The 1990 census will count 21 million Hispanics, a 44 percent increase since 1980. Hispanics now account for nearly 9 percent of Americans, up from only 5 percent ten years ago. And if the 1990 census undercounts Hispanics at the same rate as the 1980 census, the figures will fall short of the true total by about 1 million.

The number of people of "other" races (mostly Asians, as well as Pacific Islanders, American Indians, Eskimos, and Aleuts) grew the fastest during the 1980s, up by 65 percent. This growth is primarily the result of Asian immigration. Now nearing 9 million, "other" races gained as a share of the U.S. population, rising from 2 to 3 percent.

With a 16 percent increase, blacks held on to their 12 percent share of the total population. Though whites gained the greatest number of people (16 million), their 8 percent increase was not enough to maintain their share of the total population, which dropped from 86 to 84 percent.

THE 1990 CENSUS WILL SHOW THAT THE NORTHEAST HAS BECOME THE LEAST POPULOUS REGION OF THE COUNTRY.

The population of the fast-growing West squeaked past that of the slow-growing Northeast during the 1980s. Overall, states in the South and the West captured nearly 90 percent of the nation's ten-year population gain. While the Midwest was the slowest-growing region, it remains the second most populous area in the nation. The South, with 87 million people in 1990, remains solidly in first place.

California gained more people than any other state—over 5 million since 1980. The 1990 census will show that more than 29 million people live in the most populous state. Texas and Florida gained more than 3 million residents each during the 1980s, while Georgia gained over 1 million. Alaska grew the fastest during the 1980s, up by 42 percent. Arizona and Nevada follow, with gains of more than 34 percent.

Some states in the Northeast are making comebacks. The 1990 census will rank New Jersey and New York among the top 15 population gainers. New Hampshire, growing by 23 percent, was the sixth fastest growing state of the 1980s.

Fifteen states captured 81 percent of the nation's population growth. Alaska, Arizona, Nevada, and Florida each grew by more than 30 percent in the past ten years, three times as fast as the nation as a whole. Texas, New Hampshire, California, New Mexico, Utah, and Georgia grew at more than double the national rate.

The population losers of the 1980s were West Virginia and Iowa, along with the District of Columbia. During the 1970s, the District of Columbia, New York, and Rhode Island lost population.

THE 1990 CENSUS WILL SHOW A RESURGENCE IN METROPOLITAN GROWTH.

Ten years ago—as the nation looked back on a decade of unprecedented non-metropolitan growth—no one anticipated a metropolitan revival. But during the 1980s, metropolitan areas grew at nearly double the rate of nonmetropolitan areas.

While no new metros will be added to the top 25, rankings will change. The

FAST-TRACK STATES

(population and change in population, by region, division, and state, in thousands; and percent change, 1980–90)

	1990 population	1980 population	1980–90 change	1980–90 percent change
UNITED STATES	***249,870***	***226,546***	***23,324***	***10.3%***
NORTHEAST	**50,911**	**49,135**	**1,776**	**3.6%**
NEW ENGLAND	***13,134***	***12,348***	***786***	***6.4%***
Maine	*1,213*	*1,125*	*88*	*7.8*
New Hampshire	*1,133*	*921*	*212*	*23.0*
Vermont	*566*	*511*	*55*	*10.7*
Massachusetts	*5,942*	*5,737*	*205*	*3.6*
Rhode Island	*1,002*	*947*	*55*	*5.8*
Connecticut	*3,280*	*3,108*	*172*	*5.5*
MIDDLE ATLANTIC	***37,777***	***36,787***	***990***	***2.7%***
New York	*17,946*	*17,558*	*388*	*2.2*
New Jersey	*7,900*	*7,365*	*535*	*7.3*
Pennsylvania	*11,931*	*11,864*	*67*	*0.6*
MIDWEST	**59,939**	**58,866**	**1,073**	**1.8%**
EAST NORTH CENTRAL	***42,112***	***41,682***	***430***	***1.0%***
Ohio	*10,828*	*10,798*	*30*	*0.3*
Indiana	*5,556*	*5,490*	*66*	*1.2*
Illinois	*11,650*	*11,427*	*223*	*2.0*
Michigan	*9,279*	*9,262*	*17*	*0.2*
Wisconsin	*4,799*	*4,706*	*93*	*2.0*
WEST NORTH CENTRAL	***17,827***	***17,183***	***644***	***3.7%***
Minnesota	*4,333*	*4,076*	*257*	*6.3*
Iowa	*2,814*	*2,914*	*–101*	*–3.4*
Missouri	*5,184*	*4,917*	*267*	*5.4*
North Dakota	*675*	*653*	*22*	*3.3*
South Dakota	*712*	*691*	*21*	*3.1*
Nebraska	*1,603*	*1,570*	*33*	*2.1*
Kansas	*2,507*	*2,364*	*143*	*6.1*

	1990 population	1980 population	1980–90 change	1980–90 percent change
SOUTH	**87,012**	**75,372**	**11,640**	**15.4%**
SOUTH ATLANTIC	***43,578***	***36,959***	***6,619***	***17.9%***
Delaware	*658*	*594*	*64*	*10.8*
Maryland	*4,685*	*4,217*	*468*	*11.1*
District of Columbia	*622*	*638*	*–16*	*–2.4*
Virginia	*6,106*	*5,347*	*759*	*14.2*
West Virginia	*1,901*	*1,950*	*–49*	*–2.5*
North Carolina	*6,669*	*5,882*	*787*	*13.4*
South Carolina	*3,548*	*3,122*	*426*	*13.6*
Georgia	*6,557*	*5,463*	*1,094*	*20.0*
Florida	*12,832*	*9,746*	*3,086*	*31.7*
EAST SOUTH CENTRAL	***15,556***	***14,666***	***890***	***6.1%***
Kentucky	*3,768*	*3,661*	*107*	*2.9*
Tennessee	*4,954*	*4,591*	*363*	*7.9*
Alabama	*4,155*	*3,894*	*261*	*6.7*
Mississippi	*2,679*	*2,521*	*158*	*6.3*
WEST SOUTH CENTRAL	***27,879***	***23,747***	***4,132***	***17.4%***
Arkansas	*2,428*	*2,286*	*142*	*6.2*
Louisiana	*4,570*	*4,206*	*364*	*8.7*
Oklahoma	*3,316*	*3,025*	*291*	*9.6*
Texas	*17,565*	*14,229*	*3,336*	*23.4*
WEST	**52,008**	**43,172**	**8,836**	**20.5%**
MOUNTAIN	***13,881***	***11,373***	***2,508***	***22.0%***
Montana	*818*	*787*	*31*	*3.9*
Idaho	*1,019*	*944*	*75*	*7.9*
Wyoming	*515*	*470*	*45*	*9.5*
Colorado	*3,436*	*2,890*	*546*	*18.9*
New Mexico	*1,587*	*1,303*	*284*	*21.8*
Arizona	*3,656*	*2,718*	*938*	*34.5*
Utah	*1,775*	*1,461*	*314*	*21.5*
Nevada	*1,075*	*800*	*275*	*34.4*
PACIFIC	***38,128***	***31,800***	***6,328***	***19.9%***
Washington	*4,641*	*4,132*	*509*	*12.3*
Oregon	*2,758*	*2,633*	*125*	*4.8*
California	*29,030*	*23,668*	*5,362*	*22.7*
Alaska	*570*	*402*	*168*	*41.9*
Hawaii	*1,128*	*965*	*163*	*16.9*

BIG-CITY BOOM

(population of the 25 most populous metropolitan statistical areas and change, in thousands; percent change, 1980–90)

1990 rank	1980 rank	metropolitan area	1990 population	1980 population	1980–90 change	1980–90 percent change
1	(2)	Los Angeles-Long Beach, CA	8,771	7,477	1,294	17.3%
2	(1)	New York, NY	8,625	8,275	350	4.2
3	(3)	Chicago, IL	6,308	6,060	247	4.1
4	(4)	Philadelphia, PA-NJ	4,973	4,717	256	5.4
5	(5)	Detroit, MI	4,409	4,488	–79	–1.8
6	(7)	Washington, DC-MD-VA	3,710	3,251	459	14.1
7	(8)	Houston, TX	3,509	2,735	774	28.3
8	(6)	Boston, MA	2,837	2,806	31	1.1
9	(13)	Atlanta, GA	2,744	2,138	605	28.3
10	(9)	Nassau-Suffolk, NY	2,736	2,606	130	5.0
11	(15)	Dallas, TX	2,615	1,957	658	33.6
12	(10)	St. Louis, MO-IL	2,511	2,377	134	5.6
13	(14)	Minneapolis-St. Paul, MN-WI	2,460	2,137	323	15.1
14	(19)	San Diego, CA	2,375	1,862	513	27.6
15	(12)	Baltimore, MD	2,352	2,199	153	6.9
16	(16)	Anaheim-Santa Ana, CA	2,294	1,933	361	18.7
17	(24)	Riverside-San Bernardino, CA	2,265	1,558	707	45.4
18	(25)	Phoenix, AZ	2,152	1,509	643	42.6
19	(22)	Tampa-St. Petersburg, FL	2,109	1,614	495	30.7
20	(11)	Pittsburgh, PA	2,085	2,219	–133	–6.0
21	(20)	Oakland, CA	2,033	1,762	272	15.4
22	(18)	Newark, NJ	1,913	1,879	34	1.8
23	(21)	Miami-Hialeah, FL	1,853	1,626	227	14.0
24	(23)	Seattle, WA	1,842	1,608	234	14.6
25	(17)	Cleveland, OH	1,832	1,899	–67	–3.5

Note: Geography for both the 1990 and 1980 metropolitan areas is defined as of June 30, 1988

1990 census will show Los Angeles-Long Beach replacing New York City as the most populous metropolitan area. L.A. grew by 17 percent since 1980, while New York City grew by just 4 percent.

Over the decade, Los Angeles-Long Beach gained more people than any other metropolitan area—1.3 million. Despite Houston's economic woes, that area gained fully 774,000 people. Riverside-San Bernardino, which borders the L.A. metropolitan area, comes in third with a gain of 700,000 people.

Among the 25 largest metropolitan areas, Riverside-San Bernardino has been the fastest growing—up 45 percent since 1980. But Phoenix follows closely with a 43 percent gain. Dallas, Tampa-St. Petersburg, Houston, Atlanta, and San Diego all grew by more than 25 percent in the 1980s. The only losers among the top 25 metros were Pittsburgh, Detroit, and Cleveland.

THE 1990 CENSUS WILL SHOW THAT THE NUMBER OF HOUSEHOLDS GREW BY 17 PERCENT DURING THE 1980s, FASTER THAN THE POPULATION AS A WHOLE.

Average household size continues to shrink—to 2.6 people per household in 1990, down from 2.8 in 1980.

The census will show that one in four households is a person who lives alone. The number of single-person households grew 24 percent in the 1980s. In sharp contrast, the number of married couples with children under age 18 in the home fell 1 percent—the only household type to decline in number. The fastest-growing family type was families headed by women with no husband present, up 36 percent during the decade.

The number of householders who live alone or with unrelated people (nonfamilies) grew 29 percent in the 1980s, compared with a 12 percent gain for families. Among nonfamilies, the fastest-growing household type was people living with nonrelatives. Over the decade, this type of household increased by 46 percent, to 4.5 million. Nonfamily households headed by men grew faster than those headed by women.

THE 1990 CENSUS WILL SHOW THAT MEDIAN HOUSEHOLD INCOME IS NEARLY $30,000—2.7 PERCENT GREATER THAN TEN YEARS EARLIER, AFTER ADJUSTING FOR INFLATION.

The gains in household income late in the decade more than made up for an 8 percent drop between 1980 and 1981. But these income gains have not been shared equally by all age groups.

The number of householders under age 25 fell by 43 percent during the 1980s as the baby-bust generation entered adulthood. The median household

LONE LIFESTYLE

(households and change in households, in thousands; percent distribution and percent change by household type, 1980–90)

	1990		1980		1980–90	
	households	percent distribution	households	percent distribution	change	percent change
All households	93,920	100.0%	80,467	100.0%	13,453	16.7%
Family households	66,542	70.8%	59,190	73.6%	7,352	12.4%
Married couples	52,837	56.3	48,990	60.9	3,847	7.9
Without children <18	28,315	30.1	24,210	30.1	4,105	17.0
With children <18	24,522	26.1	24,780	30.8	–258	–1.0
Other family, female head	11,130	11.9	8,205	10.2	2,925	35.6
Other family, male head	2,575	2.7	1,995	2.5	580	29.1
Nonfamily households	27,378	29.2%	21,277	26.4%	6,101	28.7%
Living alone	22,879	24.4	18,202	22.6	4,677	25.7
Men	9,119	9.7	7,075	8.8	2,044	28.9
Women	13,759	14.7	11,127	13.8	2,632	23.7
Living with nonrelatives	4,500	4.8	3,075	3.8	1,425	46.3
Male householder	2,803	3.0	1,866	2.3	937	50.2
Female householder	1,696	1.8	1,209	1.5	487	40.3

income of this age group also fell, to just $17,000 in 1989—10 percent less than in 1979, after adjusting for inflation.* This median is now just 7 percent greater than that of elderly householders. Ten years earlier, it was 35 percent greater.

The number of households headed by people aged 25 to 34 grew 15 percent since the last census. The median income of this group just kept pace with inflation.

Rapid growth in the number of middle-aged householders nearing their peak earning years boosted overall median household income in the 1980s. Householders aged 35 to 44 have the second highest median income, nearly $40,000 in 1989. During the 1980s, the number of households in this segment grew by 51 percent. Householders aged 45 to 54 have the highest median income—$42,200 in 1989, nearly 5 percent greater than in 1979, after adjusting for inflation.

The number of householders aged 55 to 64 is down 2 percent since the last

* *The census asks for income in the previous year.*

MIDLIFE MONOPOLY

(households and change in households, in thousands; percent change by age of householder, 1980–90)

	1990	1980	1980–90 change	1980–90 percent change
All households	93,920	80,390	13,530	16.8%
Under 25	4,683	6,709	–2,026	–30.2
25 to 34	21,191	18,351	2,840	15.5
35 to 44	21,059	13,948	7,111	51.0
45 to 54	14,330	12,630	1,700	13.5
55 to 64	12,349	12,617	–268	–2.1
65 and older	20,307	16,134	4,173	25.9

(median household income, change in income, and percent change by age of householder, 1979–89; in 1989 dollars)

	1989 median	1979 median	1979–89 change	1979–89 percent change
All households	$29,317	$28,554	$ 763	2.7%
Under 25	17,405	19,430	–2,026	–10.4
25 to 34	30,408	30,356	52	0.2
35 to 44	39,298	37,811	1,487	3.9
45 to 54	42,218	40,361	1,857	4.6
55 to 64	30,906	31,429	–523	–1.7
65 and older	16,335	14,374	1,961	13.6

Note: Income statistics refer to annual income in the year prior to the censuses.

census. The median income of this group also fell 2 percent over the decade. The trend toward early retirement is behind this income decline.

Householders aged 65 and older enjoyed the greatest economic gains during the 1980s. Increases in Social Security and in pension participation contributed to this group's 13 percent income gain.

THE 1990 CENSUS WILL SHOW WOMEN ACCOUNTING FOR ALMOST 60 PERCENT OF LABOR FORCE GROWTH SINCE 1980.

Today, fully 58 percent of women and 75 percent of men aged 16 or older are in the labor force.

Overall, the nation's work force grew by 17 percent since 1980. But changing demographics combined with shifting labor force participation rates

BULGE IN THE MIDDLE

(civilian labor force aged 16 and older by age and sex, in thousands; participation rates, and percent change in labor force, 1980–90)

	1990		1980		1980–90
	labor force	participation rate	labor force	participation rate	percent change in labor force
Labor force, aged 16 and older	121,861	66.6%	104,450	62.5%	16.7%
MEN	67,237	75.3%	59,926	75.8%	12.2%
16 to 24	10,971	70.6	12,591	68.9	–12.9
25 to 34	19,763	93.8	16,655	93.9	18.7
35 to 44	17,090	94.3	11,609	94.8	47.2
45 to 54	11,120	90.6	9,838	90.8	13.0
55 to 64	6,493	65.2	7,256	71.9	–10.5
65 and older	1,799	14.6	1,978	20.0	–9.0
WOMEN	54,368	58.3%	44,523	50.5%	26.6%
16 to 24	10,122	63.0	10,982	58.0	–7.8
25 to 34	16,368	75.4	12,112	64.9	35.1
35 to 44	14,692	77.8	8,446	64.8	74.0
45 to 54	8,665	70.6	6,916	59.0	25.3
55 to 64	5,247	44.2	4,824	41.9	8.8
65 and older	1,274	7.4	1,243	8.7	2.4

Note: The labor force consists of persons aged 16 and older working or looking for work. The labor force participation rate is the share of the population in an age group that is in the labor force.

resulted in a sharp decline in the number of entry-level workers and a decrease in the most experienced workers.

There are 13 percent fewer men aged 16 to 24 in the labor force, and 8 percent fewer women. In contrast, the number of workers aged 25 to 34 grew by 19 percent among men and 35 percent among women.

The aging of the baby boomers produced dramatic growth in the number of workers aged 35 to 44. Over the decade, the number of men aged 35 to 44 in the labor force rose by nearly 50 percent. As the labor-force participation rate for women aged 35 to 44 leaped from 65 to 78 percent, this group experienced a 74 percent numerical increase.

The number of women aged 55 to 64 who work increased by 8.8 percent since 1980, and the number of men in this age group who work dropped by 11 percent. Although labor-force participation rates for women aged 55 to 64 rose slightly during the 1980s, men's rates fell because of early retirement. That

BETTER EDUCATED

(educational attainment of noninstitutionalized adults aged 25 or older by sex and age, 1980 and 1990, in percent)

	1990			1980	
	percent high school graduates	percent college graduates	percent completing 4 or more yrs. of college*	percent high school graduates	percent completing 4 or more yrs. of college
All adults, aged 25 and older	77.3%	18.6%	20.3%	66.9%	16.4%
MEN	77.7%	21.9%	23.9%	67.7%	20.3%
25 to 34	86.5	21.3	24.5	84.8	26.5
35 to 44	87.1	28.3	30.8	77.3	24.5
45 to 54	79.1	24.6	25.5	65.8	19.8
55 to 64	68.1	18.9	20.7	56.3	14.3
65 and older	54.6	13.4	13.6	37.5	10.0
WOMEN	76.9%	15.6%	17.0%	66.2%	12.9%
25 to 34	87.8	20.5	23.6	84.1	20.4
35 to 44	86.6	20.6	22.5	76.4	14.9
45 to 54	79.2	14.9	15.4	66.7	10.5
55 to 64	70.2	10.1	11.1	57.6	8.0
65 and older	55.2	7.9	8.0	40.1	7.2

** This category will not be included in the 1990 census. These are* American Demographics' *estimates.*

drop, combined with a smaller population in this age group, is behind an overall 3 percent decline in the experienced work force.

THE 1990 CENSUS WILL SHOW THAT THE LEADING EDGE OF THE BABY BOOM—NOW AGED 35 TO 44—IS THE MOST EDUCATED GENERATION EVER.

One in four has completed at least four years of college. Younger men, aged 25 to 34, are now less likely to have completed four years of college than were the baby boomers ten years ago. The high cost of education may be pushing young adults out of college and into the work force.

One in five Americans has completed at least four years of college, up from one in six ten years ago. But you won't be able to make this comparison using the 1990 census. That's because this census will ask for the educational degrees people have earned, rather than number of years of school they have completed. Because not everyone who completes four years of college gets a degree, the share who graduate from college will be lower than the share who have attended college for at least four years. The 1990 census will show that nearly 19 percent of Americans have at least a bachelor's degree.

The census will also show that the educational gap between men and women is narrowing. Among people aged 45 to 54, the share of men with college degrees is 10 percentage points higher than the share of women. But among people aged 25 to 34, the difference is less than 1 percentage point. While the share of young men with four or more years of college dropped since 1980, the share of young women with four or more years of college grew.

The Census Means Business

The power to analyze census data will be available to more businesses than ever in the 1990s, thanks to advances in microcomputing and digital mapping.

by Joe Schwartz

Federal Express should be excited by the 1990 census. So should McDonald's, Domino's Pizza, and L. L. Bean. Advances in microcomputing technology combined with the federal government's efforts to take the 1990 census will revolutionize the analysis of local markets in the 1990s.

The 1980 census proved its value to many businesses. But few were equipped to interpret for themselves the census information contained on the bureau's computer tape files. Most of the businesses wanting to use detailed census data had to hire other businesses to digest census data for them. The latest advances in microcomputer technology will enable even the smallest of companies to put census data to work. "Data liberation" is what Edward Spar, president of Market Statistics of New York City, calls it. Data liberation will provide opportunities not only for the businesses that use census data, but also for those that provide the hardware and software to analyze it.

IN THE PIPELINE

Taken April 1, 1990, the next census will be available to the public through the Census Bureau's Data User Services Division and the U.S. Government Printing Office in Washington, D.C. State data centers will also make census data available to the public.

Each decennial census collects the same basic information from U.S. households, such as age, sex, and race. Some questions have been added to the 1990 questionnaire, while others have been dropped. The biggest change in the 1990 census, however, is in the way its data will be distributed.

Traditionally, census information has been released in three forms: printed reports, which have been available since 1790; computer tapes, available since 1960; and microfiche, first available in 1980. The 1990 census will be available on laser disks as well, reflecting a decade of change in microcomputer technology. By putting census data on laser disks, the Census Bureau is sowing fertile ground for the private sector.

The basic medium for distributing 1990 census data will be computer tapes, as it was in 1980. The census data the bureau distributes in printed reports, in microfiche, and on laser disks will be derived from the data the bureau puts on four census "summary tape files," or STFs.

STF-1 and STF-2 will contain data from the "short" census questionnaire answered by every household in the country. The population data include household type, race, Hispanic origin, sex, age, and marital status. The housing data include the number of units in a structure, the number of rooms in a housing unit, whether the structure is owned or rented, housing value, and monthly rent. The data in STF-1 will be geographically detailed down to the city block level. STF-2 will include more data than STF-1—specifically, separate tabulations of the housing and population data by race and Hispanic origin. But the geographic detail on STF-2 will end at the census tract level.

"We plan to make STF-2 available in two versions, so you can choose to buy only A records and not have the race repeats, or buy B records, which will give you a file completely iterated by race and Hispanic origin," explains Phil Fulton, assistant division chief for census programs in the bureau's Population Division.

STF-3 and STF-4 will contain the same basic data as the first two summary files, plus the information from the "long" census questionnaire. The long form answered by a 17 percent sample of households. The additional population data derived from the long form include income, educational attainment, migration, language, disability, labor-force status, place of work, and occupation. The additional housing data will include mortgages, plumbing facilities, kitchen facilities, telephone availability, number of vehicles, and fuel used to heat the home.

STF-3 will be critically important to marketers because it will contain ZIP Code data. In 1980, this file was produced as a special tabulation paid for by a consortium of private data companies. The 1990 ZIP Code file will be paid for with tax dollars and will contain demographic data for the five-digit ZIP Codes in each state, including county portions of ZIP Code areas.

STF-4 will contain less geographic data than STF-3, but STF-4 will have more demographic detail. "STF-4, like STF-2, contains records by race and ethnicity," says Fulton. But in STF-4, "the race and ethnic iterations include the 'long-form' information and show individual Asian and Pacific Islander groups as well as individual Hispanic groups."

The bureau expects the first summary tapes, which are released on a state-by-state basis, to be available to the public by mid-1991.

WHAT'S ON PAPER?

Printed reports from the census contain only the highlights and the commonly used tables. The first report series should be available by mid-1991. It will be published as a series of state reports and will be followed by a national summary.

Each summary tape file will form the basis for several series of state reports, national summaries, and other publications. From STF-2 will come reports on the population and housing characteristics for census tracts in metropolitan areas and for block numbering areas in the remainder of the country. The printed reports from STF-3 and STF-4 will include long-form population and housing data for states, counties, places, and census tracts.

Microfiche is an alternative to the printed reports because it takes up less storage space. Also, many of the tables not included in the printed reports will be on microfiche. "We use microfiche for the block statistics because the block statistics are so voluminous," says Fulton. "Putting data on microfiche allows users who don't have access to tapes or the capability of processing tapes to get access to block statistics for a community."

DESKTOP DRAMA

For businesses, the action will be in laser disks. Also called compact disks read-only mode or CD-ROM, these have enormous potential because they can be used in desktop information systems. Each 4 5/8-inch laser disk can store as much information as three computer tapes or 1,500 floppy disks. "Laser disks have the same data as computer tapes. They are just packaged differently," Fulton says.

"The bureau has not made a final decision about which summary tape files will be on laser disks," says Fulton. "The expectation is that the most popular census files will be the first to be produced using CD-ROM technology—such as the STF-1 and STF-3 files." After the bureau produces the summary tape files for a particular state, it may transfer the data to one or more laser disks, allowing businesses to buy the entire collection of decennial census data by state.

Laser disks can hold as much information as computer tapes, and they don't require an expensive mainframe computer to process them. "With the addition of a [laser disk] reader to your microcomputer, your microcomputer becomes a slower mainframe," Fulton says. "You can use your microcomputer with a [laser disk] reader to print out any table in a summary tape file on demand. The sky is the limit if you are creative."

Despite their advantages, the bureau is not using laser disks as the basic medium for distributing 1990 census data, because as yet, there is no standardization in disk technology. Until there is standardization, as well as user-friendly software, widespread acceptance of the disks will be slowed. "Dumping data on these disks will not create demand," says Spar of Market Statistics.

MAPPING NEW GROUND

Perhaps the most revolutionary technology of the 1990 census is the TIGER digital map boundary file. Adaptable to microcomputers, TIGER (which stands for Topologically Integrated Geographic Encoding and Referencing) is "a digital street map of the country," says Don Cook, president of Geographic Data Technology in Lyme, New Hampshire. The digital mapping capabilities of TIGER—whether it is merged with census data or not—have enormous potential for businesses, from market research to site planning and logistics.

"The commercial uses of TIGER will outweigh all of the commercial value of the census data itself," Cook says. "This sounds heretical, but if you can show someone who is running a fleet that they can operate for 5 percent, 10 percent, or 15 percent less, you're talking a lot of money." Federal Express and other overnight package delivery companies, for example, will be able to use TIGER to show their fleet operators which driver is nearest to a package, and what are the most economical routing and dispatching patterns.

The Census Bureau released prototype TIGER files for all U.S. counties this year, and will release versions with 1990 census boundaries in 1991, says Robert Marx, chief of the Census Bureau's Geography Division. The bureau's preliminary plans envision TIGER boundary files for counties, census tracts, block numbering areas, and county subdivisions, according to Marx. The TIGER files currently available are only on magnetic tape, according to Marx. But, he says, "the bureau is looking at the possibility of releasing TIGER on CD-ROM as well."

TIGER files contain only geographical information—individual streets and other features digitally coded by latitude and longitude. They will not contain any 1990 census data. "That's the sort of thing that will be done by the private sector," Marx says.

The private sector is not waiting around for the 1990 census. Geographic Data Technology is marketing its "Safari" software for evaluating TIGER files. Space Time Research of Melbourne, Australia, has already merged 1980 census data with geographic boundary files on a CD-ROM for its Supermap

GEOGRAPHY TEST

The 1990 census will provide data for a variety of geographic areas, most of which are heirarchical—meaning the smaller areas are subunits of the next larger areas. These units range from the U.S. as a whole down to city blocks. Below is the geographic heirarchy in which most census data will be arranged, in descending order:

TERM	*DEFINITION*
U.S.*	The 50 states and the District of Columbia.
Region	The four regions are the Northeast, South, Midwest, and West.
Division	The four regions are split into nine divisions. Individual states combine to form divisions.
State	The 50 states and the District of Columbia are subunits of the nine divisions.
County	Counties are subunits of states. The 3,141 counties are divided into two types of subunits: minor civil divisions (MCDs) or census county divisions (CCDs); and census tracts.
Minor civil division/census county division	Minor civil divisions (MCDs) are county subunits. MCDs are defined by the municipal governments within each county. In the 21 states that are not subdivided into MCDs, the bureau creates census county divisions (CCDs). Every county is completely divided into MCDs or CCDs.
Place	Places include incorporated places and census designated places. Incorporated places are defined by the laws of states to include cities, boroughs, towns, and villages. Census designated places are created by the Census Bureau to include boundaries of closely settled population centers without corporate limits. Before 1980, census designated places were called unincorporated places. Places can cross MCD or county lines, but not state lines.
Census tract/ block numbering area	Census tracts/block numbering areas are also county subunits. Census tracts are defined by local committees and follow guidelines prepared by the Census Bureau. Block numbering areas are defined by the bureau in areas that don't have census tracts. When first defined, these areas are to contain an average of 4,000 people, having generally similar socioeconomic characteristics.
Block group	Block groups are the subunits of census tracts or block numbering areas. Block groups have an average of 1,000 people living in them. They are new versions of the 1980 block groups or enumeration districts. Block groups combine to form census tracts and block numbering areas, which combine to form counties.
Block	Roughly equivalent to a city block, census blocks are the smallest level of census geography, but they are bounded by water, roads, railroads, and other physical features. Blocks combine to form block groups, which combine to form census tracts/block numbering areas. For 1990, the entire nation is divided into blocks.

** Puerto Rico, U.S. Virgin Islands, Guam, and outlying areas in the Pacific will not be included in the U.S. totals, but the same reports will be available for these areas as those published for states.*

software. Both the census data and the digital maps are stored on a single laser disk. "Supermap frees the U.S. census from the tiny elite who have access to mainframe computers," says a spokesperson for Space Time Research. The company will release a 1990 version of Supermap that will include both TIGER files and data from the 1990 census, says Alan Fox, director of customer service at Chadwyck-Healey, the U.S. marketing representative for Space Time Research.

"Data are not the issue anymore," explains Spar of Market Statistics. "The issue is what you can do with the data."

The Census Bureau will include only the most basic software with its laser-disk products, explains Peter Bounpane, deputy director of the decennial census. "These are areas where the private sector can—and does—fill the void pretty well." The private data vendors will continue to fill this void despite "data liberation," industry officials say.

"People think that because the summary tape files are on CD-ROM they're going to get easy results," says Jim Paris, senior associate at Urban Decisions Systems, a Los Angeles-based private data company. "What they don't understand is that there are lots of data on those files that they don't need."

Analyzing the data to solve business problems is what the private data industry is all about. This will continue, with or without CD-ROM technology, another industry expert says. The bottom line is that CD-ROM will not hurt the industry. "Nobody wants to buy data. People are looking for solutions," says Keith Wardell, senior vice president for corporate product development at National Decision Systems of Encinitas, California. "The private data industry will have to deliver solutions to their clients' problems. It is the integration and analysis of data that the majority of companies will be hired to do."

Private data companies will have a market as long as their mission differs from the Census Bureau's, adds Tony Phillips, account executive with Equifax Marketing Decision Systems in Vienna, Virginia. The Census Bureau's mission is to deliver to Congress the information it needs for reapportionment and redistricting, and to supply accurate and timely data accessible to a wide range of users. "Private industry has the responsibility to take the raw data, clean them up, and package them in a way that is useful to business," Phillips says.

A Guide to the 1990 Census

Here is a guide to how and when the 1990 census data will be released

by Joe Schwartz

Don't expect instant gratification from the 1990 census. Census Bureau officials plan to distribute all census computer tapes, reports, maps, and other products on a "flow basis," beginning in 1991. The last of the census data won't be in your hands until 1993.

Census data will be released in several formats, including traditional paper reports, microfiche, computer tapes, floppy disks, and CD-ROM (compact disk-read only memory). The first information released will be "100 percent" data, or information from the short census forms sent to all U.S. households. Data gleaned from the short forms will be included in the computer tape files STF-1 and STF-2 (STF stands for summary tape file because the data are summarized for geographic areas to mask information about individuals).

But "businesses don't want to twiddle their thumbs waiting for STF-1," says Ed Spar, president of Market Statistics, a demographic data firm based in New York City. For the impatient, there is the "public law file," officially called the "Public Law 94-171 Program." This file includes the data needed to meet the constitutional requirements for congressional redistricting. By law, the Census Bureau must hand this file over to the President by December 31, 1990. The file will be distributed in early 1991 on computer tape and in printed reports. Although it holds less information than the summary tape files, it provides businesses with an important early start on the census data.

The public law file includes total population counts for each state by race and Hispanic origin cross-tabulated by all ages. The information is organized in a geographic hierarchy from the state level to the block level.

STF-1 and STF-2 include more demographic detail than the public law file. Target marketers and businesses providing custom demographic data are interested in these files' cross-tabulations of age, race, and characteristics of householders.

Information collected on the "long-form" census questionnaire, which is

COMPUTER TAPES AND CD-ROM

The Census Bureau will tabulate the 1990 census data and put them on a series of computer tapes, called "Summary Tape Files" or STFs. The Census Bureau's Data User Services Division will sell these tapes on a state-by-state basis. There may be only one reel of tape for a small state like Vermont, but several tapes for a larger state like California. The census data on CD-ROM will be derived from the summary data on the computer tapes. Here is a listing of the census tapes and disks the bureau will make available, and their release dates.

summary tape file	*population and housing data*	*geographic coverage*
STF-1A	Age, sex, race, household relationship, marital status, and Hispanic origin. Number of units in a structure, number of rooms in housing unit, whether structure is owned or rented by occupants, value of owned units, and rents paid on rental units. *Available on tape & CD-ROM:* 1991–92	State data down to block group level.
STF-1B	Same as STF-1A *Available on tape:* 1991–92 *Available on CD-ROM:* 1992	State data down to block level.
STF-1C	Same as STF-1A *Available on tape & CD-ROM:* 1992	Data for the U.S., regions, divisions, states, counties, places of 10,000 or more; minor civil divisions of 10,000 or more in selected states, metropolitan, and urbanized areas.
STF-1D	Same as STF-1A *Available on tape:* 1993 *Not available on CD-ROM*	State data on congressional districts of the 103rd Congress; separate tabulation for counties, places of 10,000 or more, and minor civil divisions of 10,000 or more (in selected states) within each congressional district.
STF-2A	Same data items as STF-1A, more detail. Separate files available for the total population and for the major race and Hispanic origin groups. *Available on tape:* 1992 *Not available on CD-ROM*	Data for each state down to the census tract and block group levels.
STF-2B	Same as STF-2A *Available on tape:* 1992 *Not available on CD-ROM*	Data for states, counties, places of 1,000 or more, minor civil divisions of 1,000 or more in selected states.

summary tape file	population and housing data	geographic coverage
STF-2C	Same as STF-2A *Available on tape:* 1992 *Not available on CD-ROM*	Data for the U.S., census regions, divisions, states, counties, places of 10,000 or more, minor civil divisions of 10,000 or more in selected states, and metropolitan and urbanized areas.
STF-3A	Same as STF-2A. Plus data from long form, such as income, educational attainment, migration, language, disability, labor force status, place of work, and occupation. Plumbing facilities, kitchen facilities, telephone, number of vehicles, heating fuel, gross rent, mortgages, and home equity loans. *Available on tape & CD-ROM:* 1992	Data on social, economic, and housing characteristics for states. Similar to STF-1A. Data for states in hierarchical order down to the block group level.
STF-3B	Same as STF-3A *Available on tape & CD-ROM:* 1993	Data by 5-digit ZIP Code areas for each state, including county portions of ZIP Code areas.
STF-3C	Same as STF-3A *Available on tape & CD-ROM:* 1993	Similar to STF-1C. Data for the U.S., regions, divisions, states, counties, places of 10,000 or more, minor civil divisions of 10,000 or more in selected states and for metropolitan and urbanized areas.
STF-3D	Same as STF-3A *Available on tape:* 1993 *Not available on CD-ROM*	State data on congressional districts of the 103rd Congress; separate tabulation for counties, places of 10,000 or more, and minor civil divisions of 10,000 or more within each congressional district.
STF-4A	Same data items as STF-3A, more detail. Plus data iterated by white, black, individual Asian groups, and individual Hispanic ethnic groups. *Available on tape:* 1992-93 *Not available on CD-ROM*	Similar to STF-2A. Data for states down to census tract and block group areas.
STF-4B	Same as STF-4A *Available on tape:* 1992-93 *Not available on CD-ROM*	Similar to STF-2B. Data by state, county, places of 2,500 or more, minor civil divisions of 2,500 or more in selected states and in minor civil divisions of less than 2,500 in New England metropolitan areas.
STF-4C	Same as STF-4A *Available on tape:* 1993 *Not available on CD-ROM*	Similar to STF-2C. Data for U.S., census regions, divisions, states, counties, places of 10,000 or more, minor civil divisions of 10,000 or more in selected states and metropolitan and urbanized areas.

sent to a 19 percent sample of the population, will be released in mid-1992. Long-form data, which are on summary tape files STF-3 and STF-4, include social, economic, and detailed housing characteristics in addition to the short-form data.

STF-3 is the "mother lode" for businesses, says Market Statistics' Spar. STF-3 includes everything on the first two summary tape files, plus socioeconomic characteristics from the long form.

This file includes "journey to work" information vital to city planners. It includes occupational, educational, employment, and detailed housing characteristics, such as the number of years a householder has lived at the residence and the age of the structure. Length of stay and age of structure provide vital information for hardware chains and other businesses supplying goods and services for renovations. STF-3 also includes demographic and socioeconomic data arranged by ZIP Code, a boon for direct marketers. STF-4 has even more detail than STF-3, but it is rarely used because it is so large.

Businesses will have to choose which census media are best for them. Some will hire demographic data firms to do their number crunching, while others may opt for detailed information on CD-ROM.

A listing of the census tapes and disks the bureau will make available and their release dates, appears on the following two pages.

CHAPTER 4

Federal Government Sources

Don't be dissuaded from using government data because you think they're too complicated to use or too out of date. Federal agencies spend a lot of time and tax dollars to ensure that the information they provide is accurate. Take advantage of their efforts.

How to Use This Chapter

The federal agencies listed here are in alphabetical order, except for the Census Bureau, which is listed first because of its overwhelming wealth of information. Read the introductory article on "Navigating the Census Bureau" and get a feel for how down-to-earth and accessible (and cheap) government data can be.

A lot of government data are available only for the U.S. as a whole, but there are a number of exceptions, notably the 1990 census. Read carefully to find if you can get current demographic or economic data for the level of geography you need.

Many government surveys have samples much larger than those conducted by commercial vendors. As a result, the data take longer to process, but sometimes it's worth the wait. (This is not to say that private vendors provide poor data. See Chapter 5 for a discussion of what to look for when buying from the commercial sector.)

THE LISTINGS:

Navigating the Census Bureau

Data from the world's largest provider of consumer information are just a telephone call away.

Most people are familiar with the census. Every ten years, the Census Bureau attempts to count everyone in the U.S. Along the way, it collects information on our socioeconomic characteristics. This information is used for Congressional reapportionment, the allocation of federal funds, site location for businesses, and much more. The data are also used as a benchmark for the annual population estimates and projections private companies produce between censuses.

The Census Bureau does much more than conduct the census. It also monitors the population through its many surveys.

Perhaps the most useful of these is the monthly **Current Population Survey,** or CPS. The bureau has conducted the CPS since 1947. To collect CPS data, the Census Bureau surveys 60,000 households each month. The survey's primary purpose is to collect employment and unemployment data for the Bureau of Labor Statistics. The CPS includes the same questions on employment every month, and some months it also includes questions asked only once a year. In September, the CPS asks about school enrollment; in June it asks about fertility; in March it asks about a variety of household characteristics, including income.

The March CPS is the standard source of household and income data used by many businesses. When you see statistics about the rise in median income and the decline of traditional families, they probably came from the last March CPS. Market research firms often use the March CPS to demographically balance their own survey samples, ensuring that they are nationally representative.

OTHER SURVEYS

The Census Bureau also conducts the ongoing **Consumer Expenditure Survey,** or CEX, for the Bureau of Labor Statistics. This survey's main purpose is to update prices for the market basket of goods used in calculating the Consumer Price Index. But the CEX also provides valuable information about the full range of household expenditures.

The CEX is really two surveys—a diary survey and an interview survey. For the diary survey, respondents keep a detailed diary of their expenditures for frequently purchased items, such as food and gasoline, for a two-week period. In the interview survey, respondents report the big-ticket items they bought during the year, including houses and cars. In the past, the CEX was conducted only every ten years. Since 1980 it has been conducted continually, and the BLS publishes the data on an annual basis.

Then there is the **Survey of Income and Program Participation,** or SIPP. As with other Census Bureau surveys, the main purpose of SIPP is to provide information on the population to government agencies. The focus of this survey, as far as the government is concerned, is to examine shifts in people's economic status. But for the business community it is an excellent source of data on wealth. SIPP has been conducted only since 1982.

The **American Housing Survey** (AHS) is taken by the Census Bureau for the Department of Housing and Urban Development. Formerly, it was called the Annual Housing Survey, but it is now conducted every other year—thus, the name change. The AHS surveys a national sample of nearly 50,000 households, including a representative sample in 11 metropolitan areas each time it's taken. In all, the bureau covers 44 metropolitan areas on a rotating basis. The survey collects structural and financial information about housing units, as well as demographic data about people who live in the units.

EVERYTHING ELSE

The Census Bureau also produces **estimates and projections of the population.** Each year, the bureau publishes population estimates by age, sex, and race for the U.S., as well as total population estimates for states, metropolitan areas, and counties. Every few years it publishes long-term projections of the U.S. population by age, sex, and race. It recently began to project the Hispanic population as well.

The bureau's **economic division** conducts economic censuses for all industries every five years. The most recent censuses were taken in 1987, and the data are just being released now. The economic division also produces reports on monthly retail sales, tracks new construction, and publishes the annual *County Business Patterns* reports.

The bureau's **geographic division** provides maps and boundary information for all types of census geography—counties, metropolitan areas, census tracts, blocks and block groups, enumeration districts, voting districts, and so on. The Census Bureau does not produce maps, or data, for noncensus geography, such as ADIs, DMAs, or utility territories.

You can get international demographic and economic data from the Census Bureau's **Center for International Research**. The center has a large collection of census and survey data from other countries and has subject specialists on each region of the world.

HOW TO GET THE DATA

Although the Census Bureau produces an overwhelming assortment of information, it's easy to keep up with it. The annual *Census Catalog and Guide* lists everything available from the bureau, from printed reports to computer tapes. The catalog is available from the U.S. Government Printing Office, Washington, DC 20402; telephone **202-783-3238.**

The most important survey results are published in the Census Bureau's *Current Population Reports* series. Population estimates and projections are in the P-25 series. Data from the Survey of Income and Program Participation are in Series P-70, "Household Economic Studies." Current Population Survey data are in several series. The P-60 series, "Consumer Income," tracks income at the household, family, and individual level. Series P-20, "Population Characteristics," covers household and family characteristics, marital status and living arrangements, geographic mobility, fertility, farm population, and voting behavior. Series P-23, "Special Studies," reports on miscellaneous topics, such as after-tax income. Data from the American Housing Survey are published in *Current Housing Reports*.

Most *Current Population Reports* are issued annually, although the timing is not always predictable. Subscriptions to these inexpensive reports are available through the U.S. Government Printing Office. Data from the Consumer Expenditure Survey, which is analyzed by the Bureau of Labor Statistics, are published in a series of occasional BLS bulletins. These are also available from the U.S. Government Printing Office.

The Census Bureau's wheels are exceedingly large, and they grind slowly. Data are often published years after they've been collected. But the bureau has a lot of information available long before it is published. Call the Public Information Office at **301-763-4040** for a free four-page telephone listing of subject specialists at the bureau. With this handy reference, you can call real people and ask them about anything from household income to the definition of the Chicago metropolitan area. They won't charge you, either. You've already paid for these services with your tax dollars.

U.S. BUREAU OF THE CENSUS

The Census Bureau has a lot more than census data. Take a look at its current surveys, estimates and projections, economic data, and international resources.

Data User Services Division
Bureau of the Census
Washington, DC 20233

Main contact:
Customer Services
301-763-4100
(See page 76 for a complete list, by subject, of the phone numbers of the hundreds of specialists who can answer your questions about everything from households and families to state population projections.)

The U.S. Census Bureau is by far the world's largest supplier of demographic data. It conducts a census of the United States once every ten years, and it monitors ongoing changes with the monthly Current Population Survey and the Survey of Income and Program Participation. It also prepares regular estimates and projections of the population by demographic characteristics such as sex, age, and race.

The Bureau also conducts many surveys for other branches of the government, and has an enormous network of specialists in population, housing, economic, and geographic areas.

For More Information

The ***Census Catalog and Guide*** is a very useful publication for understanding everything the Census Bureau offers and how to order it. Available annually from the Government Printing Office, Washington, DC 20402; phone **202-783-3238.**

To keep up with new bureau publications and other products on a more timely basis, subscribe to the monthly ***Census and You*** newsletter, also available from the GPO. You can also call the friendly and helpful Customer Services staff at the Census Bureau: **301-763-4100.**

What You Can Get From the Census Bureau

DECENNIAL CENSUS

The 1990 census was taken on April 1. But it will be at least a year before any substantial data are released from this enormous undertaking. Chapter 3 outlines a preliminary product release schedule, although you can expect this to change. To keep up with what's going on with census data, subscribe to the bureau's *Census and You* newsletter.

The census provides data for a wide variety of geographic areas on a broad range of population characteristics. It asks people about their basic demographic characteristics—sex, age, race, ethnicity, and fertility. It also covers their socioeconomic characteristics—ancestry, marital status, household composition, language, disability, geographic mobility, education, labor force status, occupation and industry, journey to work, and income. The housing portion of the census collects structural and financial data on housing units.

Census data are published in printed reports, computer tapes, maps, microdata, and now, for the first time, on CD-ROM. The 1990 census will provide data for many geographic levels, including states, counties, metropolitan areas, ZIP Codes, census tracts, and even city blocks. Not all data are available for all geographic levels, because not everyone answers all of the census questions. See Chapter 3 for a listing of what different census products will contain.

NOTE: *Neither the Census Bureau nor any other government agency collects information about religion. They are not permitted to do so, because of the U.S. constitutional separation of church and state. Go to private sources for religious information.*

BETWEEN CENSUSES—THE CURRENT POPULATION SURVEY

Between censuses, you can get up-to-date information about the population from the Current Population Survey, or CPS, at least on a national level.

The CPS is conducted each month. Its primary purpose is to collect employment data for the Bureau of Labor Statistics, but it gathers all kinds of other data along the way. Interviewers ask people in about 60,000 households across the country about their employment-related activities during the preceding week. Each household is interviewed for four consecutive months, dropped for eight months, and then interviewed over the same four months the following year.

Although the CPS sample is very large as surveys go, it is not large enough to provide data for small geographic areas. The bureau normally only publishes data for the U.S. as a whole, and sometimes for the four census regions (North, Midwest, South, and West) and the largest states and metropolitan areas, when the sample is large enough to produce valid data.

As with the decennial census, CPS data are available in

CURRENT POPULATION REPORTS

printed reports or on computer tape. The publications are known as Current Population Reports and there are three series of them:

Population Characteristics (Series P-20)

These annual reports are on education, fertility, geographic residence and mobility, households and families, marital status, Spanish origin, farm population, etc. Biennial reports examine voter registration and participation.

Consumer Income (Series P-60)

This series has tables which cross-classify income and poverty status with U.S. data on race and Spanish origin, age, farm versus nonfarm residence, sex, education, occupation, marital status, size and type of family.

Special Census Bureau Studies (Series P-23)

These reports furnish information about such topics as the older population, youth, women, metropolitan and nonmetropolitan residents, etc. For a complete list of P-23 reports that are available, see the *Census Catalog and Guide*.

A subscription to the three series of reports is $96 a year and can be ordered from the Government Printing Office; **202-783-3238.** Each of these series also contains reports that show research/developmental results. They are designated "RD" and contain research results rather than official Census Bureau figures.

Tapes from the regular part of the survey, which gathers data for the Department of Labor's monthly report on employment and unemployment, are usually available within two months of the survey. Tapes for supplementary questions to the survey, which gather the data for the Current Population Reports, are usually not ready until at least six months after the survey. Order from Customer Services at the Census Bureau.

POPULATION ESTIMATES AND PROJECTIONS *(Series P-25 & 26)*

The Census Bureau regularly provides current estimates and projections of the U.S. population, which are published in Current Population Reports Series P-25 and P-26. The series include estimates of:

- *total U.S. population (monthly)*
- *population by age, sex, and race (annual midyear)*
- *population of states by age (annual)*
- *population of counties and metropolitan areas (annual)*
- *population and per capita income for counties and incorporated areas (every two years, series P-26)*

The series also include long-range projections of the population by age, race, and sex. The latest volume in the series covers the years 1988 to 2080, and includes data by single years of age; a report projecting the voting-age population appears in alternate years before each Congressional election.

A subscription to series P-25 costs $20 a year and can be ordered from the Government Printing Office, as can individual reports in the P-26 series.

SURVEY OF INCOME AND PROGRAM PARTICIPATION (SIPP)

SIPP is a longitudinal survey that was designed to collect information on the economic, demographic, and social situations of Americans. Each individual in a sample of households is interviewed at four-month intervals for a period of 2-1/2 years.

Core questions, which are repeated at each interview, cover labor force activity, types and amounts of income, and participation in various cash and noncash benefit programs for each month of the four-month reference period. Data for employed persons include hours and weeks worked and earnings, and weeks without a job. In addition to income derived from working, data for nearly 50 other types of income are collected, including government and transfer payments, pensions, and income from assets.

Topical modules with questions on other specific topics are included during various waves. They include questions on child care arrangements, child support agreements, health insurance and coverage, fertility, marital, and migration history, assets and liabilities, welfare history, pension coverage, employment history, education, health status, and others.

For general information about the SIPP, order the *Survey of Income and Program Participation Users' Guide,* which contains general information on the survey content, sample design, and procedures for estimation and calculation of sampling variability, as well as a glossary of selected terms; $10 from Customer Services at the Census Bureau.

Get printed data from the SIPP in the *Household Economic Studies* (Series P-70). These publications cover data on income, labor force activity, participation in government assistance programs, and other related subjects collected in the SIPP's topical modules (see above listing).

The series of occasional reports is available for $11 a year from the Government Printing Office.

Related printed reports from the SIPP include working papers written by Census Bureau staff, compilations of papers presented at annual meetings of the American Statistical Association, articles appearing in the *Journal of Economic and Social Measurement,* and conference proceedings. Contact the bureau's Customer Services office for a free listing.

SIPP computer tapes are available on a "wave-by-wave" basis, meaning that the four months of a given round of interviews are on one tape. These files are suitable for cross-sectional analysis. Researchers can also create longitudinal files by matching the waves for an entire panel. Tapes can be ordered from Customer Services at the Census Bureau.

SIPP data are also available as Full Panel Microdata Research Files, which contain monthly observations for a subset of the data from the individual wave files, generally providing 32 monthly observations of household composition, labor force activity, income, and participation in various cash and noncash benefit programs. They are available through the SIPP Research and Coordination Staff (Office of the Director).

SPECIAL CENSUSES

The Census Bureau takes special population censuses at the request and expense of city or other local governments. Periodic summaries showing population figures for all the censuses conducted during the period are available in *Current Population Reports Series P-28,* as are individual reports issued for areas of 50,000 or more, showing population by age, sex, and race. Order from the Government Printing Office.

MAPS

At this point, census maps generally show boundaries as of January 1, 1980, and they fall into three categories: outline maps in the publications, outline maps sold separately, and display maps. With the advent of the TIGER file, however, a new generation of maps will appear. See page 43 for more about this important advance in census technology.

Outline maps in data publications show only the areas to which data can be related, and do not show any data themselves. They cover congressional districts, county subdivisions, MSA blocks, state blocks, state and U.S.

MSAs, and urbanized areas. Outline maps sold separately come in five basic types: counties, Indian reservations, places, place-and-vicinities, metropolitan vicinities. Display maps sometimes include demographic or economic data. They are described in detail in the *Census Catalog and Guide*.

To order maps, or for more information, contact Customer Services. To order maps that are out of print or to order individual maps, contact the Data Preparation Division, Geography Branch, Bureau of the Census, Jeffersonville, IN 47132; **812-288-3213.**

ECONOMIC DATA

The Census Bureau is part of the Department of Commerce, and has an economic division that conducts economic censuses of all industries every five years. The most current data available are from the 1987 census. The division also collects and disseminates data on monthly retail sales, residential construction and a variety of other subjects. See the phone listing on page 82 for more information about what the economic division provides.

INTERNATIONAL DATA

The bureau's Center for International Research provides a huge array of demographic information for other countries. See page 255 for a full description of this group.

U.S. BUREAU OF THE CENSUS

Telephone Contact Listing

U.S. Department of
Commerce
Washington, DC 20233

CENSUS HELPLINES
(most frequently called numbers)

General Information (Data User Services) *Customer Services Staff*	**301-763-4100**
Office of Congressional Affairs *Mark Neuman, Chief*	**763-2446**
Public Information Office *Staff*	**763-4040**

DEMOGRAPHIC PROGRAMS

Center for Demographic Studies *James R. Wetzel, Chief*	**763-7720**
Center for International Research *Barbara Boyle Torrey, Chief*	**763-2870**
Center for Survey Methods Research *Elizabeth A. Martin, Chief*	**763-3838**
Decennial Operations Division *Arnold A. Jackson, Chief*	**763-2682**
Decennial Planning Division	**763-7670**
Demographic Surveys Division *Thomas C. Walsh, Chief*	**763-2776**
Geography Division *Robert W. Marx, Chief*	**763-5636**
Housing Division *Acting Chief*	**763-2863**
International Statistical Programs Center *Robert O. Bartram, Chief*	**763-2832**
Population Division *Paula Schneider, Chief*	**763-7646**
Statistical Methods Division *Preston Jay Waite, Chief*	**763-2672**
Statistical Research Division *Acting Chief*	**763-3807**

	Statistical Support Division *Acting Chief*	**763-4072**
	21st Century Decennial Census Planning	**763-8601**
POPULATION & HOUSING SUBJECTS	**Age and Sex** (states and counties) *Staff*	**763-5072**
	Age and Sex (U.S.) *Staff*	**763 -7950**
	Age Search *Census History Staff*	**763-7936**
	Aging Population *Arnold Goldstein*	**763-7883**
	Apportionment *Robert Speaker*	**763-7962**
	Child Care *Amara Bachn*	**763-5303**
	Citizenship: Foreign Born/Stock, Country of Birth *Staff*	**763-7955**
	Commuting: Means of Transportation, Place of Work *Phil Salopek/Celia Boertlein*	**763-3850**
	Consumer Expenditure Survey *Gail Hoff*	**763-2063**
	Crime Surveys: Victimization, General Information *Larry McGinn*	**763-1735**
	Current Population Survey *Ronald Tucker*	**763-2773**
DECENNIAL CENSUS	**Content & Tabulations–Program Design** *Patricia Berman*	**763-7094**
	Count for Current Boundaries *Joel Miller*	**763-5720**
	Count Questions–1990 Census *Ed Kobilarcik*	**763-4894**
	Content (General) *Al Paez*	**763-4251**
	Tabulations and Publications (General)	**763-3938**
	Special Tabulations: Housing Data *Bill Downs*	**763-8553**

***Census Bureau:* POPULATION & HOUSING SUBJECTS** *(continued)*	**Decennial Census** *(continued)*	
	Special Tabulations: Population Data *Rosemarie Cowan*	**301-763-7947**
	User Defined Areas Program (UDAP) *Adrienne Quasney*	**763-4282**
DISABILITY	**Disability** *Jack McNeil*	**763-8300**
EDUCATION	**Education, School Enrollment and Social Stratification** *Staff*	**763-1154**
EMPLOYMENT	**Employment, Unemployment, Labor Force** *Thomas Palumbo*	**763-8574**
FARM POPULATION	**Farm Population** *Don Dahmann/Diana DeAre*	**763-5158**
FERTILITY	**Fertility/Births, Number of** *Martin O'Connell/Amara Bachu*	**763-5303**
HEALTH	**Health Surveys** *Robert Mangold*	**763-5508**
HOMELESSNESS	**Homeless Population** *Cynthia Taeuber*	**763-7883**
HOUSEHOLDS	**Household Estimates for States & Counties** *Campbell Gibson*	**763-5221**
	Household Wealth *Enrique Lamas*	**763-8578**
	Households and Families *Staff*	**763-7987**
HOUSING	**American Housing Survey** *Edward Montfort*	**763-8551**
	Components of Inventory Change Survey *Jane Maynard*	**763-8551**
	Information, Decennial Census *Bill Downs*	**763-8553**
	Market Absorption/Residential Finance *Anne Smoler/Peter Fronczek*	**763-8552**
	New York City Housing & Vacancy Survey *Margaret Hooper*	**763-8552**
IMMIGRATION	**Immigration** (Legal/Undocumented), **Emigration** *Karen Woodrow*	**763-5590**

INCOME	**Income Statistics** *Staff*	**301-763-8576**
	Income Surveys *Chester Bowie*	**763-2764**
	Institutional Population *Denise Smith*	**763-7883**
INTERNATIONAL STATISTICS	**Africa, Latin America, Asia, Oceania & North America** *Frank Hobbs*	**763-4221**
	China, People's Republic of *Judith Banister*	**763-4012**
	Europe Godfrey Baldwin	**763-4022**
	Health *Peter Way*	**763-4086**
	International Data Base *Peter Johnson*	**763-4811**
	Soviet Union *Barry Kostinsky*	**763-4022**
	Women in Development *Ellen Jamison*	**763-4086**
JOURNEY TO WORK	**Journey to Work** *Phil Salopek*	**763-3850**
LANGUAGE	**Language, Current: Mother Tongue** *Staff*	**763-1154**
LONGITUDINAL SURVEYS	**Longitudinal Surveys** *Ronald Dopkowski*	**763-2767**
MARITAL STATUS	**Marital Status, Living Arrangements** *Arlene Saluter*	**763-7987**
MIGRATION	**Migration and Geographic Mobility** *Diana DeAre*	**763-3850**
OCCUPATION STATISTICS	**Occupation and Industry Statistics** *John Priebe/Wilfred Masumura* *(see also Economic Subjects)*	**763-8574**
PLACE OF BIRTH	**Place of Birth** *Kristin Hansen*	**763-3850**
POPULATION	**General Information, Published Data from Censuses, Surveys, Estimates, and Projections** *Staff*	**763-5002** or **763-5020 (TTY)**

Census Bureau: POPULATION & HOUSING SUBJECTS

POPULATION *(continued)*

Population Estimates, Projections, Methodology & Research

Counties (total), MSAs, Places, Congressional Districts Methodology — **301-763-7722**, **763-7964**
Staff

Experimental County Estimates — **763-5072**
Sam Davis

National Population Estimates & Projections — **763-7950**
Staff

Race Estimates Research — **763-7964**
David Word

State Population Projections — **763-1902**
Staff

States and Outlying Areas Estimates Research — **736-5072**
Staff

Hispanic and Other Ethnic Populations — **763-7955**
Staff

Race Statistics — **763-2607**
Staff — **763-7572**

OTHER POPULATION AND HOUSING SUBJECTS

Postcensal Net Migration Estimates — **763-7722**
Staff

Poverty Statistics — **763-8578**
(Decennial Census & Current Surveys)
Staff

Prisoner Surveys: National Prisoner Statistics — **763-1735**
Larry McGinn

Reapportionment/Redistricting — **763-3856**
Marshall Turner/Cathy Talbert — **763-4070**

School District Data — **763-1154**
Paul Siegel

Social Stratification — **763-1154**
Paul Siegel

Special Population Censuses — **763-7854**
George Hurn

Special Surveys — **763-2767**
Ronald Dopkowski

Survey of Income & Program Participation — **763-2764**
Staff

Travel Surveys — **763-5468**
John Cannon

POPULATION & HOUSING SUBJECTS *(continued)*	**Undercount** (Demographic Analysis)	**763-5590**
	Gregg Robinson	
	Veterans Status	**763-8574**
	Thomas Palumbo/Selwyn Jones	**763-8576**
	Voting and Registration	**763-4547**
	Jerry Jennings	
	Women	**763-7883**
	Denise Smith	
GEOGRAPHIC CONCEPTS & PRODUCTS	**Area Measurement**	**763-5720**
	Don Hirshfeld	
	Boundaries of Legal Areas:	**763-3827**
	Annexations, Boundary Changes	
	Nancy Goodman	
	State Boundary Certification	**763-3827**
	Louise Stewart	
	Census Geographic Concepts	**763-5720**
	Staff	
	1980 Counts for Census Boundaries	**763-1996**
	Joel Miller	
	Census Tracts:	
	Address Allocations	**763-5720**
	Ernest Swapshur	
	Boundaries, Codes, Delineation	**763-3827**
	Cathy Miller	
	Centers of Population	**763-5720**
	Don Hirschfeld	
	Congressional Districts:	
	Address Allocations	**763-5692**
	Ernie Swapshur	
	Boundaries, Component Areas	**763-5720**
	Robert Hamill	
	GBF /DIME System	**763-1580**
	Staff	
MAPS	**1980 Census Map Orders**	**812-288-3192**
	Leila Baxter	
	1990 Census Maps	**301-763-4100**
	Customer Services Staff	
	Cartographic Operations	**763-3973**
	Staff	
	Computer Mapping	**763-3973**
	Fred Broome	
	Metropolitan Areas (MSAs)	**763-5158**
	Richard Forstall/Jim Fitzsimmons	

Census Bureau: GEOGRAPHIC CONCEPTS & PRODUCTS *(continued)*

Outlying Areas — **763-2903**
Staff

Statistical Areas — **763-3827**
Staff

TIGER System Applications — **763-1580**
Larry Carbaugh

TIGER System Products — **763-4100**
Customer Services Staff

Urban/Rural Residence — **763-7962**
Staff

Voting Districts — **763-3827**
Cathy McCully

ZIP Codes — **763-4667**
Rose Quarato

ECONOMIC & AGRICULTURE PROGRAMS

Agriculture Division — **763-8555**
Charles Pautler, Chief

Business Division — **763-7564**
Howard Hamilton, Chief

Center for Economic Studies — **763-2337**
Robert McGuckin, III, Chief

Construction Statistics Division — **763-7163**
W. Joel Richardson, Chief

Economic Census Staff — **763-7356**
Thomas Mesenbourg, Chief

Economic Programming Division — **763-2912**
Barry M. Cohen, Chief

Economic Surveys Division — **763-7735**
Vacant

Foreign Trade Division — **763-5342**
Don L. Adams, Chief

Governments Division — **763-7366**
Gordon Green, Chief

Industry Division — **763-5850**
Gaylord E. Worden, Chief

AGRICULTURE STATISTICS

Crop Statistics — **763-8567**
Donald Jahnke

Data Requirements and Outreach — **763-8561**
Douglas Miller

AGRICULTURE STATISTICS *(continued)*

Farm Economics **301-763-8566**
James A. Liefer
General Information **763-1113**
Tom Manning
Irrigation and Horticulture Statistics **763-8560**
John Blackledge
Livestock Statistics **763-8569**
Linda Hutton
Puerto Rico, Virgin Islands, Guam, North Marianas **763-8564**
Kent Hoover

BUSINESS STATISTICS

Business Owner's Characteristics, Minority and Women-Owned Businesses **763-5517**
Donna McCutcheon
Finance, Insurance, and Real Estate **763-1386**
Sidney Marcus
Retail Trade:
Advance Monthly Sales, Annual Sales, and Monthly Inventories **763-5294**
Ronald Piencykoski
Census **763-7038**
Anne Russell
Monthly Retail Trade Report **763-7128**
Irving True
Service Industries:
Census **763-7039**
Jack Moody
Current Selected Services Reports **763-5528**
Thomas Zabelsky
Utilities, Communications, and Transportation **763-2662**
Dennis Shoemaker
Wholesale Trade:
Census **763-5281**
John Trimble
Current Sales and Inventories **763-3916**
Dale Gordon

CONSTRUCTION STATISTICS

Census of Industries **763-7546**
Bill Visnasky
Construction Authorized by Building Permits (C40 Series) **763-7244**
Linda Hoyle

Census Bureau: ECONOMIC SUBJECTS

CONSTRUCTION STATISTICS *(continued)*	**New Residential Construction:**	
	Characteristics, Price Index, Sales (C25/27 Series) *Steve Berman*	**301-763-7842**
	Housing Starts (C20 Series) and Completions (C22 Series) *David Fondelier*	**763-5731**
	In Selected MSAs (C21 Series) *Dale Jacobson*	**763-7842**
	Survey of Expenditures for Residential Upkeep and Improvements (C50 Series) *George Roff*	**763-5705**
	Vacancy Data *Wallace Fraser*	**763-8165**
	Value of New Construction Put in Place (C30 Series) *Allan Meyer*	**763-5717**
COUNTIES	**County Business Patterns** *Zigmund Decker*	**763-5430**
EMPLOYMENT	**Employment/Unemployment Statistics**	
	Thomas Palumbo	**763-8574**
ENTERPRISE	**Enterprise Statistics** *Johnny Monaco*	**763-1758**
FOREIGN TRADE	**Foreign Trade Data Services**	
	Staff	**763-5140**
	Haydn Mearkle	**763-7754**
GEOGRAPHIC TOPICS	**Geographic Areas of the Economic Censuses** *Staff*	**763-4667**
GOVERNMENTS	**Criminal Justice Statistics** *Diana Cull*	**763-7789**
	Eastern States Government Sector *Genevieve Speight*	**763-7783**
	Employment *Alan Stevens*	**763-5086**
	Federal Expenditure Data *David Kellerman*	**763-5276**
	Finance *Henry Wulf*	**763-7664**
	Government Organization *Diana Cull*	**763-7789**

GOVERNMENTS *(continued)*	**Single Audit** *William Fanning*	**301-763-4403**
	Taxation *Gerard Keffer*	**763-5356**
	Western States Government Sector *Ulvey Harris*	**763-5344**
INCOME	**Income/Poverty** (see *Demographic Subjects: Income Statistics and Income Surveys*)	
INDUSTRY	**Industry and Commodity Classification** *Alvin Venning*	**763-1935**
INVESTMENT	**Investment in Plant Equipment** *John Gates*	**763-5596**
MANUFACTURING	**Industry Data:** *John P. Govoni*	**763-7666**
	Durables *Kenneth Hansen*	**763-7304**
	Nondurables *Michael Zampogna*	**763-2510**
	Products Data: *Robert Tinari*	**763-1924**
	Durables (Current Industrial Reports) *Malcolm Bernhardt*	**763-2518**
	Nondurables (Current Industrial Reports) *Thomas Flood*	**763-5911**
	Special Topics:	
	Concentration, Exports from Manufacturing Establishments and Water Use *Bruce Goldhirsch*	**763-1503**
	Fuels/Electric Energy Consumed *John McNamee*	**763-5938**
	Monthly Shipments, Inventories, Orders *Ruth Runyan*	**763-2502**
	Research and Development, Capacity, Production Index, Pollution Abatement *Elinor Champion*	**763-5616**
MINERALS	**Mineral Industries** *John McNamee*	**763-5938**
	Puerto Rico, Virgin Islands, Guam, and Northern Marianas	
	Censuses of Retail Trade, Wholesale Trade, Selected Service Industries, Agriculture, Construction, and Manufactures *Odell Larson/Kent Hoover*	**763-8226** **763-8564**

Census Bureau: ECONOMIC SUBJECTS: *(continued)*

Quarterly Financial Report *Paul Zarrett*	**763-2718**
Accounting and Related Issues *Ronald Lee*	**763-4270**
Classification *Frank Hartman*	**763-4274**
Shippers' Declaration *Hal Blyweiss*	**763-5310**
Transportation: Commodity Transportation Survey, Truck Inventory and Use *William Bostic*	**763-2735**

USER SERVICES, STATISTICAL STANDARDS & METHODOLOGY

Data User Services Division *Marshall L. Turner Jr., Chief*	**763-5820**
Field Division *vacant*	**763-5000**
Age Search–Access to Personal Census Records *Census History Staff*	**763-7936**
Catalog, Bureau of the Census *John McCall*	**763-1584**
CENDATA (online access service) *Staff*	**763-2074**
Census and You (monthly newsletter) *Neil Tillman*	**763-1584**
Census Awareness Products & Programs (Regional Offices) *Staff*	**763-4683**
Census Curriculum Support Project *Staff*	**763-1510**
Census Procedures, History of *Frederick Bohme*	**763-7936**
Clearinghouse of Census Data Services *Larry Carbaugh*	**763-1580**
Data User Training *Staff*	**763-1510**
Exhibits, Conventions *Joanne Dickinson*	**301-763-2370**

USER SERVICES, STATISTICAL STANDARDS & METHODOLOGY
(continued)

Guides and Directories *Gary Young*	**763-1584**
Historic Statistics *Staff*	**763-7936**
Monthly Product Announcement *Bernice L. Baker*	**763-1584**
Public-Use Microdata Samples *Carmen Campbell*	**763-2005**
Sampling Methods, Current Programs *Preston J. Waite*	**763-2672**
Sampling Methods, Decennial Census *Henry Waltman*	**763-1840**
State Data Center Program *Larry Carbaugh*	**763-1580**
Statistical Abstracts: *Glenn King*	**763-5299**
County & City, State & Metropolitan Area Data Books *Wanda Cevis*	**763-1034**
Statistical Research for Demographic Programs *Lawrence Ernst*	**763-7880**
Statistical Research for Economic Programs *Nash J. Monsour*	**763-5702**
Undercount Research and Post-Enumeration Surveys *Howard Hogan*	**763-1794**

U.S. BUREAU OF THE CENSUS

Regional Assistance

ATLANTA

James F. Holmes, Dir.	404-347-5443
Census Awareness & Products	404-347-2274

BOSTON

Arthur G. Dukakis, Dir.	617-421-1421
Census Awareness & Products	617-565-7078

CHARLOTTE

William F. Hill, Dir.	704-521-4400
Census Awareness & Products	704-371-6142

CHICAGO

Stanley D. Moore, Dir.	312-531-1990
Census Awareness & Products	312-353-0980

DALLAS

John Bell, Dir.	214-767-7488
Census Awareness & Products	214-767-7105

DENVER

William F. Adams. Dir.	303-969-7750
Census Awareness & Products	303-969-7750

DETROIT

Dwight P. Dean, Dir.	313-354-1990
Census Awareness & Products	313-354-4654

KANSAS CITY

Marvin Postma, Dir.	816-891-7470
Census Awareness & Products	816-891-7562

LOS ANGELES

John Reeder, Dir.	818-904-6514
Census Awareness & Products	818-904-6339

NEW YORK

Sheila Grimm, Dir.	212-997-1990
Census Awareness & Products	212-264-4730

PHILADELPHIA

LaVerne Vines Collins, Dir.	215-597-1990
Census Awareness & Products	215-597-8313

SEATTLE

Leo C. Schilling, Dir.	206-728-5300
Census Awareness & Products	206-728-5314

AGRICULTURE, Department of

The USDA covers more than farms and nutrition. It looks at family economics, too.

1301 New York Ave, NW
Washington, DC 20005

Main contact:
Ben Blankenship
202-786-1504

There are three groups in the Department of Agriculture that are of interest to marketers: the Population Group, which provides information about the population of farms, rural areas, and small towns; the Family Economics Research Group, which studies families nationwide, not just those that live on farms or in rural areas; and the Consumer Nutrition Center, which conducts the Nationwide Food Consumption Survey to see whether the nutritional needs of the population are being met. Each of these groups provides a wealth of data on their respective areas.

For more information

- ***Agricultural Chartbook,*** available annually. Call **800-999-6779** for prices.
- ***Agricultural Statistics,*** available from the Government Printing Office; **202-783-3238.**
- ***Reports,*** lists new publications from the Agricultural and Rural Economics Division of the Economic Research Service. To get on the free mailing list, call **800-999-6779.**

Telephone contacts

Economic Research Service *James Sayre*	**202-786-1512**
Family Economics Research *Helene Gutman*	**301-436-8461**
Group Childraising Costs *Nancy Schwenk*	**301-436-8461**
Human Nutrition Information Service *Laura Sims*	**301-436-8474**
Income Studies Group *Thomas Carlin*	**202-786-1527**
Information Division *Ben Blankenship*	**202-786-1504**
Population Group *Calvin Beale*	**202-786-1534**
Savings & Investment **Household Production** *Colien Hefferan*	**301-436-8461**

What You Can Get From the Department of Agriculture

Continuing Survey of Food Intake by Individuals

Conducted in 1985-86, this is a dietary study of men and women aged 19 to 50 and their children under age 5. It is available from the GPO.

Family Economics Review

The quarterly journal of the Family Economics Research Group covers factors that affect the decisions people make about life's big events—getting married, having children, buying a house, deciding to retire. It also reports on such topics as how much it costs to raise a child, and household savings and credit use. An annual subscription is $5, single issues are $2, and it can be ordered from the GPO.

Hired Farm Working Force

An annual report profiling farm workers—who they are, where and when they work, and what kind of work they do.

National Food Review

The quarterly journal of the Economic Research Services covers economic issues of the food industry, not including farm production. There is also an annual issue on food consumption, expenditures, and prices. Call **800-999-6779** for subscription information.

Nationwide Food Consumption Survey

A periodic survey that examines foods commonly eaten by individuals, the amount per day and per eating occasion. Reports on regions are available, and data from the 1987-88 survey are now available from the GPO.

Other Reports Available

The Consumer Nutrition Center uses the information it gathers to estimate how much it should cost to eat at home each month for families of different sizes and individuals of different ages. These estimates are based on four food plans the center staff has made, depending on the household's income level. For prices and ordering information write to: Human Nutrition Information Service, Federal Building, Hyattsville, MD 20782.

ECONOMIC ANALYSIS, Bureau of

Income data from the BEA are different from Census Bureau data. The BEA is the source for an important economic indicator—per capita income.

U.S. Department of Commerce
1401 K Street, NW
Washington, DC 20230

Main contact:
Barbara Howenstine
202-523-0777

The Bureau of Economic Analysis provides the only ongoing annual measure of economic activity at the regional and local levels. It examines principal sources of personal income, including transfer payments and rental income, dividend and interest income, wages, salaries, and the industries that supply them.

BEA data differ from those of the Census Bureau in that the Census Bureau, using a narrower concept of income, surveys people to learn their income and then averages the responses, while the BEA first determines the total personal income of a county or state and then divides it by the population.

For more information

User's Guide to BEA Information; available for free from the Bureau of Economic Analysis Public Information Office.

Telephone contacts

Public Information Office **202-523-0777**
Barbara Howenstine

Economic Projections, State & Metropolitan Areas **202-523-0971**
Kenneth Johnson

Personal Income & Employment, State, MSA & County Data Requests **202-523-0966**
Economic Information Staff

What You Can Get From the Bureau of Economic Analysis

Survey of Current Business

This monthly publication provides four valuable series of income data:

1. Quarterly estimates of personal income for states, which appear in the January, April, July, and October issues.
2. Preliminary annual estimates of personal income for states appear in the April issue; revised estimates appear in August.

3. Annual estimates of per capita disposable personal income for states are in the August issue.
4. Estimates of personal income for counties for two years earlier appear in the April issue.

The *Survey of Current Business* is $18 a year from the Government Printing Office; **202/783-3238.**

Local Area Personal Income

An annual publication that provides detailed income data and tabulations for the six most recent years for many geographic regions:

Volume 1. Data for the U.S., regions, states, MSAs.

Volumes 2-8. County data and maps for the eight BEA geographic regions (New England, Mideast, Great Lakes, Plains, Southeast, Southwest, Rocky Mountain, and Far West).

These volumes, which come out every July, vary in price and can be ordered from the GPO.

BEA Regional Projections

Published every five years, these projections forecast demographic and economic characteristics for regions, states, and MSAs by:

1. Three age groups: 0-14, 15-64, and 65 and over
2. Personal income by source
3. Employment and earnings for 57 industrial sectors.

The two volumes in this set are for sale from the Government Printing Office; **202-783-3238.** An order form is available from the Regional Economic Analysis Division, Projections Branch, 1401 K Street, NW, Washington, DC 20230, or from the GPO.

Tabulations

Tabulations can be requested for counties or combinations of counties and can be ordered on tape, disk, or hard copy. For this service, which the BEA provides relatively quickly, call **202-523-0966.**

Data About a Particular State

State and local economic information can be had by joining a Bureau of Economic Analysis user group. The user groups are listed for each of the states under the heading *Economic Sources* in Chapter 7.

EDUCATIONAL RESEARCH AND IMPROVEMENT, Office of

(National Center for Education Statistics)

One out of four Americans is involved in the educational process, as a student or teacher. The NCES covers all aspects of this huge industry.

Information Services
Education Information Branch
U.S. Dept. of Education
555 New Jersey Ave., NW
Washington, DC 20208

Main contact:
Fred Beamer
800-424-1616
Metro Washington area
202-626-9854

Since 1867, the Department of Education has been responsible for information on the "condition and progress of education." It provides a wealth of statistical and research information through its Office of Educational Research and Improvement. The National Center for Education Statistics (NCES), OERI's statistical unit, conducts a wide variety of surveys covering all levels of education.

For more information

- ***OERI Publications Catalog*** lists the wide range of statistical reports that are available, many of them free.

Write: Education Information Branch, Information Services, U.S. Department of Education, Washington, DC 20208; **800-424-1616;** in Washington call **202-626-9854.**

Telephone contacts

General Information	**1-800-424-1616**
In metro Washington area	**202-626-9854**
Fred Beamer/Norman Brandt	
Vance Grant/Richard Whalen	
Common Core of Data	**202-357-6335**
John Sietsema	
Data Tapes/Computer Products	
Imelda Smallwood	**357-6528**
John Dusatko	**357-6522**
Elementary & Secondary Education	**357-6614**
Paul Planchon	
Longitudinal Studies	**357-6774**
Dennis Carroll	
International Education	**357-6740**
Larry Suter	
Library Surveys	**357-6642**
Lawrence LaMoure	

Post-Secondary Education	**202-357-6354**
Samuel Peng	
Private Schools	**357-6333**
Jeffrey Williams	
Projections	**357-6581**
Debra Gerald	
School District Tabulation	**1-800-424-1616**
Richard Cook	

What You Can Get From NCES

Digest of Education Statistics and Condition of Education

These annual publications contain a wide range of education statistics gathered from the National Center for Education Statistics' own surveys and a variety of other sources. Available from the Government Printing Office; **202-783-3238.** The 1989 edition of the *Digest* was released in December 1989.

Longitudinal Surveys

Thecenter has been tracking the accomplishments of high school students, beginning with seniors in 1972 for the National Longitudinal Study (NLS), sophomores and seniors in 1980 for the High School and Beyond (HS&B) Study, and eighth graders in 1988 for the National Education Longitudinal Survey (NELS). These surveys follow up on the education and labor force experience of individuals over time. Publications are produced periodically and data are available on tape.

National Assessment of Educational Progress (NAEP)

NAEP is popularly known as the Nation's Report Card. It tracks the achievement levels of children aged 9, 13, and 17 in a variety of academic subjects.

Integrated Postsecondary Education Data Systems (IPEDS)

The center conducts an annual census of all colleges and universities, gathering data on enrollment, faculty, faculty salaries and tenure, degrees conferred, finances, and student costs. Annual reports and data tapes are available from Information Services, Educational Information Branch.

Projections of Education Statistics

The center periodically issues ten-year projections of enrollment, graduates, teachers, and expenditures for elementary, secondary, and higher education institutions. *Projections of Education Statistics to 1999-2000* were released in December 1989.

Targeted Forecasts

The center's Projections Branch also issues five-year projections of key education statistics and highlights projected data for the coming term. The reports are published annually, and are available from the Education Information Branch at no charge.

Decennial Census

Although the center does not disseminate decennial census data, it does provide a list of Census Bureau state data centers which provide census data and maps by school district *(see Chapter 7 for a complete list of these data centers).*

Computer Reports and Other Services

The center gives people access to more detailed data than its publications contain via computer tape, computer printouts, and microfiche.

It also does special tabulations, although it advises anyone wanting extensive analysis to buy the tapes and do it themselves.

Finally, Information Services produces mailing labels from the survey tapes for businesses that sell products to schools. Call Jack Dusatko at **202-357-6522** for further information.

ENERGY INFORMATION ADMINISTRATION

As we enter a new era of environmental awareness, the EIA tells us how Americans use energy.

National Energy Information Center
Forrestal Building
1000 Independence Avenue, SW
Washington, DC 20585

Main contact:
Nancy Nicoletti
202-586-1174

The Energy Information Administration (EIA) is an independent statistical agency of the U.S. Department of Energy, serving as the government's collector, processor, interpreter, analyst, and disseminator of energy information. In 1989, EIA conducted more than 70 surveys to collect information on supply, consumption, and cost of all major forms of energy; it also maintained approximately 35 forecasting models to provide analyses of possible future trends in energy use.

What You Can Get From the EIA

Monthly Energy Review

The most widely read of its 79 periodicals and reports, the *Monthly Energy Review* presents current data on production, consumption, stocks, imports, exports, and prices of the principal energy commodities in the U.S. These data are also available on disk, as are state data, grouped by census regions.

Other Publications

Certain publications, such as EIA directories, are available free of charge, but most must be purchased by subscription or as individual copies. All publications are free to government agencies and repositories, and to academic institutions.

EQUAL EMPLOYMENT OPPORTUNITY COMMISSION (EEOC)

Women and minorities will account for five out of six net additions to the labor force in the 1990s. The EEOC tracks the status of these workers.

EEOC Survey Division
Office of Program Research
1800 L St., NW, Rm. 9608
Washington, DC 20507

Main contact:
James S. Neal
202-633-4920

The Equal Employment Opportunity Commission surveys employment in private industry every year, and its reports are categorized by sex, race, ethnic group, and broad job categories. Results are published for MSAs and larger geographical units.

What You Can Get From the EEOC

Job Patterns for Minorities and Women

The following reports were available in early 1990:

1. **Job Patterns for Minorities and Women in Private Industry, 1988**
2. **Job Patterns for Minorities and Women in Referral Unions, 1983**
3. **Job Patterns for Minorities and Women in State and Local Government, 1985**
4. **Job Patterns for Minorities and Women Elementary and Secondary School Staffing** (using most current data)
5. **Job Patterns for Minorities and Women in Colleges and Universities** (using most current data)

Single copies of the reports are available free of charge from the EEOC Survey Division.

HEALTH STATISTICS, National Center for

The NCHS provides data on Americans' health. It's also the place to go for vital statistics.

Scientific and Technical Information Branch
National Center for Health Statistics
U.S. Department of Health and Human Services
3700 East-West Highway, Room 157
Hyattsville, MD 20782

Main contact:
Jack Mounts
301-436-8500

The National Center for Health Statistics was founded in 1960 to collect and disseminate data on health in the United States. Some of the center's statistics come from local registrations of births and deaths, marriages and divorces, but most come out of an extensive program of national surveys, usually conducted for the center by the Census Bureau or private survey firms.

There are two main types of data available from the NCHS. The first is vital statistics—births, deaths, marriages, and divorces. Much of these data are compiled from administrative records—i.e., certificates. Others are collected through surveys. Most NCHS data are published in its series of *Vital and Health Statistics* reports.

What You Can Get From the National Center for Health Statistics

Vital Statistics

The *Monthly Vital Statistics Report* provides monthly and cumulative data, with brief analyses, on births, deaths, marriages, divorces, and infant deaths for states and the U.S. The final statistics are released about a year later in *Advance Reports*, available from the Center at no charge.

Annual Volumes, Vital Statistics of the United States contain final figures tabulated by natality, mortality, marriage and divorce for states, counties, metropolitan areas, and cities with populations of 10,000 or more. The data, which are published four years after they are collected, can be ordered from the Government Printing Office; **202-783-3238.**

Additional Vital Statistics Publications:

Since the information contained on a birth, death, or marriage certificate is necessarily limited, the center supplements it by taking four broad surveys, the results of which are published in *Vital and Health Statistics:*

1986 National Mortality Followback Survey

Covers risk factors associated with premature death, health services received and their cost during the last year of life, and lifestyles; e.g., diet, exercise, etc. Data from this survey became available in late 1988. For more information, call the Center at **301-436-7107.**

National Mortality Survey (Series 20)

Mortality surveys, conducted annually from 1961 through 1968 and again in 1986, collected data on such topics as the smoking habits of people who had died between the ages of 35 and 84. Call the Center at **301-436-8954** for more information.

National Natality Survey (Series 21)

The birth survey periodically studies pregnancy history, birth expectations, family composition, employment status, health insurance coverage, and related topics. Data from 1980 are currently available, and another survey was taken in 1988.

National Survey of Family Growth (Series 23)

This survey, which was conducted in 1973, 1976, 1982, and 1988, gathers statistics about the dynamics of population change, family planning, and maternal and child health. Data on birth intentions and a range of demographic and economic variables are also reported. For more information call **301-936-8731.**

Health:

The NCHS also conducts surveys regarding American's health and publishes the results in several series of *Vital and Health Statistics* publications:

Health Interview Survey (Series 10)

This annual survey is the principal source of information on the health of Americans. It obtains statistics on health and demographic factors related to illness, injuries and disability, and the costs and uses of medical services.

Health and Nutrition Examination Survey (Series 11)

The data in this survey are collected through physical examinations as well as through interviews. The center sends out a mobile examination unit made up of specially constructed truck-drawn rooms. This way the center ensures that all examinations are uniform in temperature and humidity control for exercise tests and in noise levels for hearing tests.

Hispanic Health and Nutritional Examination Survey (Series 11)

This one-time survey of a sample of 16,000 Hispanics was conducted in 1982-84, and information from it was released in separate reports. Because the information published is so diverse, it is organized by topic, such as "cholesterol levels" or "periodontal disease."

Hospital Discharge Survey (Series 13)

This survey collects information annually on hospital patients' demographic characteristics, how long they stayed in the hospital, and the purpose of their visit.

National Ambulatory Medical Care Survey (Series 13)

A complement to the *Hospital Discharge Survey,* this survey is a continuous sample of patients' visits to doctors' offices. Doctors fill out forms for a sample of their patients, including their age, race, sex, principal problem, diagnosis, and prescribed treatment.

Nursing Home Survey (Series 13)

This national, intermittent survey collects data on nursing home residents, staff, and facilities. The information is used for evaluating present legislation, such as Medicare and Medicaid, and for planning new legislation. The last survey was conducted in 1985-86 and data from it were released in 1987.

Computer Tapes Available

Computer tapes containing detailed data are available, and the center will also answer requests for unpublished data if it has already made the tabulations or, for a fee, it will make special tabulations. For further information call the Scientific and Technical Information Branch at **301-436-8500.** To order tapes, contact the National Technical Information Service, 5285 Port Royal Road, Springfield, VA 22161; **703-487-4650.** Most tapes are available at an average cost of $160.

HOUSING AND URBAN DEVELOPMENT, Department of

The HUD's principal data product is the biennial American Housing Survey.

451 Seventh Street, NW
Washington, DC 20410

Main contact:
John Murphy
202-708-2374

An enormous amount of valuable data is provided by HUD's American Housing Survey, which updates changes in the housing stock and the demographic characteristics of occupants. Conducted nationally every other year, separate samples of 11 of 44 selected MSAs are taken every year. Unlike the Census Bureau's Current Population Survey, the American Housing Survey returns to the same housing units, a practice that makes it possible to check for changes in structures and occupants.

What You Can Get From HUD

American Housing Survey Reports

Published reports from the American Housing Survey National Sample (Series H-150) cover six basic subjects, each of which provides data for the U.S. and regions:

A. General Housing Characteristics
This report provides data on tenure, vacancy rates, number of rooms, household race and composition, characteristics of newly constructed units, etc.

B. Indicators of Housing and Neighborhood Quality
Organized by financial characteristics, this report covers structural characteristics of dwelling units, such as water damage in roofs and basements, cracked and peeling paint or plaster, and holes in floors, ceilings, or walls.

C. Financial Characteristics of the Housing Inventory
Cross-tabulations of structural characteristics and occupants' demographic characteristics by family and individual income.

D. Housing Characteristics of Recent Movers
Reports data for households that moved into a unit within the previous 12 months. Reasons for moving and characteristics of the previous and current housing unit are presented.

E. Rural and Urban Housing Characteristics

F. Energy-Related Housing Characteristics

Other Reports

Other reports include the *Summary of Housing Characteristics for Selected Metropolitan Areas* (Series H-170), a supplementary report that shows selected occupancy, vacancy, utilization, structural, and financial characteristics. Printed reports from the 1987 survey are the latest currently available; order from the Government Printing Office, Washington, DC 20402.

Computer Tapes

Computer tapes from the 1987 American Housing Survey can be ordered from the Customer Services Branch, Data User Services Division, U.S. Bureau of the Census, Washington, DC 20233; **301-763-4100.**

Computer tapes with individual response records are available from both the MSA and national samples. However, because of confidentiality guidelines, the tapes are available only for areas with large samples. Contact the Data User Services Division for more information.

Other Data Available

Before ordering tapes, you may also want to check with the Census Bureau for unpublished data, which are available either in paper photocopies or on microfiche. An index of what you can get is available free of charge from the Housing Division, U.S. Department of Commerce, Washington, DC 20233.

IMMIGRATION AND NATURALIZATION SERVICE

By the year 2028, 100 percent of U.S. population growth may come from immigration. The INS tracks the multitudes who enter the U.S. each year.

Statistical Analysis Branch
425 Eye Street, NW,
Room 5020
Washington, DC 20536

Main contact:
Christine Davidson
202-376-3066

Part of the Department of Justice, the Immigration & Naturalization Service is the source of data about population change due to international migration. It gathers a wide array of data about immigrants, nonimmigrants, refugees, people becoming naturalized citizens, and children claiming citizenship through the naturalization of their parents.

Telephone contacts

Deportations, Required Departures & Exclusions , *John Bjerke* — **202-376-3015**

Emigration — **376-3008**
Robert Warren

Immigrants — **376-3066**
Michael Hoefer

Nonimmigrants — **376-3015**
Mark Herrenbruck

Refugees, Naturalization & Derivative Citizenship, *Christine Davidson* — **376-3046**

What You Can Get From the Immigration & Naturalization Service

Nonimmigrant Statistics

This quarterly bulletin compares nonimmigrant and arriving visitor statistics with data from the same quarter of the previous fiscal year. Includes port of entry statistics by classification and port of departure. Order through the Immigration & Naturalization Service.

The Statistical Yearbook

An annual yearbook which provides data about population change due to international migration. Demographic data include age, country of birth, occupation, country of last permanent residence, marital status, sex, nationality, and ZIP Code of intended residence. The data also include when, where, and under what status the individual entered the country. Order from the National Technical Information Service, 5285 Port Royal Road, Springfield, VA 22161; **703-487-4650.**

Tapes Available

The branch also puts together public-use tapes, which go back ten years, making it easy to analyze trends. Available from the National Technical Information Service.

INTERNAL REVENUE SERVICE

IRS data are useful for more than tax and income information. They can be used to examine migration and population trends between censuses.

Statistics of Income Division, R:S
1111 Constitution Avenue, NW
Washington, DC 20224
202-376-0216

Main contact:
David Jordan
202-233-1755

The IRS Statistics of Income Division's annual report of individual income is a good source of demographic data between censuses. Income by income source, tax deductions, and tax exemptions are all reported by the marital status of the taxpayer. Researchers can often infer household composition from the filing status of the taxpayer and the number of exemptions claimed. Exemptions can also be used in making population inferences for years between censuses, and researchers can match (identity-stripped) records to track migration from one year to another.

What You Can Get From the IRS

Statistics of Income (SOI) Bulletin

This quarterly report is where the division first reports statistics based on individual income tax returns for the year just past. It is more useful for discerning general trends, rather than levels of change in individual income. The *Bulletin* also provides estimates on the personal wealth of the nation's top wealthholders, tabulated by age, sex, and marital status. Selected data by state are also included. The *SOI Bulletin* is available for $20 from the Superintendent of Documents, Government Printing Office, Washington, DC 20402.

Individual Income Tax Return File

The microdata available in these public-use computer tapes often provide more detailed information than the printed publications, but some of the data are edited to protect the identity of individual taxpayers. Researchers can buy the file of individual income tax returns from the IRS, which also sells two sets of files containing county-level migration statistics. Microdata files for individual states are also available.

JUSTICE STATISTICS, Bureau of

Crime is an important concern for many people. The BJS provides data about crime and criminals in the U.S.

633 Indiana Avenue, NW
Washington, DC 20531
202-724-7759

Main contact:
Sue Lindgren
202-724-7759

Part of the Department of Justice, the Bureau of Justice Statistics provides data on both the victims of crime and its perpetrators.

For more information

- ***Data Center Clearinghouse for Drugs & Crime Statistics;*** call **800-666-3332** for information and research service.
- ***Justice Statistics Clearinghouse;*** call **800-732-3277** for information and research service.
- ***Telephone Contacts*** lists a wide range of criminal justice topics and the names and telephone numbers of subject specialists. Available for free from the Government Printing Office; **202-783-3238.**
- ***How to Gain Access to BJS Data*** describes the Bureau's programs and how to obtain data and services from it. Also available for free from the GPO.

Telephone contacts

Correctional Statistics *Larry Greenfield*	**202-724-7755**
Judicial Statistics *Patrick Langan*	**724-7774**
Law Enforcement Statistics *Paul White*	**724-7770**
National Crime Survey *Patsy Klaus*	**724-7774**

What You Can Get From the BJS

Correctional Statistics

This survey collects age, race, sex, income, marital status, education, criminal, and drug use history data every five years on state prisoners and jail inmates.

National Crime Survey

Every six months, the National Crime Survey asks a sample of 49,000 Americans aged 12 and older in urban, suburban, and rural areas about their experience during the previous six months with rape, robbery, assault, household burglary, personal and household larceny, and motor vehicle theft.

The survey provides data about the victim's demographics, where and when the crime occurred, the extent of injury and economic loss, the relationship between the victim and the person committing the crime, and whether or not the crime was reported and why. The survey also asks whether the offender was on drugs and asks victims to describe their experience with the criminal justice system.

Report to the Nation on Crime and Justice, Second Edition

This excellent publication is a non-technical report on crime and justice, and was regarded as a landmark document when first published in 1983; the second edition came out in 1988.

Sourcebook of Criminal Justice Statistics

This annual book incorporates criminal justice data from virtually every source of national data, including public opinion surveys, the FBI, and the court system.

How to Order Reports

There are many other BJS reports available, and they're all free from the Justice Statistics Clearinghouse, Box 6000, Rockville, MD 20850. Outside of Maryland and Washington, DC, call toll-free **800-732-3277;** Maryland and Washington, DC, call **301-251-5500.**

Tapes Also Available

The Bureau of Justice Statistics places public-use tapes in the Criminal Justice Archive and Data Network of the Inter-University Consortium for Political and Social Research at the University of Michigan. Data tapes from the annual surveys are archived there too.

To order machine-readable data files, call the archive staff at **313-763-5010**, or write CJAIN, P.O. Box 1248, Ann Arbor, MI 48106. This organization also puts out a free quarterly newsletter, the *ICPSR Bulletin*.

LABOR STATISTICS, Bureau of

It may come as a surprise that the BLS—known for its employment and unemployment information—also provides some of the best consumer spending data around.

441 G Street, NW
Washington, DC 20212
202-523-1221

Main contact:
Veola Kittrell
202-523-1221

Most of the statistics that people need to assess what is going on in the economy—trends in prices, earnings, employment, unemployment, consumer spending, wages, and productivity—come from the Bureau of Labor Statistics.

For more information

The following reports are free and can be obtained from the Office of Inquiries and Correspondence, U.S. Bureau of Labor Statistics, 441 G St., NW, Rm. 2831A, Washington, DC 20212; **202-523-1221** or **-1222:**

• ***Major Programs of the Bureau of Labor Statistics,*** which describes each of the agency's activities in detail and lists relevant publications.

• ***BLS Update,*** a quarterly publication which lists all new publications and tells how to get them.

• ***Telephone Contacts for Data Users,*** which lists the names and telephone numbers of all subject-matter specialists.

Telephone contacts

Inquiries & Correspondence — **202-523-1221**
Veola Kittrell

Recorded Message: — **523-9658**
Consumer Price Index (CPI), Producer Price Indexes (PPI), & Employment Situation

Consumer Expenditure Survey — **272-5060**
Data & Tapes
Stephanie Shipp

Consumer Expenditure Surveys — **272-5156**
Eva Jacobs

Consumer Price Index Detail — **523-1239**

Demographic Studies — **523-1944**
Paul Flaim

Economic Growth and Employment Projections — **272-5328**
Howard Fullerton

Family & Marital Characteristics of Labor Force, *Howard Hayghe*	**523-1371**
Industry Occupational Employment Matrix, *Delores Turner*	**272-5283**
Local Area Unemployment Statistics *Carol Utter*	**523-1002**
Microdata Tapes & Analysis *Robert McIntire*	**523-1776**
Occupational Employment Statistics Survey, *Michael McElroy*	**523-1684**
Occupational Outlook *Michael Pilot*	**272-5282**
Occupational Projections—National *Neal Rosenthal*	**272-5382**
Producer Price Index Detail	**523-1765**
State & Local Area Demographic Data *Edna Biederman*	**523-1002**

What You Can Get From the BLS

Consumer Expenditure Survey

This is the most detailed source of data on consumer spending, consisting of interviews and diaries from some 10,000 households which keep detailed records of their purchases for two-week periods distributed throughout the year. Tables and tapes of the survey data are available on an annual basis, and people who are interested in getting data should contact the BLS to be put on the mailing list.

Current Population Survey (CPS)

Conducted every month by the Census Bureau, this survey is the bureau's major source of employment and demographic data. The CPS also gathers quarterly information on people's weekly earnings by demographic group and occupation. There are separate labor force reports for blacks and Hispanics, as well as for women. (For more details about the Current Population Survey, see page 71.) Available from the Government Printing Office; **202-783-3238.**

Labor Force Projections

Every other year, the BLS projects the size and characteristics of the labor force as well as the demand for people in particular occupations and industries. Demographics include age, sex, and race. Summaries of these projections are published in *Monthly Labor Review* (see periodicals below), while detailed occupational forecasts appear in the

Occupational Outlook Handbook. The most recent projections go to the year 2000 and were published in November 1989.

Occupational Employment Statistics Survey

This annual survey covers each major industry division on a three-year cycle and the data are published in bulletins entitled "Occupational Employment in (Industry Division)." Available from the Government Printing Office; **202-783-3238.**

Periodicals

The BLS publishes six periodicals. Described below, they're all available from the Government Printing Office.

The Monthly Labor Review

This venerable economics and social sciences publication features articles on employment, wages, prices, and productivity. Recent articles include "Projections of Occupational Employment: 1988-2000" and "Consumer Expenditures in Different-Size Cities"; $20 a year.

Employment and Earnings

Gives current employment and earnings statistics for the U.S., individual states, and over 200 areas. Included are household and establishment data, seasonally and not seasonally adjusted. Available for $25 a year, which includes an annual supplement.

Current Wage Developments

Reports on wage and benefit changes from collective bargaining agreements. Includes data on strikes or lockouts, major agreements expiring, and compensation changes; $15 a year.

CPI Detailed Report

Provides the monthly consumer price indexes and rates of change. It also includes data on commodity and service groups for 27 cities; $21 a year.

Occupational Outlook Quarterly

Helps students and guidance counselors learn about new occupations, training opportunities, salary trends, and career counseling programs. Written in nontechnical language and illustrated in color; $5 for four issues.

Producer Price Indexes

Includes price movement of industrial commodities and farm products each month. The $29 price includes an annual supplement.

Other Useful BLS Reports

The BLS publishes a number of other useful data in a series of Bulletins. Titles include "Handbook of Labor Statistics," "Employee Benefits in Medium and Large Firms," "Employment in Perspective: Women in the Labor Force," "Employment in Perspective: Minority Workers," and the quarterly "Usual Weekly Earnings of Wage and Salary Workers." Order them from the Government Printing Office.

Tapes Available

BLS Data Files on Tape is available from the Bureau of Labor Statistics, Division of Special Publications, Washington, DC 20212; **202-523-1090.** Requests for these tapes, which are available for the cost of duplication, should be addressed to the Bureau of Labor Statistics, Division of Financial Planning and Management, Washington, DC 20212.

News Releases Online

The BLS makes its news releases available online through a commercial contractor. There is no charge for the data; users pay only for actual computer time, which is about $7.50 an hour for local access and $20 an hour for access anywhere in the country. For more information write to the BLS Electronic News Release Service, 441 G St. NW, Rm. 2822, Washington, DC 20212.

NATIONAL PARK SERVICE

Millions enjoy the parks and other sites maintained by the NPS—which also keeps tabs on its visitors.

Denver Service Center,
T-N-T
P.O. Box 25287
Denver, CO 80225

Main contact:
Kenneth E. Hornback
303-969-2060

The National Park Service, part of the Department of the Interior, administrates the national parks, memorials, monuments, battlefields, historics, recreation, and other areas designated by the U.S. Congress. The NPS collects, edits, and publishes data about public use of the areas—recreation visits, backcountry use, tent camping, recreational vehicle use, and concession lodging.

What You Can Get From the NPS

The audit controlled data collection efforts by parks are unique in the realm of federal data in that they are edited and available within three weeks of the close of each month. Data are available in preliminary monthly reports showing parks by NPS region, and final data are published in the annual *National Park Service Statistical Abstract*.

NATIONAL TECHNICAL INFORMATION SERVICE

The NTIS acts as a clearinghouse for government data.

5285 Port Royal Road
Springfield, VA 22161

Main contact
Stuart Weisman
703-487-4807

The National Technical Information Service sells information the government produces that can help U.S. businesses. Perhaps for this reason, NTIS is run like a business: It gets no money from Congress and must support itself from the sale of its products.

Customers can charge orders to their VISA, MasterCard, or American Express accounts, and for an extra fee you can get publications within 24 hours.

For more information

NTIS General Catalog, available for free from NTIS Promotions Division, 5285 Port Royal Road, Springfield, VA 22161; **703-487-4650;** ask for item PR-827.

What You Can Get From the NTIS

Published Searches

Published searches are economical, annotated bibliographies that summarize completed research from the U.S. government and worldwide sources. Users get an annually updated bibliography in the areas of their interest. For a free *Master Catalog of Published Searches,* call **703-487-4650** and ask for item PR-186.

How to Access the NTIS Database

To access the NTIS bibliographic database, contact one of the commercial online services listed below. They will give you a password and instructions on how to use the database. If you don't have a personal computer, check with your local academic or public library—most have access to these services:

BRS Information Technologies	**800-345-4277**
DATA-STAR	**800-221-7754**
DIALOG Information Services, Inc.	**800-334-2564**
ORBIT Search Service	**800-421-7229**
In Virginia:	**703-442-0900**
STN International	**800-848-6533**
In Ohio and Canada:	**800-848-6538**

Batch searching and SDI service is available from NERAC, Inc.; **203-872-7000.**

The NTIS database is also available on CD-ROM. It covers the last six years and is updated quarterly. You will need a personal computer and a CD-ROM reader. Contact the following companies for more information:

DIALOG Information Services		**800-334-2564**
SilverPlatter Information, Inc.		**800-343-0064**
Online Computer Library Center, Inc.		**800-848-5878**
(OCLC)	*In Ohio:*	**800-848-8286**

NTIS Abstract Newsletter

The NTIS database is updated every two weeks, and people can keep up by subscribing to the weekly *NTIS Abstract Newsletter* in their area of interest, such as "Business and Economics," "Behavior and Society," and "Problem Solving Information for State and Local Governments." Whatever method you choose for finding out what material NTIS has, you can order their reports in printed or micro form.

Computer Software and Data Files

NTIS's Federal Computer Products Center sells computer software and data files useful to business and the scientific community. It has more than 1,800 software and 1,300 data files from more than 100 federal agencies including the National Energy Software Center, National Library of Medicine, and Environmental Protection Agency. Subjects covered include: demography, banking and finance, energy, health statistics, and more.

Call the Federal Computer Products Center at **703-487-4763** for more information about any of its products and services. To receive the free newsletter, call the sales division at **703-487-4650** and ask for item PR-838.

SOCIAL SECURITY ADMINISTRATION

Social Security isn't just for retired people; SSA programs, and data, cover a broader audience.

Office of Research & Statistics
U.S. Department of Health & Human Services
4301 Connecticut Ave, NW
Washington, DC 20008

Main contact:
Lelia Findley
202-282-7137

One of the best sources of data on America's growing elderly population is the Social Security Administration, which puts out regular reports on the Old Age, Survivors, and Disability Insurance Program (Social Security), as well as the Supplemental Security Income (SSI), and Aid to Families with Dependent Children (AFDC) Programs.

For more information

The *SSA Research and Statistics Publications Catalog* and single copies of all documents in the catalog are available from the Office of Research and Statistics Publication staff.

What You Can Get From the Social Security Administration

Biennial Reports:

Available from the Government Printing Office; **202-783-3238.**

Social Security Programs in the United States

Issued biennially, this is a layman's guide to the nation's network of publicly funded cash and in-kind income-maintenance programs provided by the Social Security Act. It discusses the history and current provisions of the OASDI program, Medicare, unemployment insurance, workers' compensation, and the temporary disability program.

Social Security Programs Throughout the World

This biennial publication describes in chart format the Social Security systems of 141 countries. It provides perspectives on methods used by different countries in designing and applying income-maintenance measures.

Income of the Population 55 or Older

This biennial publication presents a broad economic picture of a cross-section of the population aged 55 and older. The major focus is on sources of income and amounts received from various sources.

Annual Reports:	Available from the SSA.
OASDI Beneficiaries by State and County	This report has information on the number of persons receiving OASDI benefits by type and amount.
Supplemental Security Income State and County Data	Statistical data on the distribution of federally administered SSI payments to aged, blind, and disabled adults, and disabled children are contained in this report.
Earnings and Employment Data for Wage and Salary Workers Covered Under Social Security by State and County	This report presents data on employment for wage and salary workers including number of persons, amount of taxable wages, amount of Social Security contributions, as well as age, sex, and race of worker. The population includes those in the armed forces and in U.S. territories.

VETERANS AFFAIRS, Department of

The U.S. has 27 million living veterans. VA tracks the status of this special group, especially its health.

Office of Planning and Management Analysis Statistical Service (043C2)
810 Vermont Avenue, NW
Washington, DC 20420

Main contact:
Lynne Heltman
202-233-6802

The Office of Planning and Management Analysis in the Department of Veterans Affairs produces and maintains a wealth of statistical data on the veteran population, including demographic, socioeconomic, and medical care information. *Publications from the Statistical Service* describes the many reports that are available from VA. All reports are free and can be ordered by writing to the above address.

Telephone contacts

Secretary of Veterans Affairs Annual Report, *Carolyn Wong*	**202-233-2525**
Patient Treatment File & Annual Patient Census, *Susan Gee Krumhaus*	**233-6807**
Population Estimates & Projections *Lynne Heltman*	**233-6802**
Surveys of Veterans *Stephen Dienstfrey*	**233-6811**
Veterans Receiving Compensation or Pension & Veterans Receiving Educational Benefits, *Mike Wells*	**233-6815**
Veterans Unemployment, Labor Force Status, Income, *Rob Klein*	**233-6813**

What You Can Get From the Department of Veterans Affairs

Below is a sample of reports available from VA.

Veteran Population Estimates and Projections

An annual report with estimates of the number of living veterans by period of military service, state of residence, sex, and age. Projections are made to the year 2040.

State and County Veteran Population

This annual report presents county-level estimates and forecasts of the veteran population.

1987 Survey of Veterans

This survey collected data from some 10,000 veterans nationwide on their income, assets, and liabilities, as well as their health status, medical conditions, and use of veteran programs.

Personal and Family Income of Male Veterans and Nonveterans

This analysis of March 1988 Current Population Survey data from the Census Bureau contrasts the family and personal income of veterans and nonveterans for 1987.

Disability, VA Programs, and Labor Force Status Among Vietnam Era Veterans

This report examines the relationships among disability, labor force status, employment characteristics, and use of VA job programs.

Usage of VA Medical Facilities by Service-Connected Veterans, Pensioners, and Other Veterans

This report is based on the 1983 Survey of Aging Veterans conducted for VA by Louis Harris and Associates. It presents a comparison of three groups of aging veterans, focusing on their health care needs and utilization of services.

Patient Treatment File

The PTF contains information on all episodes of patients discharged from VA medical centers, nursing homes, or domiciliaries during a given fiscal year. The file includes detailed data on patient characteristics as well as clinical data.

Secretary of Veterans Affairs Annual Report

Every key subject area on veterans is discussed in this report, and data are included on population, health care, compensation and pension, education benefits, cemeteries and memorials, and veterans assistance.

Annual Patient Census

The Office of Planning and Management Analysis collects and disseminates information on the veteran population in this yearly sample of 20 percent of VA hospital inpatients and residents of domiciliaries, and a complete count of all patients in VA nursing homes. The data collected pertain to the numbers of patients and their characteristics as of one particular day in the year. Standard data items collected include date of birth, compensation and pension status, disability rating, period of service, date of admission, sex, marital status, race/ethnicity, and principal diagnosis.

CHAPTER 5

Private Sources

Private firms are usually the best source for current estimates and projections of small geographic areas such as ZIP Codes, counties, and even customized market areas. They also often combine demographic indicators with consumer media and purchase behavior. The turnaround time is usually immediate for this information. However, it can be expensive.

How to Use This Chapter

The companies listed here are divided into seven categories. But the consumer information industry is getting more complex all the time and products and services often overlap. Read the introduction on "Who Owns Who and What It Means to You" for an overview of the rapid changes taking place, and see the subject index at the back of this book for a complete guide to the information you need. Also note the areas of specialty listed for each firm.

In general, the private sector offers up-to-date demographic information for smaller levels of geography than are available from the government. It also provides the business and consumer information so vital to most marketing efforts, as well as tools for analysis—software, consulting services, and so on. In many cases, these firms are able to provide a level of service and support unavailable from busy government staff—for a price, of course.

THE LISTINGS:

Who Owns Who and What It Means to You

Merger mania has struck the consumer information industry. It may be good news for your bottom line.

by Joe Schwartz

The consumer information industry once resembled a hardware store. It sold its customers an assortment of marketing tools, such as demographic profiles fashioned from the decennial census.

Today, the consumer information industry is changing rapidly. It depends less on the decennial census and more on large national surveys linked to scanner data, credit-card transaction records, and other sources. Companies that once prospered by crunching census figures no longer sell just numbers—they sell solutions.

The information industry is using desktop demographic systems to link databases together, explains Gary Hill, president of the Consumer Marketing Information Group of VNU, a Dutch-owned publishing and information company. A growing number of companies can match demographic "cluster" systems with media behavior studies by Arbitron or Nielsen to determine a neighborhood's radio-listening or television-viewing habits, for example. The same demographic database, linked to Birch/Scarborough reports, reveals newspaper readership. When combined with surveys by Mediamark Research or Simmons, it can target magazine readers. Linking these databases gives researchers a comprehensive look at consumer media habits and buying behavior.

"There is a proliferation of databases, and they become extremely powerful when you tie them together," Hill says.

These linkages represent a new direction for the consumer information industry. Data vendors are realizing that their clients don't really want to know where there are concentrations of 50-to-64-year-olds with household incomes of $50,000 or more. What businesses want to know is where to put their stores, where to mail their catalogs, and where to send their credit-card applications.

"Selling data is like selling hammers," observes Ben Addoms, director of business development at National Demographics and Lifestyles in Denver. "You can still buy hammers and boards, but companies want people who can build houses."

WHAT'S HAPPENING

"This is a classic example of a maturing industry," says Dana Simmons, senior vice president of sales and marketing for National Planning Data Corporation. New growth must come from selling information within specific industries. The larger consumer information companies are now targeting department stores, supermarkets, and banks, for example.

"Vertical marketing is taking hold," observes John Rougeou, executive vice president of Equifax Marketing Services in Atlanta, Georgia.

VNU subsidiary Claritas is targeting the financial services industry, while R. L. Polk's acquisition of National Demographics and Lifestyles means that Polk can now target the manufacturers of consumer durables. Equifax has positioned itself to provide consumer information to smaller banks and insurance companies. Buying Mediamark Research has allowed MAI plc of Great Britain to go after packaged-goods manufacturers, magazines, and advertising agencies.

"There's a difference between growing big and growing profitable," says National Demographics and Lifestyles' Addoms. "As consolidation continues, you will see people acquiring industry-specific databases, merging them into companies, and focusing on specific industries."

VNU's Hill sees a growing split in the consumer information industry. Small- and medium-size vendors of demographic data will continue to sell numbers, just as they have for nearly 20 years. But competition probably will increase after the 1990 census, resulting in lower prices for the basic building blocks of consumer information systems.

Another side of the industry consists of large consumer information companies that will become even bigger in the 1990s. "Here you'll find the more mature companies such as Claritas, National Decision Systems, and Donnelley Marketing Information Services," Hill says.

VNU's Consumer Marketing Information Group includes Claritas and National Planning Data Corporation, two of the early demographic data companies; Birch/Scarborough, for newspaper and radio research; part of Market Metrics, which focuses on the packaged-goods and food industries; and 10 percent of Urban Decision Systems, another early demographic data company. Equifax, a major holder of consumer credit histories, also owns a demographic data company, Equifax Marketing Decision Systems. Dun &

Bradstreet owns Donnelley Marketing Information Services and A. C. Nielsen. R. L. Polk, in addition to owning National Demographics and Lifestyles, also owns part of Wiland Services, a direct-mail company, and Geographic Data Technology, a mapping company.

"All of these companies are moving from demographics to the measurement of marketing performance," says Addoms of National Demographics and Lifestyles.

STRENGTH IN NUMBERS

Consolidation in the consumer information industry is happening for several reasons. First, many companies are buying the talent and resources they need to target a specific industry better. Second, pooling resources gives companies the ability to maintain massive databases of individual consumers. "There is higher investment, higher risk, and higher rewards," says VNU's Hill. "This is why you need an Equifax, a Dun & Bradstreet, and a VNU. Only they have the resources to make the types of investments that have to be made."

The cost of maintaining large databases will limit the number of firms that can offer them. It also may spawn consumer information franchises, where big companies will license smaller firms to use their databases.

Without access to the few large databases, smaller companies could have a difficult time competing with multinationals backed by huge financial and marketing resources. Ken Needham, senior vice president of Urban Decision Systems, notes that VNU's 10 percent share in his company is essential: "We have to do our work with a larger corporation in order to achieve our objectives."

Competition within the maturing consumer information industry is the driving force behind consolidation. In the years ahead, businesses will enjoy a complete range of choices in consumer information—from raw demographic data to tailor-made marketing solutions.

Multi-Service Demographic Firms

CACI

Specialties: desktop demographic system, cluster system, international data

Paul Davies
Director, Marketing Information Products
9302 Lee Highway, #310
Fairfax, VA 22031
800-292-2224
703-218-4400

CACI Marketing Systems is a single source for international demographic information. With North American headquarters in the metropolitan Washington, DC area and European headquarters in London, CACI offers services, products, and systems in the U.S., United Kingdom, Canada, Finland, Norway, Germany, and France.

CACI's U.S. databases contain demographic information for the current year and a five-year forecast, with 1980 census data as a benchmark. Data are available through online services as well as the **SITELINE** Call-in Order Service. Over 30 reports are available for any area of the U.S., defined by both standard and custom geography. Reports include demographic, retail sales potential, and ACORN—A Classification of Residential Neighborhoods—information.

ACORN is CACI's U.S. cluster system, which categorizes neighborhoods into 44 unique market types. In the United Kingdom, **ACORN Lifestyles** classifies 81 types of neighborhoods. ACORN reports are specifically designed for businesses interested in targeting customers in a variety of areas such as finance, insurance, and restaurant services.

Now available in North America, **Insite•USA** is a PC-based geographic information system for site location, trade area analysis, direct marketing, competitive analysis, and media planning. It combines demographic, purchasing, and business databases, and ACORN segmentation information in a desktop marketing system. The system can also be used with popular spreadsheet, database management, mapping, and graphics software.

CACI also publishes the annual **Sourcebook of ZIP Code Demographics** and the **Sourcebook of County Demographics.** These volumes provide current-year estimates and five-year forecasts of key demographics. You can also get disks with selected demographic and sales potential information for states and metropolitan areas.

CLARITAS/NPDC

Specialties: desktop demographic system, cluster system, financial services

Mike Reinemer
Director of Communications
201 N. Union Street
Alexandria, VA 22314
703-683-8300

Claritas/NPDC develops national target marketing databases and software systems designed to meet the specific marketing needs of various industries, including automotive, banking, consumer products, health care, media, and utilities. With six offices throughout the U.S., Claritas is one of 16 information firms of VNU Business Information Services, Inc.

Compass is a PC-based targeting system used for product development and profiling, site location, strategic planning, media planning, and direct marketing. The desktop system combines and analyzes diverse types of data—clients' customer information files, as well as cartographic data, syndicated surveys, demographic indicators, and Claritas' PRIZM and P$YCLE segmentation systems. Compass is customized for each user, and allows the creation of unique applications. Claritas/NPDC provides on-site training and unlimited telephone support free of charge.

PRIZM is a market segmentation cluster system that was first introduced in 1974. It classifies all U.S. households into 40 neighborhood types at the census block group level. Originally modeled using census demographics combined with millions of customer records, PRIZM is updated anually.

Claritas/NPDC offers several products specifically for the financial services industry. **P$YCLE** is a segmentation system. **LifeP$YCLE** is an insurance consumer database. Claritas/NPDC also offers the **Claritas/Accountline** market audit database.

DATAMAP, INC.

Specialties: small-area demographics, software, insurance, mapping

Richard Byers
National Sales Manager
6436 City West Parkway
Eden Prairie, MN 55344
800-533-7742
612-941-0900

Datamap has offered custom mapping and data services since 1975. In recent years, the firm has added geodemographic software and geographic information services to its line of products.

Datamap specializes in small-area geography and demographics, to the postal carrier route level—a grouping of 300-500 households. Demographics are available for other levels of geography, including state, county, metropolitan area, ADI, ZIP Code, census tract, and block group, as well as custom geography.

CAM-1+ is a software and data system that aids in site analysis, target marketing, strategic planning. Users can access data for metropolitan areas, ZIP Codes, and custom geography. The system also offers customized buying power indices, spreadsheet capabilities, importation of customer and other user data, and exportation of data to Atlas*Graphics mapping software *(see Strategic Mapping, Inc., page 153).*

GUS (Geographic Underwriting System) links small-area geography with insurance risks. **Lightning Locator** and **Appoint-Plus** are software/service products for in-bound telemarketing that assist callers in finding products or making appointments based on geographic location.

DONNELLEY MARKETING INFORMATION SERVICES

Specialties: desktop demographic system, cluster system

Howard (Skip) Hunt
Vice President & General Manager
70 Seaview Avenue
Stamford, CT 06904
800-866-2255
203-353-7474

DMIS is a company of The Dun & Bradstreet Corporation. Donnelley provides a variety of demographic and business data in formats ranging from printed reports to analytical software.

CONQUEST is Donnelley's desktop marketing system. Using CD-ROM technology, it offers Donnelley's demographic estimates and projections, as well as **ClusterPLUS,** the firm's neighborhood cluster system. Other data available include retail sale estimates, Dun's business data, syndicated survey data from Simmons and Mediamark on media use and product purchases, Nielsen ratings and cable data. Users can also access industry-specific data for use in automotive, financial, health care, grocery, and shopping centers.

Demographic On-Call provides access to hundreds of standard demographic and business reports, as well as mapping and other marketing analysis, through a toll-free number, **800-866-2255**. Analytic Services provide custom analysis for marketing problems.

EQUIFAX NATIONAL DECISION SYSTEMS

Jon Voorhees
Vice President, Marketing
539 Encinitas Boulevard
Encinitas, CA 92024
800-877-5560
619-942-7000

Specialties: desktop demographic system, cluster system

EMDS produces **Infomark**, a PC system with over 20 databases on three CD-ROM disks—over 1.6 gigabytes of information. Data include demographics, daytime and business populations, media and product usage, industry-specific data, consumer expenditures, and geographic coordinates for mapping. Users can also add their own data to the system. Infomark generates maps and tabular reports, and operates on an upgraded IBM/AT/XT or PS/2.

EMDS also provides a line of market analysis/site selection tools and a cluster system called **MicroVision-50**, which classifies all 19 million ZIP+4 neighborhoods in the U.S. into 50 market segments, using census and individual data from the Equifax Consumer Marketing Database. The system is updated annually.

MARKET STATISTICS

Specialties: small-area demographics, software

Robert M. Katz
Sr. Vice President
633 Third Avenue
New York, NY 10017
212-986-4800

Market Statistics, producers of the annual **Survey of Buying Power** published in *Sales & Marketing Management,* specializes in sales and marketing analysis using demographic, economic, retail trade, and business-to-business data.

The **Market Statistics Data Bank** has annually updated information and projections for the U.S., metropolitan areas, television markets, counties, cities, ZIP Codes, and custom geography. Data are available as printed reports or on computer tape and disks.

The firm provides customized Buying Power Index (BPI) programs to help companies measure market potential and evaluate sales performance. Market Statistics also offers sales territory management and quota analysis, site selection, and a demographic modeling geographic information system.

Your Marketing Consultant (YMC) is an inexpensive bundled data/software package that allows users to analyze Market Statistics data on a PC.

NATIONAL PLANNING DATA CORPORATION

(See also Claritas/NPDC)

Specialties: small-area demographics, mapping, desktop demographic system

(Call for the name of the nearest sales representative)
P.O. Box 610
Ithaca, NY 14851-0610
607-273-8208

Claritas/NPDC provides current-year estimates and five-year projections of a variety of key demographic and business indicators. The firm has several databases which combine its proprietary data with census data. **PrimeLocation** is a desktop consumer information system incorporating satellite images in registration with demographic data, for use in target marketing, site location, and strategic planning. **Consumer CLOUT** provides demand forecasting for over 300 product categories by geography. It is based on data from the Bureau of Labor Statistics' Consumer Expenditure Survey, the Census Bureau's Census of Retail Trade, and proprietary Claritas/NPDC databases. The **Yellow Pages Data System** adds business information by SIC code. Reports are available through a call-in service or by tapping the MAX Online Demographic System.

MAXpc MapAnalyst is a thematic mapping PC package which downloads data from the MAX database.Claritas/ NPDC offers training seminars for its MAX and MapAnalyst systems.

The firm also offers special reports on a variety of subjects, including the 55+ market, health care market, and the labor force.

URBAN DECISION SYSTEMS, INC.

Specialties: small-area demographics, financial services

Elliott Steinberg
Sales Manager
2040 Armacost Avenue
P.O. Box 25953
Los Angeles, CA 90025
800-633-9568
213-820-8931

UDS's main product is its demographic updates, including current-year estimates and five-year forecasts of over 100 demographic and business indicators. All data are available as printed reports, or on disk or tape.

The firm also offers business data from the Census Bureau and Dun's National Business List. **Retail Potential** data estimate consumer spending potential based on demographic and socioeconomic characteristics of specified geographic areas. UDS also offers Claritas' **PRIZM** cluster data and new **Consumer Behavior** lifestyle system.

Another new database is **TRW Credit Profile and Purchasing Power** data, which has credit information to the census tract and ZIP Code level, as well as current-year income distribution by age of householder.

UDS also produces **COLORSITE Grid Images,** which display data through a network of equal-sized squares colored according to the density of the selected variable. They are available for geographic areas from the neighborhood to the state level.

Economic Forecasters

DATA RESOURCES, INC.

Specialty: population and economic projections

(Call for the name of the nearest sales representative)
24 Hartwell Avenue
Lexington, MA 02173
617-863-5100

DRI has more than 125 databases covering a broad range of financial, industrial, economic, and international topics.

Consumer Markets Forecasts examines personal expenditures for a variety of durable and nondurable categories, discretionary income, retail stores, and nondurable goods stores.

The **Regional Model Forecast** projects data for employment and production by industry, personal and disposable income, prices and wages, housing starts, population and households, and retail sales for regions and states. The **Metropolitan Area Forecasts** project employment, income, population and households for all metropolitan statistical areas. The **County Forecast** projects employment, income, population and households, and births, deaths, and migration trends for counties.

NPA DATA SERVICES, INC.

Specialty: population and economic projections

Nestor E. Terleckyj
1424 16th Street, NW
Suite 700
Washington, DC 20036
202-265-7685

NPA Data Services produces an annual **Regional Economic Projection Series,** or REPS, which produces long-range projections for regions, states, metropolitan areas, and counties, including population by age and sex, and employment, earnings, and personal income by industry. You can access the data through printed reports, on disks (for IBM and Macintosh), and online.

THE WEFA GROUP

Wharton Econometric Forecasting Associates

Specialties: population and economic projections, consulting

Sungchul Kim
Manager, Direct Marketing
150 Monument Road
Bala Cynwyd, PA 19004
215-896-4927

The WEFA Group provides economic projections, including the **Long-Term Service** which examines demographic shifts, technology developments, and other changes anticipated in the next decade. It also offers consulting services, including alternative scenarios, product-line forecasts, and market-potential assessment.

WOODS & POOLE ECONOMICS

Specialty: population and economic projections

Sallie L. Poole
Vice President, Marketing
1794 Columbia Road, NW
Washington, DC 20009
202-332-7111

Woods & Poole offers annually updated demographic and economic estimates and forecasts to the year 2010 for the U.S., regions, states, metropolitan areas, and counties. Population data include age, sex, race, personal income by source, and households. Economic data include employment and earnings by industry, and retail sales by kind of business. Data are available in printed reports, on disk, and on tape. The firm also does consulting and provides custom forecasts.

Media Specialists

THE ARBITRON COMPANY

Specialty: media and purchase behavior

Thom Mocarsky or
Katy Bachman
142 West 57th Street
New York, NY 10019
212-887-1300

Arbitron measures audiences in hundreds of television and radio markets. The firm provides estimates for specific television programs and for any radio or television daypart. Data are available for geographic areas such as metropolitan area, county, ZIP Code, or Arbitron's own ADIs (Areas of Dominant Influence). They're also available segmented by demographic, socioeconomic, lifestyle, and purchasing characteristics.

ScanAmerica is a relatively new division that offers single-source data through the use of people meters, which electronically measure television viewing of individuals in a household in combination with portable UPC scanners to record product purchases.

Arbitron recently acquired **SAMI,** which tracks product movement for packaged goods advertisers and retailers.

DIRECTORY DATA

Specialty: media behavior

Jim Sotzing
Director
One Post Road
Fairfield, CT 06430
203-254-1410

Directory Data is a new division of Survey Sampling *(see page 158)* that offers a nationally syndicated audience measurement service, providing audience estimates for 167 products/services and major media. Subscribers receive reports on the top 80 markets, regionally and nationally.

INFORMATION RESOURCES, INC.

Specialty: single-source media and purchase data, packaged goods, desktop marketing system

Alan Hill
Vice President, Retail Product Management
150 N. Clinton Street
Chicago, IL 60606
312-726-1221

IRI offers **BehaviorScan,** a single-source system which links purchase information collected through UPC scanners and television watching measured by people meters. The firm also provides demographic and purchase information for a large national household panel through its **Infoscan** service, which does sales and market share tracking for products, categories, and departments, promotion planning and evaluation, price comparison measurement, and more. Clients can buy printed reports or do their own analysis with **pcInfoscan for Retailers,** a desktop system.

MEDIAMARK RESEARCH, INC.

Specialty: media and purchase behavior, software

708 Third Avenue
New York, NY 10017
212-599-0444

MRI conducts an annual syndicated survey of 20,000 adults in the 48 continental states, collecting data on demographic and socioeconomic characteristics, media usage, and purchase behavior. Data are available in printed reports and online. **MEMRI** is a PC-based system that allows custom analysis of survey data. MRI also combines its media and product data with all four U.S. geodemographic (cluster) systems for lifestyle analysis.

MENDELSOHN MEDIA RESEARCH, INC.

Specialties: media behavior, affluent market

Jacqueline Toback
Senior Vice President, Director of Marketing
352 Park Avenue South
New York, NY 10010
212-684-6350

Mendelsohn's annual **Survey of Adults and Markets of Affluence** is conducted among adults with household incomes of $60,000 or more in 48 states. The six-volume report and data tape contain audience data for publications, broadcast television viewing and radio listening by daypart, and cable television access and viewing. The survey also provides demographic and purchase data. Mendelsohn provides large samples of super-affluent adults having incomes of $150,000 or more and $200,000 or more.

NIELSEN MEDIA RESEARCH

Specialty: television behavior

(Call for the nearest sales representative)
Nielsen Plaza
Northbrook, IL 60062-6288
708-498-6300

Nielsen estimates broadcast and cable television audiences through the **Nielsen Television Index,** which provides national network ratings by using electronic people meters in a nationwide sample of households. The **Nielsen Station Index** supplies viewing reports for each of 220 local television markets at least four times a year. These reports reveal who watches television and when.

Segment Specialists

AMERICAN SPORTS DATA, INC.

Specialty: sports market

Harvey Lauer
234 North Central Avenue
Hartsdale, NY 10530
914-328-8877

This company conducts an annual mail survey of 15,000 households on sports and leisure activities. Respondents are asked about activities ranging from aerobics to tennis, as well as health club membership. Results are available in summary reports and for each activity.

ANALYSIS AND FORECASTING, INC.

Specialty: household projections

John R. Pitkin
President
P.O. Box 415
Cambridge, MA 02138
617-491-8171

A&F provides estimates, projections, and reports for households and housing for the U.S., regions, states, metropolitan areas and counties. Data characteristics include type of household, presence of children, number of earners, and type of housing.

In collaboration with Cambridge Systematics, A&F also specializes in the implications of future population trends for business and government.

CENTER FOR CONTINUING STUDY OF THE CALIFORNIA ECONOMY

Specialty: California market

Aviva Bernstein
Marketing Director
610 University Avenue
Palo Alto, CA 94301
415-321-8550

CCSCE specializes in demographic and economic studies for public and private sector clients, reporting on subjects ranging from house income and spending power to population by ethnic group and age. It publishes a series of annual reports on the population and economy of California by region and county, including projections.

The firm also conducts seminars and management briefings on the impact of national trends on California and the outlook for the California economy.

DANTER COMPANY

Specialty: real estate

J. Terry Hall
40 West Spruce Street
Columbus, OH 43215
614-221-9096

The Danter Company is a real estate research firm that conducts market feasibility studies for commercial and housing development. In addition to on-site project and development analysis, the firm conducts telephone and intercept surveys to establish tenant buyer profiles in real estate markets throughout the U.S., including key demographic factors and attitudes. Analyses are available for client-specified sites based on published information and an online database.

What's Hot and What's Not is an annual ranking of housing development potential in the nation's 150 largest metropolitan areas.

DEMO-DETAIL

Specialty: county population estimates

Richard Irwin
Director
2303 Apple Hill Road
Alexandria, VA 22308
703-780-9563

Demo-Detail provides annual population estimates for all counties in the U.S. by age, sex, and race. You can get the data in printed reports, on disk, or the entire national file dating back to 1980 on tape.

ELECTION DATA SERVICES, INC.

Specialty: political services

Kimball W. Brace
President
1522 K Street, NW
Suite 626
Washington, DC 20005
202-789-2004

EDS provides research and consultation for all levels of government, candidates, political organizations, labor unions, trade associations, and others interested in the electoral process. Its emphasis is on developing databases for political and demographic analysis. **GeoPol** is a campaign database and targeting system that combines election, census, and geopolitical data. The system is available online and can produce maps. EDS also has special programs for designing and analyzing redistricting plans.

FULTON RESEARCH, INC.

Specialty: real estate

George A. Fulton
President
11351 Random Hills Road
4th floor
Fairfax, VA 22030
703-359-1720

Fulton Research offers a variety of research and consulting services for those involved in real estate development, such as market area analysis, specific site analysis, planned unit development studies, and pricing and consumer studies. The firm also conducts an annual survey of over 2,000 homeshoppers and provides its findings on a national and regional basis.

LINK RESOURCES CORPORATION

Specialty: consumer electronics consulting

Andy Bose, Vice President
79 Fifth Avenue
New York, NY 10003
212-627-1500

Link is a market research and consulting firm specializing in the electronic information, electronic services, telecommunications, and home electronics industries. Annual surveys include the **HomeMedia Consumer Survey** of 2,500 households and the **Small Business Survey** of 1,000 small businesses, and **Medium-Large Business Survey** (200 companies).

The firm offers annual syndicated continuous research services for various industries including Electronic Entertainment, Consumer Teleservices, Home Office, and Consumer Personal Computer Market. Additionally, Link **Multivariate Cluster Analysis** offers residential segmentation for targeting home electronics markets based on past product purchases and future buying intentions. Data are collected on age, education, presence of children, marital status, occupation, race, home value, mobility, credit card usage, and media behavior. Link also offers information for specialty areas such as CD players, VCRs, cable television, fax machines, camcorders, videogames, etc.

MARKETING EVALUATIONS TVQ, INC.

Specialty: brand-name-oriented consumers

Steven Levitt
President
14 Vanderventer Avenue
Port Washington, NY
11050
516-944-8833

This firm monitors the demographics of people who favor specific actors, cartoon characters, athletes, brand names, movies, fashion designers, and TV and cable programs. It also offers a 35,000-member nationally representative household panel for mail and telephone surveys.

MARKET METRICS

Specialty: supermarket retailing, desktop marketing system

Jerry Clapp
Executive Vice President
P.O. Box 10097
Lancaster, PA 17605-0097
717-397-1500

Market Metrics provides **Supermarket Solutions,** a desktop marketing system for food retailers. The combination data/software package includes data from the company's annual **In-Store Survey of Supermarkets,** as well as store-specific demographics and expenditures, and links to Mediamark survey data on purchase behavior by demographics *(see page 133)*. Users can also add their own data to the system, which handles tasks such as estimating product potential across stores, site evaluation, and measurement of store performance.

PRI ASSOCIATES, INC.

Specialties: labor force, affirmative action

Harold Thompson
Director of Marketing
1905 Chapel Hill Road
Durham, NC 27707
919-493-7534

PRI (formerly Personnel Research Inc.) offers labor force data by sex and age for over 514 detailed occupations from the Census Bureau's EEO Special File, to be used for relocation analysis and affirmative action planning. Data are available for the U.S., states, counties, metropolitan areas, and large cities in print, on disk or CD-ROM, or tape. PRI also offers **AAPlanner** and **Work Force/Job Group Analyst,** two PC software programs that perform affirmative action planning calculations.

PRIMELIFE MARKETING

Specialty: mature market

Jeff Ostroff
Partner, PrimeLife Marketing Division
The Data Group
2260 Butler Pike, Su. 150
Plymouth Meeting, PA 19462
215-834-3003

PrimeLife Marketing is a division of The Data Group which provides expertise in marketing to the 45+ consumer. It offers a wide range of marketing research, communications, and advisory products and services.

RUNZHEIMER INTERNATIONAL

Specialty: employee relocation and travel, international cost of living

Peter D. Packer
Runzheimer Park
Rochester, WI 53167
414-534-3121

Runzheimer International conducts research on a wide variety of topics related to doing business in the U.S. and abroad, particularly in regard to employee relocation and travel costs. In this capacity it offers a variety of publications by subscription, including monthly publications which cover surveys and issues of interest to professional employee relocation and travel managers. A semi-annual report covers the costs of meals, lodging, and other comparative living costs for 300 U.S. and international locations.

SLATER HALL INFORMATION PRODUCTS

Specialties: government data on CD-ROM, software

Courtenay Slater
1522 K Street, NW
Washington, DC 20005
202-682-1350

SHIP offers government databases on CD-ROM with its proprietary Searcher software, with which users can retrieve, rank, analyze, and export data for other uses. Five disks are currently available: **County and City Statistics** includes a variety of demographic and economic information from the Census Bureau's COSTAT database as well as data for over 900 cities; **Population Statistics** has 1980 census data for states, metros, counties, and places of 10,000 or more, as well as current population and per capita income estimates for counties and places, and state population projections through the year 2010; **County Income and Employment** has annual data on employment and earnings by industry for states and counties from 1969 on; **Business Indicators** is updated monthly and includes income and employment by industry for states, as well as the National Income and Product Account from 1929 to the present, plus economic time series from the Survey of Current Business; and **Agricultural Statistics** contains the 1982 and 1987 Censuses of Agriculture, plus farm income data.

SOCIOECONOMICS

Specialty: real estate

Jack Lessinger
President
17004-26th Avenue, NE
Seattle, WA 98155
206-382-9658

This firm locates prime areas for real estate investment based on migratory patterns, economic trends, and social attitudes and their affect on property values, for use in site location, investment, and marketing strategy.

STRATEGY RESEARCH CORPORATION

Specialty: Hispanic market

Richard D. Roth
Vice President
100 NW 37th Avenue
Miami, FL 33125
305-649-5400

Strategy Research is a full-service marketing firm which specializes in the Hispanic market, although it also conducts general market research. Its quarterly **Hispanic Omnibus** survey is based on personal interviews with 1,500 Hispanic adults. SRC also conducts the **Anglo** and **Black Omnibuses** for comparative purposes. Services include bilingual focus groups and cover a broad variety of areas such as health care, real estate/site location, financial services, and political polls and campaign strategies.

TEENAGE RESEARCH UNLIMITED

Specialty: youth market

Peter Zollo
President
601 Skokie Boulevard
Northbrook, IL 60062
708-564-3440

TRU conducts the syndicated **Teenage Media/Market Study.** The research is fielded twice a year and measures teenagers' purchases in 250 product categories, as well as collecting data on media use, grocery shopping behavior, attitudes, and participation in sports and leisure activities.

TRU also offers custom research on the youth market using personal interviews, focus groups, and telephone and mail surveys. TRU is associated with McCollum/Spielman International and Child Research Services.

U.S. TRAVEL DATA CENTER

Specialty: travel market

Survey Research Department
1133 21st Street, NW
Washington, DC 20036
202-293-1040

The U.S. Travel Data Center is a private organization that studies the travel market extensively. Since 1979 it has conducted a monthly telephone survey of of 1,500 Americans' travel intentions and activities. The **National Travel Survey** collects information on 19 trip characteristics such as duration, transportation, lodging, destination, and purpose. Survey data are published in **The Monthly Travel Monitor,** which also tracks other sources of travel industry data. The seasonal and annual **Travel Market Close-Up** provides charts and detailed crosstabulations of current survey data, while the **Travel Executive Briefing** contains summary text and graphics of trend data. Subscribers can also tap into an extensive database containing data from1984 to the present for custom analysis.

The Center has also conducted a monthly **Survey of Business Travelers** since 1984, drawn from the National Travel Survey sample. Data are published annually. **Discover America 2000**, a special report published in 1988, is a compilation and synthesis of demographic statistics, consumer surveys, and observations from social analysts and futurists. The report addresses how the population will change towards the turn of the century and what effect these changes will have on the travel industry.

Canadian Specialists

CANADIAN MARKET ANALYSIS CENTRE (CMAC)

Specialties: Canadian market, cluster system

Dan Huck
International Institute for Market Analysis
3430 Mansfield Road
Falls Church, VA 22041
800-829-3004
703-824-0200

Canada address:
P.O. Box 2749
Station "A"
Toronto, Ontario
CANADA M5W 9Z9

CMAC is a division of the International Institute for Market Analysis that offers database and software products for target marketing applications in Canada. The **Target Marketer's Guide on Canada** is a 600-page statistical reference book with demographic and market information for three-character postal codes and the top 130 metropolitan areas. The Guide is also available on disk.

Mosaique is a geodemographic system for targeting approximately 50 lifestyles by geography. The **Quick*Site** ordering services offers demographic reports for any geographic area, as well as graphs and maps.

COMPUSEARCH MARKET AND SOCIAL RESEARCH LIMITED

Specialties: Canadian market, cluster system

Kelly Woodcock
Senior Marketing Manager
330 Front Street West, Suite 1100
Toronto, Ontario M5V 3B7
Canada
416-348-9180

Compusearch offers a complete line of services for the Canadian market, including its **Lifestyles Market Segmentation** cluster system, census data, population estimates and projections, consumer spending, and shopping center and other business data. Data are available for all geographies on-line, in printed reports, and for microcomputers, and can be linked to proprietary data.

TETRAD COMPUTER APPLICATIONS LIMITED

Specialty: Canadian desktop demographic system, cluster system

Wilson Baker
1445 West Georgia Street
Vancouver,
British Columbia
Canada V6G 2T3
604-685-2295

Tetrad offers **PCensus** and **PSearch** desktop demographic software and data for the 1986 Canadian census. PCensus provides geographic access to over 300 demographic variables. PSearch locates target areas that match a user-defined lifestyle. Other databases include family expenditures, household facilities, and **Mosaique** lifestyles.

Market, Public Opinion, and Lifestyle Research

FIND/SVP

Specialties: market research, baby boom

Peggy Koenig
Director, Marketing Communications
625 Avenue of the Americas
New York, NY 10011
212-645-4500

Find/SVP has offered business and competitive intelligence to clients for over 20 years. Eighty research consultants answer over 7,000 inquiries a month through the company's **Quick Information Service,** accessing over 1,500 online databases, 11,000 company and subject files, and 2,000 periodicals. The Strategic Research Division handles in-depth requests.

FIND publishes about 40 syndicated market research reports annually in areas such as demographics, food/beverages, technology, health care, and consumer durables. It also publishes two monthly newsletters—**The Boomer Report** (on baby boomers) and **Ice Cream Reporter.**

FROST & SULLIVAN, INC.

Specialties: health and beauty aids, international

Kathy Palagonia
106 Fulton Street
New York, NY 10038
212-233-1080

Frost & Sullivan publishes market research studies for the health care and beauty aids industries in the U.S. and Europe. Reports are updated every 2 years or so and cover topics such as skin care, home health care, private-label cosmetics, and generic drugs.

THE GALLUP ORGANIZATION

Specialty: public opinion research

Diane Colasanto
Senior Vice President
100 Palmer Square
Suite 200
Princeton, NJ 08542
609-924-9600

Gallup's Opinion Research Division conducts **The Gallup Poll**—a weekly syndicated news service that tracks American lifestyles and public reaction to current events. The division also conducts custom research on public opinion regarding social and policy issues for clients in media, trade associations, public relations, advertising, and other businesses, in both the U.S. and internationally. Other divisions of the company conduct market research for hospitals, broadcasters, financial institutions, and consumer products companies.

Gallup provides national personal interview and telephone omnibus services to which clients can add customized questions. Both are conducted each month using a nationally representative sample of 1,000 adults. Gallup has 46 affiliates worldwide and does research in 76 nations on 6 continents.

IMPACT RESOURCES

Specialty: market research

Michelle Becker
Director of
Public Relations
125 Dillmont Drive
Columbus, OH 43235
614-888-5900

Impact Resources conducts annual non-commissioned consumer studies in over 50 major markets nationwide. The **MA*RT Consumer Intelligence System** offers profiles of over 280,000 consumers and more than 1,000 retailers, including demographics, lifestyle characteristics, media habits, shopping behavior, reasons for store choice, automobile ownership, and banking/financial activities. The monthly **MarkeTrend: Micro Market News** offers summaries of MA*RT research.

Other products include custom reports and **Market Opportunities in Retail** reports of important consumer groups, such as Hispanics and Asians, which are published jointly with Deloitte and Touche TRADE.

LANGER ASSOCIATES, INC.

Specialties: qualitative research, lifestyles

Judith Langer
President
19 West 44 Street
New York, NY 10036
212-391-0350

Langer Associates specializes in qualitative studies of social and marketing issues. **The Langer Report** is a syndicated newsletter on changing values and lifestyles. **TrendSpotter** studies identify emerging trends. The firm gathers information through focus groups, as well as personal and telephone interviews, and offers consulting services.

MANAGEMENT HORIZONS

Specialty: international market research and consulting

Dennis Anspach
570 Metro Place North
Dublin, OH 43017
614-764-9555

Management Horizons is a divison of Price Waterhouse which provides international market research and consulting. It offers a nationally representative database of over 3,000 shoppers by demographics, shopper typology, media preferences, shopping behavior, and store appeals. The firm offers an annual **Consumer Expenditure Forecast** and several reports related to specific issues and trends in consumer markets. Subscribers to the **Retail Intelligence System** can produce an unlimited number of reports using raw data, others may purchase custom reports on an individual basis.

MARKET OPINION RESEARCH

Specialty: market research

James Leiman
Vice President
243 West Congress
Detroit, MI 48226
314-963-2414

MOR provides marketing research services for a variety of industries. It has two telephone data collection systems with over 100 CATI-equipped stations. It also offers computer models, databases, and software, as well as a variety of studies in the fields of hospital positioning, health screening research, money management and investor services, customer service, public affairs and communications, and media. MOR also does geodemographic analysis and other research for political campaigns.

NFO RESEARCH, INC.

Specialty: household panel

Melanie A. Mumper
Marketing Support
2700 Oregon Road
Box 315
Toledo, OH 43691-0315
419-666-8800

NFO conducts research through its 400,000-plus household panel, which is balanced for a variety of demographic characteristics within the nine census divisions. This allows researchers to select samples that match their requirements. NFO conducts virtually any type of data collection for a wide variety of industries, the results of which can be combined with major psychographic and cluster systems.

THE NPD GROUP, INC.

Specialty: market research

Claire Hamilton
Corporate Communications Manager
900 West Shore Road
Port Washington, NY 11050-0402
516-625-2302

The NPD Group offers syndicated tracking services, which include mail/diary panels and retail/POS databases for a variety of industries, including automotive, consumer electronics, food, petroleum, restaurant, soft goods, sporting goods, and toys.

HTI Custom Research conducts proprietary mail and telephone surveys. This division also offers marketing models featuring **ESP, Brand*Star, Brandscape,** and **Brandlab.**

OPINION RESEARCH SERVICE

Specialty: public opinion research

Dennis Gilbert
President
P.O. Box 9076
J.F.K. Station
Boston, MA 02114
617-482-1534

Opinion Research publishes the annual **American Public Opinion Index.** This reference book lists questions asked in other firms' surveys alphabetically by topic. Sources include national opinion research firms and media polls as well as a broad range of state and local polling organizations. Subjects include business and economics, communications, crime, current events, education, family and social life, government and politics, health, religion, and so on. **American Public Opinion Data** provides summary data on microfiche for all questions listed in the Index, as well as exact question wording and survey methodology.

PACKAGED FACTS

Specialty: market research

David A. Weiss
274 Madison Avenue
Suite 202
New York, NY 10016
212-532-5533

Packaged Facts provides custom research in a variety of formats for market researchers, advertising agencies, and others. It also publishes **Consumer Market Studies** for specific food, beverage, durables, health care, personal care, demographic, and household markets.

THE ROPER ORGANIZATION

Specialties: market and public opinion research, international

Thomas A.W. Miller
Senior Vice President
205 East 42nd Street
New York, NY 10017
212-599-0700

The Roper Organization is the nation's oldest market/opinion research firm. Its custom research division specializes in consumer behavior analysis, new product development, corporate public affairs/issues management, and legal evidence surveys. Its syndicated research division publishes **Roper Reports,** tracking consumer/public opinion through 10 surveys (2,000 respondents each) a year, and **The Public Pulse,** a monthly newsletter of market/opinion analysis and forecast. Its **Limobus** service fields proprietary questions through Roper's shared cost, in-person omnibus every month. Roper's international division conducts research in over 60 countries worldwide.

SIMMONS MARKET RESEARCH BUREAU

Specialties: media and purchase behavior, youth market, affluent market, international

Ellen Cohen
President
420 Lexington Avenue
New York, NY 10017
212-916-8900

Simmons' Syndicated Studies Division conducts the annual **Study of Media & Markets,** which personally interviews 20,000 adults nationwide. This division also conducts the **Exclusive Set** survey of 3,000 adults with household incomes of $75,000 or more and the biennial **Teen Age Research Study** (STARS). All surveys collect information on detailed media usage and over 800 product/service categories, as well as demographic and socioeconomic characteristics. Subscribers can get data through printed reports, online services, or the **CHOICES** PC system, which allows custom crosstabulation of the survey data.

The Custom Media Studies Divison conducts subscriber, newsstand, and specialized studies for print media (magazines and newspapers). It also publishes the biennial **Food Industry Study** and **Top Management Insights.**

Custom Studies is a division of Simmons/MRB Group which provides full-service research in the U.S. and over 90 countries worldwide for consumer and non-consumer markets. It offers particular expertise in promotions testing, pricing research using the **PriceSet** model, sponsorship, market segmentation, produce and service modeling using **Micro Modeler** and **SIMALTO**, customer research, and corporate image and trade research. Contact David Pring, President of Custom Studies, at **212-916-8933.**

VALUES AND LIFESTYLE (VALS) PROGRAM

Specialty: lifestyle research

Deborah Moroney
SRI International
Director of Marketing
333 Ravenswood Avenue
Menlo Park, CA 94025-3493
415-859-4324

VALS 2 is a new consumer segmentation built on the basic forces driving consumer choices. Using two dimensions—self-orientation and resources—VALS 2 defines eight segments of adult consumers with different attitudes and who display distinctive behavior and decision-making patterns. Each segment represents a viable target.

The VALS program offers subscribers an all-inclusive package of products and services. **Leading Edge Reports** cover psychological and consumption patterns of the segments, as well as social trends, applications of the system, and analyses of specific markets.

VALS 2 is also linked to syndicated media studies, consumer panels, and geodemographic (cluster) services. Other services include orientation training sessions, consultation, and use of the VALS 2 classification questions for use in producing customized segmentation.

YANKELOVICH CLANCY SHULMAN

Specialty: lifestyle research

Robert Shulman
8 Wright Street
Westport, CT 06880
203-227-2700
212-752-7500

Yankelovich Clancy Shulman is known for **The Monitor,** which interviews 2,500 adults in order to gauge consumers' social values and attitudes. It currently tracks 55 trends and segments the population into six groups—New Autonomous, Gamesmen, Scramblers, Traditionals, American Dreamers, and Aimless. The **Senior Monitor** follows the same procedure in classifying the 50+ market. They also publish the **Hispanic Monitor.**

Other services include **Perceptual Scan,** which tracks customer attitudes towards clients' products. **Data Recast** analyzes customer data, and **Litmus Optimization** defines and solves a variety of marketing problems using a mathematical model.

Geographic Specialists

CHADWYCK-HEALEY

Specialties: mapping, software

Michael J. Fischer
Geographer
1101 King Street
Alexandria, VA 22314
800-752-0515

This firm offers **Supermap,** a CD-ROM program with which users can retrieve, manipulate, and display 1980 census and other more current demographic data. Users can also enter their own data for reporting and mapping.

GEOGRAPHIC DATA TECHNOLOGY, INC.

Specialty: geographic services

Molly Hutchins
National Sales Manager
13 Dartmouth College Highway
Lyme, NH 03768-9713
603-795-2183

GDT supplies boundary and street network files for use with mapping software on mainframe and microcomputers. **DYNAMAP/USA II** is a national database of digitized street segments and non-street features, and is the basis for a line of many of the cartographic products and services offered by other firms. **GeoSpreadSheet** is an integration of spreadsheet software with a computerized map for use in site analysis, thematic mapping, and territory planning. **HandShake/GDT** is a software package that assists telephone operators in referring callers to the nearest outlets for goods and services.

HAWTHORNE SOFTWARE COMPANY, INC.

Specialty: mapping software

Linda A. Lido
P.O. Box 35
Hawthorne, NJ 07507
201-304-0014

PINMAP is a PC mapping software program for plotting ZIP Code and county level data. Users can access data from spreadsheets or database programs, and display them at six levels—five-digit zip, three-digit zip, county, state, city, and user-defined areas. The package includes **Dr. HALO III** from Media Cynbernetics which allows users to customize maps for printer, plotter, or slide presentations.

INTELLIGENT CHARTING, INC.

Specialty: mapping services

John Butkus
National Sales Manager
600 International Drive
Mt. Olive, NJ 07828
201-691-7000

Intelligent Charting offers custom-generated maps in sizes ranging from 3x3 inches to 3x4 feet. You can map demographic and industry data available through the firm or provide your own data. Geographies available include states, counties, ZIP Codes, metropolitan areas, DMAs, ADIs, census tracts, carrier routes, as well as custom territories and marketing areas. Overnight delivery is available for requests.

MPSI SYSTEMS, INC.

Specialties: geographic information system, international

Joe Perrault
Senior Manager
Marketing/Planning
8282 South Memorial Drive
Tulsa, OK 74133
918-250-9611

MPSI is an international firm which specializes in computer software and information services. It offers the **Geographic Information System,** which links data to geography—from counties down to road networks—and provides results through tabular reports and maps. Users can combine their own data with MPSI's databases on retail sales, land use, and traffic counts. MPSI will also generate customized geographic files for trade areas and distribution networks.

RAND MCNALLY

Specialty: geographic services

Mike Kelly
8255 North Central Park Avenue
Skokie, IL 60076-2970
800-332-7163
312-673-9100 x3477

Rand McNally is known for its annual **Commercial Atlas & Marketing Guide,** which has state maps, and population and economic statistics. A new publication is the **ZIP Code Market Atlas & Planner,** which combines the firm's national, regional, and local-level road atlas maps with clear film overlays delineating five-digit ZIP Code boundaries.

RANDATA is a database that links various levels of geography through three files. **Geolink** provides data for places sorted by city, county, or ZIP Code. **Ziplink** has ZIP and county codes in combination with latitude and longitude coordinates with ZIP Code centers. **International** is an index to almost 93,000 places worldwide.

SAMMAMISH DATA SYSTEMS

Specialty: geographic information systems

Rod Clark
Director of Marketing
1813 130th Avenue, NE
Suite 216
Bellevue, WA 98005-2240
206-867-1485

Sammamish Data has two Geographic Information Systems specifically designed for use in marketing research and sales territory management. **GeoSight** integrates, displays, and analyzes multiple databases with respect to multiple geographic layers, and produces customized maps or reports for any user-defined areas. The **Territory Management System** interactively defines and modifies sales territories, marketing regions, and distribution zones, using census blocks or tracts, ZIP Codes, counties, or other geographic areas.

Market Statistics *(see page 127)* offers both systems for use with its demographic and economic databases.

STRATEGIC MAPPING, INC.

Specialty: mapping software

Stephen Poizner
President
4030 Moorpark Avenue
San Jose, CA 95117
408-985-7400

Strategic Mapping (formerly Strategic Locations Planning) provides **ATLAS*GRAPHICS,** a software program that maps census geography, ZIP Codes, and market areas on PCs. Users can also enter their own data and create customized geographic areas. The firm also offers **ATLAS*DRAW** for creating and editing boundary files, and **ATLAS*MapMaker,** a thematic mapping software program for the Apple Macintosh.

TYDAC TECHNOLOGIES, INC.

Specialty: geographic information systems

Joe Francica/Terry Moloney
1655 North Fort Myer Drive, Suite 320
Arlington, VA 22209
703-522-0773

TYDAC offers **SPANS**, a comprehensive geographic information system for use on personal computers. SPANS includes data modeling, networking, address matching, and overlay analysis, as well as interfaces to public and private databases of all kinds, and to statistical and database management software.

WESTERN ECONOMIC RESEARCH COMPANY, INC.

Specialty: ZIP Code maps

C. Michael Long
President
8155 Van Nuys Boulevard
Suite 100
Panorama City, CA 91402
818-787-6277

WER provides pre-packaged research aids in the form of maps, reports, and disks. They are known particularly for their ZIP Code maps and demographic estimates.

Consultants and Tools for Analysis

ECONOMIC RESEARCH SERVICES, INC.

Specialty: labor force consulting

Leonard T. Elzie
4901 Tower Court
Suite 200
Tallahassee, FL 32303
904-562-1211

The economists at ERS develop computerized databases to monitor corporate employment and compensation practices, develop and update affirmative action plans. They also serve as expert witnesses in the areas of labor economics, employment discrimination, and wage forecasts.

THE FUTURES GROUP

Specialties: consulting, software

Charles Perrottet
80 Glastonbury Boulevard
Glastonbury, CT
06033-1264
203-633-3501

for Consumer Markets:
Sandra Shaber/David Cross
202-347-8165

for StatPlan IV: Diane Bernier
203-633-3501

The Futures Group performs strategic analyses, market studies, and technology assessments intended to help make strategic decisions for an uncertain future. Techniques include environmental scanning, decision and simulation modeling, forecasting, and trend analysis.

The firm offers **Consumer Markets,** a subscription and consulting service providing analysis of trends in consumer spending, household income distribution, demographics, and lifestyles. Monthly reports are supplemented by semi-annual strategic reviews. **StatPlan IV** is a PC statistical software package with forecasting capability and graphic display.

GMI/UNI-MAIL

Specialty: direct marketing services

Ken Altman
President
352 Park Avenue South
New York, NY 10010-1709
212-679-7655

GMI/Uni-Mail offers a database called **Agebase** which has the names and addresses of over 140 million adults and children. Each name is matched with exact date of birth. The file also contains 300 socioeconomic indicators including income (via ZIP Code, block group, or census tract), householder designation, type of dwelling, and ethnicity.

METRODIRECT

Specialty: direct marketing services

Shari Gridley
Account Executive
901 West Bond Street
Lincoln, NE 68521-3694
800-228-4571

MetroDirect is a divison of Metromail which offers address and telephone listings for a variety of demographic and household characteristics. Its database of nearly 78 million households can be segmented by house size, length of residence, age of members, ethnic or religious surname, income, response to direct mail solicitations, and other items.

MODERN BUSINESS APPLICATIONS, INC.

Specialty: software

J.F. Squillante
67 GAR Highway
Somerset, MA 02725
508-672-2398

MBA produces **Select.Site,** a PC system which allows you to call up a metropolitan area, draw any shape area on it and obtain a demographic profile for the custom area. Data come from NPDC *(see page 128)* and include current-year estimates and five-year forecasts for a variety of demographic and socioeconomic characteristics such as sex, age, race/ethnicity, income, and housing value. Select.Site can be custom designed to meet the specific needs of users.

NATIONAL DEMOGRAPHICS & LIFESTYLES, INC.

Specialties: direct marketing services, lifestyles

corporate office:
1621 Eighteenth Street
Denver, CO 80202-1211
800-525-3533
303-292-5000

One Madison Avenue
New York, NY 10010
212-481-9220

701 Palomar Airport Road
Carlsbad, CA 92009
619-931-4790

NDL builds individual-level databases using self-reported and detailed demographic and lifestyle information voluntarily provided by consumers. NDL offers the 18-million name **Lifestyle Selector,** and rents targeted mailing lists to all reputable direct marketers.

R.L. POLK & CO.

Specialty: direct marketing services

Jerry Helmicki
Manager, List Services
6400 Monroe Blvd.
Taylor, MI 48180-1814
313-292-3200

R.L. Polk has **List X-1,** which is compiled through vehicle registrations, telephone lists, birth and school information, questionnaires, and other means. It includes names and addresses broken out by sex, income, homeownership, occupation, presence of children, and other demographic variables which can be further segmented by geography.

The firm also provides **Geoplus**, a main frame software system which assigns census tract codes to ZIP Codes so addresses can be further enhanced by cluster analysis. **Household Mail Response Analysis** applies demographic factors to your customer lists and compares results to the X-1 list, allowing clients to determine and rank responsiveness of households in their file.

SALES EVALUATION ASSOCIATES

Specialty: consulting

David Glazer
President
780 Third Avenue
Suite 1603
New York, NY 10017
212-758-2990

SEA helps businesses in consumer products and services, trade associations, and business-to-business markets to build and use demographic databases, analyze sales, and allocate advertising budgets. It applies demographic and business data to measure clients' sales potential and performance. SEA also designs and implements marketing information systems for the Yellow Pages industry.

SMARTNAMES, INC.

Specialties: direct marketing services, real estate

Jan L. Davis
Vice President
176 Second Avenue
Waltham, MA 02154
800-424-4636
617-890-8900

SmartNames offers **HOMES**, a direct mail list with information about home market value, age, size, and construction type, as well as homeowner demographics. The **Consumer** list is broken down by age, income, sex, dwelling type, education, and so on. Both lists are available segmented by a variety of demographic and geographic characteristics.

SmartNames also provides research services, profiling and analysis, modeling, and custom database development.

STATISTICAL INNOVATIONS, INC.

Specialties: consulting, statistical software

Jay Magidson
President
375 Concord Avenue
Belmont, MA 02178
617-489-4490

SI is a consulting firm which develops response models and conducts training seminars for direct marketers on segmentation analysis, log-linear modeling, and other advanced statistical techniques. The firm also offers **SI-CHAID,** a PC-based program that analyzes response to test mailings and identifies target segments. The program is also available as a SAS procedure for mainframe computers.

SURVEY SAMPLING, INC.

Specialty: survey samples

Gwen Kaplan
Account Group Manager
One Post Road
Fairfield, CT 06430
203-255-4200

SSI provides custom-drawn telephone samples for any type of geography and a variety of household profiles and business categories. **Super Samples** is a random-digit database that identifies residential telephones, whether listed or unlisted. **Listed Telephone Samples** includes only residential telephones listed in directories. **Business and Industrial Samples** use SIC codes to classify companies. **Targeted Samples** allow the selection of household listings by income, race, and ethnicity, and age of members (including children).

SSI also offers a Yellow Pages audience measurement service through its Directory Data division *(see page 133)*.

WALONICK ASSOCIATES

Specialty: statistical software

Leon Storm
Sales Manager
6500 Nicollet Ave., South
Minneapolis, MN 55423
612-866-9022

Walonick offers **Stat-Packets,** an alternative to full-fledged statistical analysis software. It consists of low-priced PC software modules which analyze data directly from spreadsheet files. They perform a variety of statistical functions, from simple crosstabulation to multivariate analysis, and you can purchase them separately or in any combination.

Walonick also offers **StatPac Gold,** a full-fledged statistical program that can handle more than 32,000 cases and up to 500 variables.

CHAPTER 6

Academic, Industry, & Nonprofit Sources

Sometimes you can't get what you need from standard sources like the Census Bureau or your favorite private vendor. If the information you're after seems too obscure or unique for anyone to have, don't be so sure that it doesn't exist. It may take some digging, but there is probably someone out there doing research on your topic.

How to Use This Chapter

The hodgepodge of sources listed here are divided into two main types—academic and industry. The academic sources include survey research centers and scholarly associations. The industry sources include trade associations, magazines, and nonprofit organizations. Each has an area of specialty which is identified in parentheses after the title.

Most of these groups provide data, publications, and other information to the general public, although members often get substantial price discounts.

THE LISTINGS:

Academic Sources

CENTER FOR HUMAN RESOURCES RESEARCH

Specialty: labor force

Gale James
Coordinator
NLS Public Users Office
Suite 200
921 Chatham Lane
Columbus, OH 43221
614-442-7300

Since 1966, the Department of Labor and Ohio State University have been following thousands of men and women through the National Longitudinal Surveys of Labor Market Experience. Longitudinal data are valuable because they track individuals over time, uncovering the experiences of different groups of people throughout their work lives.

You can learn about early retirement trends from the **Survey of Older Men,** which studies the withdrawal from the labor force of over 5,000 men who were aged 45 to 59 in 1966. Data were collected for these men from 1966 to 1983, and they are scheduled to be reinterviewed in 1990.

To learn how women move in and out of the labor force during childraising years, look at the **Survey of Mature Women.** This survey tracks more than 5,000 women who were aged 30 to 44 in 1967. Data are currently available through 1986 and data from the 1987 interviews are due for release in 1990.

The **Surveys of Young Men** and **Young Women** have been tracking more than 10,000 adults who were aged 14 to 24 in 1966 (men) and 1968 (women). Data for men are available through 1981 and for women through 1987.

These cohorts may seem too old to track trends in today's young work force. This is why a new panel of nearly 13,000 young men and women was added to the NLS in 1979. In order to capture valid information on growing minority groups in the labor force, blacks and Hispanics were oversampled in this **National Longitudi-**

nal Survey of Youth (NLSY). Data for 1979 through 1987 are available and the 1988 data will be released in 1990.

In 1986 and 1988, **Children of the NLSY** women were surveyed for various cognitive, socioemotional, and physiological measures. Contact the CHRR for a free copy of the *NLSY Child Handbook 1989*.

NLS data sets are available on computer tape, and the NLSY is also available on CD-ROM. Contact the above address for a free copy of **The NLS Handbook,** which lists the publications, services, and data sets available from the CHRR.

CENTER FOR MATURE CONSUMER STUDIES

Specialty: mature market

George P. Moschis
College of Business Administration
Georgia State University
University Plaza
Atlanta, GA 30303
404-651-4177

CMCS was founded in 1986 as an activity of the Gerontology Center of Georgia State University, but it operates under its own board of directors. Research activities include national and regional studies of older consumers and market reports on consumer behavior in the areas of financial services, insurance, travel and leisure, health care, housing, food, retail, technology and telecommunications, and others.

CMCS publishes a quarterly newsletter on developments in the mature market, as well as bimonthly strategic marketing technical reports. An annual research report summary is based on syndicated market studies. CMCS also maintains a research library and advisory service, sponsors an annual conference, and provides custom research and data analysis on the mature market.

JOINT CENTER FOR URBAN POLICY RESEARCH

Specialty: housing

George Sternlieb
Hickman Hall, Room 309
Rutgers University,
Douglas Campus
New Brunswick, NJ 08903
201-932-6703

The Joint Center publishes annual data on population, employment, housing starts and prices, and income levels for municipalities of the 31-county greater New Jersey-New York-Connecticut (Gold Coast) area.

POPLINE

Specialty: demography

Population Information Program—School of Hygiene and Public Health
Johns Hopkins University
624 North Broadway
Baltimore, MD 21205
301-955-8200

Popline is the largest bibliographic demographic database in the world. It has items related to family planning and policy, as well as demography, fertility, education, migration and health care. Popline is updated monthly, and covers the period from 1970 to the present. It is available online through the National Library of Medicine's **MEDLARS** system. To open an account, contact the National Library of Medicine, MEDLARS Management Section, 8600 Rockville Pike, MD 20209; **301-496-6193.**

POPULATION ASSOCIATION OF AMERICA

Specialty: demography

Jean Smith
1722 N Street, NW
Washington, D.C. 20036
202/429-0891

The Population Association of America is the professional organization of demographers and others interested in population data. Membership includes a subscription to the quarterly journal **Demography,** which covers the full range of demographic topics including population estimates and projections, regional shifts, changing lifestyles, ethnic diversity, and international comparisons. The quarterly **Population Index** is a bibliographical guide to the world's population literature, primarily academic.

The PAA holds an annual meeting at which the world's premier demographers present research and studies on a wide variety of topics. The Business and Applied Demography committee of the PAA conducts at least one session in which the business aspects of demography are explored. The Committee also publishes an occasional newsletter to keep members informed of its activities.

PRINCETON-RUTGERS CENSUS DATA PROJECT

Specialty: census data

Judith S. Rowe
Princeton University
Computer Center
87 Prospect Avenue
Princeton, NJ 08540
609-452-6052

Gertrude Lewis
Rutgers University
Center for Computer and
Information Services
P.O. Box 879
Piscataway, NJ 08854
201-932-2483

This organization provides a full range of demographic data services, including creating extracts, printing data from computer tapes, merging files, creating custom disks, providing statistical analysis using mainframe and microcomputers, and producing computer graphics including maps.

THE ROPER CENTER FOR PUBLIC OPINION RESEARCH

Specialty: public opinion archives

Lois Timms-Ferrara
P.O. Box 440
Storrs, CT 06268
203-486-4440

The Roper Center is the only comprehensive library of public opinion and survey data. Over 40 survey organizations regularly contribute their polls to the center. Polling material is indexed by subject and is available by calling the center. The data can be accessed online as well. Clients can request special tabulations of survey questions. Fees vary by academic and membership status.

SURVEY RESEARCH CENTER

Specialty: survey of consumers

Richard Curtin
Institute for Social
Research
P.O. Box 1248
University of Michigan
Ann Arbor, MI 48106
313-763-5224

SRC conducts the monthly **Survey of Consumers,** which regularly repeats core questions covering three broad areas of consumer sentiment—personal finances, business conditions, and buying conditions. Consumers provide their attitudes regarding both short-term and long-term economic expectations, at both the personal and national level, for subjects ranging from the probable purchase of large durables, cars, and homes to unemployment and inflation rates. Demographics include age, sex, income, education, marital status, and geographic region.

Survey Research Centers

These university research centers conduct opinion polls and other survey research, usually for the state in which they are located. Some provide data to the public, others conduct proprietary research. The following is just a sampling of those who offer such research. The best way to find out about, and keep up with, the research going on nationwide is to get the quarterly ***Survey Research*** newsletter which lists the activities of these centers. For subscription information, contact the Survey Research Laboratory, University of Illinois, 1005 West Nevada Street, Urbana, IL 61801.

Jan W. Kuzma
Survey Research Center
Loma Linda University
Nichol Hall, Room 1911
Loma Linda, CA 92350
714-824-4590

The Loma Linda SRS is a full-service organization that designs and carries out surveys on education, health, religion, and consumer behavior, primarily in the southwestern U.S. Most reports are proprietary.

Dr. Bernard Goitein
Center for Business and Economic Research
1501 West Bradley Avenue, Baker 202
Peoria, IL 61625
309-677-2278

This center conducts ongoing surveys of consumer sentiment in the Peoria MSA and maintains a business and economic database for the Peoria MSA. It publishes quarterly updates and a biannual **Consumer Confidence** report. There is a nominal fee to subscribe to these databases. The center also conducts contract research for special market and economic studies.

Susan M. Hartnett, Manager
Northwestern University Survey Laboratory
625 Haven
Evanston, IL 60208
708-491-8759

Beginning in 1990, the laboratory will conduct an **Annual Chicago Area Survey.** The core set of questions will collect data on demographics and other social indicators and will be generally available. In addition, public and private sector clients can add questions to the core questionnaire.

Dr. James Hougland, Jr., Director
Survey Research Center
University of Kentucky
12 Porter Building
Lexington, KY 40506-0205
606-257-4684

The SRC collects demographic, socioeconomic, and attitudinal information through telephone surveys, mail questionnaires, and personal interviews. Research can be national in scope, but most research focuses on Kentucky, and the center has two recurring surveys. The **Kentucky Survey** began in 1979 and the **Kentucky Health Survey** began in 1988. Clients may have exclusive use of data for a limited time, but all data end up in the public domain.

Elizabeth Sale
Survey Research Unit
Center for Metropolitan Studies
University of Missouri
8001 Natural Bridge
St. Louis, MO 63121
314-553-5135

This center conducts research for public agencies and nonprofit organizations, including attitude surveys and public opinion polls, mainly for the St. Louis metropolitan area and the state of Missouri.

Dr. Lloyd D. Bender
Survey Research Center
Montana State University
1108 Wilson Hall
Bozeman, MT 59717
406-994-4481

The MSU SRC provides services to researchers in Montana. It operates a full-service mail and telephone survey research service, including design and analysis of studies. Recent studies include home health care, needs of the aging population, and entrepreneurial training. While studies are contracted by individual clients, most research is available to the public.

Dr. Donald Carns, Director
Center for Survey Research
Univ. of Nevada, FDH 616
Las Vegas, NV 89154
702-739-3322

The center does state-wide polls of Nevada adults, with subsamples for the Las Vegas and Reno metropolitan areas. It collects data on demographics, and tracks attitudes towards social, economic, environmental, and legislative issues. Data are available to the general public in news releases, statistical tables, and on disk.

Kathy Vaccariello
Center for Social and Demographic Analysis
State University of New York at Albany, SS340
Albany, NY 12222
518-442-4905

The CSDA conducts a full range of demographic and survey research, but one of its specialties has been demographic trends affecting New York State. Research results are published in occasional reports. The center also maintains a census data archive and telephone survey facility.

Richard A. Rehberg
Program in Survey Research
Center for Education and Social Research
State University of New York at Binghamton
Binghamton, NY 13901
607-777-2116

The center conducts periodic surveys for local media on issues such as the environment and abortion. Data are available from the sponsors.

Rick Shields
Center for Urban Affairs and Community Services
North Carolina State University, Box 7401
Raleigh, NC 27695
919-737-3211

The center's Applied Research Group (ARG) produces a wide variety of research assistance—from project design to report analyses—to federal, state, and local agencies. Projects include **Service Needs for Small Businesses** and **Child Care Study.**

John Shelton Reed, Director
Institute for Research in Social Science
Univ. of North Carolina
Chapel Hill, NC 27599-3355
919-962-3061

In cooperation with the University of North Carolina School of Journalism, IRSS conducts the twice-yearly **Carolina Poll,** an omnibus telephone survey of North Carolina households. In addition, IRSS houses the **Louis Harris Data Center,** the national repository for public opinion surveys by Louis Harris and Associates. IRSS also redistributes polls by the *Atlanta Journal-Constitution* and *USA Today,* and has major holdings of census and other demographic data. Poll data are available through a no-charge online service. Data tapes are available for a nominal fee, and printed summaries of the North Carolina polls are available on request.

Dr. Robert W. Oldendick
Survey Research Laboratory
Institute of Public Affairs
Columbia, SC 29208
803-777-8157

The SRL conducts statewide surveys in South Carolina that cover a variety of public policy issues. Topic areas vary from survey to survey, but generally include the most important problem facing South Carolina, state budget priorities, and other issues under consideration by the governor and state legislature. The surveys are conducted twice a year and collect demographic information such as age, race, sex, education, and income. Data are available on tape and disk; some information may be proprietary.

Scott Keeter
Survey Research Laboratory
Virginia Commonwealth University
Richmond, VA 23284-3016
804-367-8813

The VCU SRL conducts mail and telephone surveys for government and nonprofit clients, with extensive experience in the areas of health care, business, and special populations. SRL also conducts a quarterly statewide omnibus telephone survey of the public.

H. Sharp, Director
Wisconsin Survey Research Laboratory
610 Langdon Street, Suite 109
Madison, WI 53703
608-262-3122

The laboratory conducts national, statewide, and community telephone and mail surveys. It covers a variety of subjects, but specializes in health care. Data are proprietary for a period of time, then become publicly available. Annual reports list all available projects.

University Data Centers

These centers specialize in census data

The following university research and computing centers are members of the National Clearinghouse for Census Data Services, which means that they own tapes from the decennial census and can provide copies of tables or tapes of census data, as well as extract data from them. They all provide data for anywhere in the U.S. These centers are primarily service bureaus, although some do more extensive research, for themselves and outside clients.

Edward Ratledge and Phyllis Raab
Center for Applied Demography and Survey Research
University of Delaware
Newark, DE 19716
302-451-8406

Ray Jones
Census Access Program
University of Florida Libraries
Department of Reference
University of Florida
Gainesville, FL 32611
904-392-0361

Anders C. Johanson
Michigan State University
Computer Laboratory
East Lansing, MI 48824
517-355-4684

M. El-Attar
Mississippi State University
Department of Sociology
P.O. Box Drawer C
Mississippi State, MS 39762
601-325-2495

John G. Blodgett
University of Missouri-St. Louis
Computer Center
8001 Natural Bridge Road
St. Louis, MO 63121
314-553-6014

Marta Fisch
CUNY Data Service
Graduate School and University Center
City University of New York
33 West 42nd Street, Room 1446
New York, NY 10036
212-642-2085

Lew Alvarado
Memphis State University
Bureau of Business and Economic Research
Memphis, TN 38152-0001
901-678-2281

Industry and Nonprofit Organizations

AMERICAN CHAMBER OF COMMERCE RESEARCH ASSOCIATION

Specialty: cost of living

4323 King Street
Alexandria, VA 22302
703-998-4172

The ACCRA has been publishing the **Cost-of-Living Index** since 1968. These quarterly reports provide comparative cost-of-living indexes for hundreds of U.S. cities, which participate on a voluntary basis. The ACCRA calculates indexes for each of six categories—grocery items, housing, utilities, transportation, health care, and miscellaneous goods and services. The products and services used to calculate the indexes are defined in great detail to ensure comparability from city to city.

AMERICAN INSTITUTE OF FOOD DISTRIBUTION

Specialty: food

Jack Rengstorff
28-12 Broadway
Fair Lawn, NJ 07410
201-791-5570

Founded in 1928, the American Institute of Food Distribution is a nonprofit information and reporting association, whose basic function is to help inform members in all segments of the food industry. It publishes the weekly **Food Institute Report,** as well as special studies such as the annual **Food Business Mergers and Acquisitions.** Other recent studies include **Demographic Directions for Food Marketing** and **Food Retailing Review.**

AUTOMOTIVE MARKETING

Specialty: automotive

Rosemarie Kitchin
201 King of Prussia Road
Radnor, PA 19089
215-964-4395

Automotive Marketing magazine publishes an annual report called **Consumer Automotive Repair Study (CARS).** It examines the product purchase and installation behavior of do-it-yourselfers, as well as their basic demographics including age, income, occupation, and marital status. The **Product/Aftermarket Retail Trade Study (PARTS)** also is published annually, and covers the retail aspect of automotive parts and accessories. Both reports are sent to the magazine's controlled circulation; individual requests are considered as made.

THE CONFERENCE BOARD

Specialty: consumer behavior

Fabian Linden, Director
Consumer Research Center
845 Third Avenue
New York, NY 10022
212-759-0900

The Conference Board is a nonprofit membership organization whose Consumer Research Center is dedicated to the analysis of consumer spending. One of its best known products is **A Marketer's Guide to Discretionary Income**—an occasional report jointly produced with the Census Bureau. This publication provides the only consistent analysis of discretionary income available for households by demographic characteristics such as age, race, region, number of earners, and occupation.

The Consumer Research Center publishes **How Consumers Spend Their Money,** an analysis of the government's Consumer Expenditure Survey. The two-volume reports contain data on household spending for over 400 specific products and services by a number of demographic characteristics. The center also provides detailed cross-tabulations of data from the Census Bureau's annual demographic file (from the March Current Population Survey—*see page 67 for more information*).

The monthly **Consumer Confidence Survey** newsletter reports the results of a nationally representative survey of 5,000 households. The **Consumer Market Watch** newsletter carries current income, employment, expenditure, and price data. It also contains results from the Consumer Confidence Survey and a consumer confidence index showing present and future expectations of economic conditions and planned purchases of large durables. The **Consumer Market Guide** is a statistical compendium of consumer data.

EMPLOYEE BENEFIT RESEARCH INSTITUTE

Specialty: labor force

Stephanie Poe
2121 K Street, NW
Suite 600
Washington, DC 20037
202-659-0670

In the face of a diversifying work force, the EBRI studies a broad variety of issues of increasing concern to employers and employees alike. It publishes a number of periodicals and other reports focusing on these concerns.

Employee Benefit Notes and **EBRI Issue Briefs** are monthly newsletters that examine issues from child care to health insurance to retirement policies. EBRI also publishes the **Quarterly Pension Investment Report,** the biannual **Washington Bulletin,** a series of **Special Reports,** and occasional books. **EBRI.Net** is an online service offering access to the organization's publications and other resources. EBRI also conducts primary research through the Gallup Organization *(see page 145).*

HISPANIC BUSINESS

Specialty: Hispanic market

Joseph Wells
360 South Hope Avenue
Suite 300c
Santa Barbara, CA 93105
805-682-5843

Hispanic Business magazine collects and collates statistics on various aspects of Hispanic businesses and markets. The 1990 schedule includes topics such as Hispanics and cars, the Hispanic market in Chicago and the Midwest, Hispanics in law, and the demographics, marketing strategies, product preferences, and buying habits of Hispanics. All requests for information are honored at no charge.

MARKETING SCIENCE INSTITUTE

Specialty: market research

1000 Massachusetts Ave.
Cambridge, MA
02138-5396
617-491-2060

This nonprofit organization was founded in 1961 in order to advance marketing practice and knowledge. MSI solicits and funds research projects conducted by academic scholars. Research is reported through conferences and a variety of published reports, including working papers, technical working papers, monographs, conference summaries, and special reports. Recent titles include **Building an Information Strategy for Scanner Data** and **Toward Understanding and Controlling Customer Dissatisfaction with Waiting.** Call the Publications Department for a catalog.

MATURE MARKET INSTITUTE

Specialty: mature market

Lee M. Cassidy
20 Chevy Chase Circle, NW
Washington, DC 20015
202-363-9644

The Mature Market Institute is a non-profit business membership organization which acts as a resource for information on the population aged 50 and older. Members receive a bimonthly newsletter. The MMI also publishes other reports, which are available to non-members, and access to a network of sources and contacts.

Beginning in 1990, the MMI will offer **Discretionary Income Among Mature Americans** (DIAMA) research.

NATIONAL ASSOCIATION OF HOME BUILDERS

Specialty: housing

Economic Division
15th and M Streets, NW
Washington, DC 20005
800-368-5242
202-822-0292

The NAHB offers several monthly periodicals for the housing industry. **Current Housing Situation** provides up-to-date data from government and financial sources, including annual, quarterly, and monthly data for over 250 housing market variables. **Housing Economics** examines current and future economic conditions, housing starts, monthly employment and permit data for all states and over 100 metropolitan areas, and regular features on industry and consumer issues. **Forecast of Housing Activity** includes monthly estimates for census regions and divisions, as well as biannual long-term forecasts of housing starts by geographic area and type of dwelling, housing completions, home sales and prices, employment and income, and interest rates. Economists are available to update information as warranted by unexpected changes in economic conditions.

NATIONAL OPINION RESEARCH CENTER

Specialty: The General Social Survey

Patrick Bova
1155 East 60th Street
Chicago, IL 60637
312-702-1200

data tape available from:
The Roper Center
University of Connecticut
Storrs, CT 06268
203-486-4882

NORC has been conducting the **General Social Survey** (GSS) since 1972. This annual survey covers a wide variety of social, familial, and political topics. Some questions are asked year after year, others are added as deemed relevant. For example, the 1988 survey included a set of questions on AIDS, and a topical module on religious background and beliefs. The cumulative database is available on computer tape for analysis of trends in socioeconomic characteristics and attitudes over time. NORC publishes **GSSNEWS,** an annual newsletter, but doesn't produce other survey reports. All materials are in the public domain, and there are no restrictions on data use.

NATIONAL RESTAURANT ASSOCIATION

Specialty: food

1200 17th Street, NW
Washington, DC 20036
800-424-5156; 202-331-5900

The National Restaurant Association (NRA) is the trade association for foodservice companies and restaurants. It publishes a number of reports, all of which are available to non-members, although members receive discounts. A publications catalog is available on request. **Restaurants USA** is a monthly publication and **Foodservice Information Abstracts** is biweekly. The NRA also has annual reports on **Foodservice in Review, Restaurant Industry Operations Report,** and **Foodservice Industry Forecasts.** Monographs include consumer studies on dinner decision making, ethnic food preferences, beverage preferences, and consumer attitudes towards fast food, family restaurants, take-out food, and nutrition.

The NRA also has an annual trade show and holds nationwide seminars on various aspects of foodservice and restaurant management. Members have access to a 5000-volume library and reference service from staff.

NATIONAL SPORTING GOODS ASSOCIATION

Specialty: sports

Thomas B. Doyle, Director of Information & Research
1699 Wall Street
Mt. Prospect, IL 60056
708-439-4000

The NSGA conducts annual surveys of sports participation and of purchases of sports equipment, footwear, and clothing. The **Sports Participation** studies, begun in 1984, track participation in 47 activities, from aerobics to water-skiing. Reports crosstabulate activities by demographic characteristics such as age, sex, household composition, income, and geographic region.

The **Sporting Goods Market** studies, begun in 1976, track purchases in 26 sports. These reports also include demographics, as well as 12 lifestyle segments based on Claritas' PRIZM system. The NSGA has also studied those who are not physically active, by surveying "couch potatoes" in the **National Fitness Study.** All reports are available to non-members, although NSGA members receive discounts.

NEWSPAPER ADVERTISING BUREAU

Specialty: media

Julie S. Newhall
1180 Avenue of the Americas
New York, NY 10036
212-921-5080

The NAB conducts research on issues of interest to the newspaper/advertising community, and to others interested in media-related consumer behavior. Reports are available to members, as well as to editors, advertisers, and advertising agencies on request.

POINT-OF-PURCHASE ADVERTISING INSTITUTE

Specialty: media

Susan D. Evans
Education Relations Manager
66 North Van Brunt Street
Englewood, NJ 07631
201-894-8899

POPAI is the trade association for those who do in-store advertising. It conducted a **Supermarket Consumer Buying Habits Study** in 1987 and a **Drug Store Consumer Buying Habits Study** in 1983. Both studies are available to non-members. It also offers an audio tape of a presentation called **The Consumer of Tomorrow: A Look at Demographic Changes.**

THE POPULATION RESOURCE CENTER

Specialty: research

Jane S. DeLung, President
500 East 62nd Street
New York, NY 10017
212-888-2820

Nancy McConnell, Vice President
1725 K Street, NW
Suite 1102
Washington, DC 20006
202-467-5030

Using the services of the nation's leading authorities in demography, economics, and related fields, the center organizes briefings, workshops, conferences, and commissioned research to analyze the relationship between demographic trends and key social and economic issues.

PREVENTION MAGAZINE

Specialty: health

Tom Dybdahl
33 East Minor Street
Emmaus, PA 18098
215-967-5171

Prevention Magazine publishes **The Prevention Index,** an annual survey of Americans' health and safety habits, conducted by Louis Harris and Associates. The Index acts as a report card for Americans' health behavior, and provides data on various aspects of health behavior such as diet, exercise, auto safety, and purchase of health-related products. Copies of the reports are generally available for no charge.

PROGRESSIVE GROCER

Specialty: food

Vining Sherman, Progressive Grocer

Scott Wright, Trade Dimensions

Peter Featherstone, Monitor and Retail Tenant Directory

Maclean Hunter Media, Inc.
Four Stamford Forum
Stamford, CT 06901
203-325-3500

Progressive Grocer is a monthly magazine for the retail grocery industry. **Trade Dimensions** provides store-by-store retail data for the supermarket industry. **Monitor, the Shopping Center Industry Magazine** is a monthly research-based publication providing facts and figures of importance to retailers and developers. The **Retail Tenant Directory** lists retailers who tenant shopping centers and malls. Database information is available on a custom basis, and in PC format.

SUNSET'S WESTERN MARKET ALMANAC

Specialty: western region

Corrine Anderson, Director of Research Services
Lane Publishing Company
80 Willow Road
Menlo Park, CA 94025
415-321-3600

Sunset's Western Almanac is a comprehensive source of marketing information on the 13 western states, published by Lane Publishing Company, producers of Sunset books and **Sunset Magazine.** The Almanac covers demographics, attitudes, lifestyles, and product preferences, making statistical and graphic comparisons of the West with other regions and the nation. Categories include: automotive; travel; recreation, sports and leisure; housing, home equipment and furnishings; finance, banking and insurance; grocery; gardening; and media use. Other chapters discuss Pacific Basin influences and trends in population, commerce, employment, income, and retail sales.

THE TRAFFIC AUDIT BUREAU FOR MEDIA MEASUREMENT

Specialty: outdoor advertising

Ken Sammon
President
114 East 32nd Street
Suite 802
New York, NY 10016
212-213-9640

TAB is the national circulation authority for outdoor advertising, providing an **Annual Computer Summary** of over 800 markets. Most information is proprietary to members, but individual market data on specific billboard locations are available to advertisers and agencies.

THE UNITED WAY OF AMERICA

Specialty: volunteering/charity

Martha Taylor
Director, Market Research Products & Services
701 North Fairfax Street
Alexandria, VA
22314-2045
703-836-7100

Lu Anne Fischman
Director,
Environmental Analysis
United Way Strategic Institute

The United Way provides a variety of studies which examine charitable giving and volunteering behavior, attitudes, and related demographics. It maintains a database which links demographic and socioeconomic characteristics with fund raising and fund distribution patterns in communities. Summaries of these data are available to the general public.

The United Way Strategic Institute is the think tank and strategic planning arm of the United Way of America. Its products are available to all. The monthly newsletter, **United Way Soundings,** reports on trends in philanthropy. The **Soundings** database, updated continually, contains abstracts of articles from over 150 publications that deal with charity and related issues.

The Institute also publishes a biannual report on **What Lies Ahead.** The 1989 edition is titled **Countdown to the 21st Century** and covers social, economic, political, technological and other trends that affect charitable giving. The Institute also publishes other occasional reports and issues papers.

THE URBAN INSTITUTE

Specialty: urban affairs

2100 M Street, NW
Washington, DC 20037
202-833-7200

The Urban Institute studies the social and economic problems of the nation's urban communities and government programs and policies designed to alleviate such problems. Its **Demographic Studies Program** emphasizes policy issues related to changing family and household demographics, international migration to the U.S., and interrelations between population growth and economic development in developing countries.

The **Dynamic Simulation of Income Model (DYNASIM)** projects the income and demographic characteristics of a nationwide sample of families. Unlike the Census Bureau's projections, which are only available aggregated, DYNASIM forecasts how demographic changes will affect individual families over time.

WOMEN'S RESEARCH & EDUCATION INSTITUTE

Specialty: women

Betty Dooley
Executive Director

Paula Ries
Director of Research

1700 18th Street, NW,
Suite 400
Washington, DC 20009
202-328-7070

WREI publishes an annual report on **The American Woman,** which examines the social, economic, and political characteristics of women and their families. A statistical appendix presents tables and charts on topics such as education, family status, income, poverty, employment, and child care. A biennial **Directory of Selected Research and Policy Centers Working on Women's Issues** lists who's doing what in the realm of research on women's and family issues in more than 45 centers nationwide. WREI also publishes occasional policy papers which pull together statistics on a wide variety of issues dealing with women and work.

WORLD FUTURE SOCIETY

Specialty: futurist

Edward Cornish
President
4916 Saint Elmo Avenue
Bethesda, MD 20814
301-656-8274

The World Future Society acts as an impartial clearinghouse for ideas about the future. The society publishes several periodicals that deal with forecasts and trends on a wide variety of topics. **The Futurist** is a bimonthly general-interest magazine, the **Future Survey** is a monthly journal of future-related abstracts, and the **Futures Research Quarterly** is a scholarly journal.

CHAPTER 7

State & Local Sources

When looking for small-area data, sometimes it's best to go to "the source"—the local area itself.

How to Use This Chapter

The sources listed here alphabetically by state fall into three main categories—state data centers, economic sources, and local information. The Census Bureau has a network of ***state data centers****—usually local government agencies or university research centers—which provide census and other data. They also often have population estimates and projections.*

The ***economic sources*** *are also usually government agencies that primarily provide employment and earnings data for states and local areas.* ***Local information*** *is offered by journalists who are willing to provide local demographic information as it becomes available to them; some even conduct primary research.*

The introduction, "How to Get to the Grass Roots," suggests ways for finding and evaluating local information.

How to Get to the Grass Roots

If you need information about a local market, ask local sources.

by Judith Waldrop

Cities and counties change rapidly as neighborhood populations shift, often in just a few months. One of the best ways to keep up with local population change is to go to the source.

While many federal agencies generate small-area statistics, local sources frequently have more up-to-date and detailed data. The variety of local sources can be overwhelming, however. Here's a guide to navigating the bureaucracy.

If you're interested in several localities in one state, start by calling the state data center. These agencies serve as clearinghouses for Census Bureau data. State data centers can give you census data for the areas you're interested in as well as information from more recent surveys. Some data centers produce estimates and projections of the populations of cities within their state, and many also distribute local data collected by other state agencies. For a current list of state data centers, call the Bureau of the Census at 301-763-1580.

Other state agencies that might be useful in your quest for local information are state departments of economic development, vital statistics, health, and transportation. In some areas, interstate agencies will also have valuable information. Some examples of these agencies are the Tennessee Valley Authority, the New York Port Authority, and the Metropolitan Washington Council of Governments.

CLOSER TO HOME

At the local level, city or county planning departments are most likely to collect demographic data and track development. They may also aggregate building-permit data and generate population and employment forecasts. The planning departments in larger cities will do more data collection and compilation than those in smaller cities.

Locate the agency that handles transportation planning in an area. These agencies must develop and maintain sophisticated databases, according to Connie Blackmon, data services director of the Atlanta Regional Commission (ARC). Since 1982, the ARC has been selling data to businesses through its Decision Resources Center. Prices range from $10 for a report on regional population growth to $140 for a diskette on housing. The Decision Resources Center also develops customized databases for businesses needing data for irregular pieces of geography. Blackmon has confidence in the center's numbers because the researchers live in the area. "We're here," she says, "so we don't have to extrapolate."

Once you've investigated what data the local planning departments have, check with the building departments, housing authorities, health departments, employment offices, boards of realtors, industrial and downtown development boards, and school boards for additional information. If you plan to visit an area, call ahead and make appointments. A few telephone calls will direct you to the most knowledgeable local experts.

TRUST, BUT VERIFY

The best source of information on an area is firsthand experience. A lot of construction in an area means investors are committed to growth. But find out if developers are building on speculation or with contracts. At public meetings, pay attention to what people say about local development, and take note of who's making the most noise.

Local experts are the most knowledgeable about local developments. But be aware that boosterism is commonplace among people intensely involved in their community. Be sure you know the methodology behind local estimates. Gather data from as many different sources as possible. Then evaluate those data in light of what you know about the community.

Look for clues to back up your assumptions. If you're interested in children, for example, school enrollment figures provide a good proxy. Data on the number of children in each grade by race and sex may be available from the school board. Remember to take private-school enrollment into account. Large private-school enrollments in a district can selectively remove students from the public-school rolls.

Utility-company data can help you estimate an area's overall population growth, and traffic counts can approximate daytime populations. Employment figures can help you identify economic change that can affect migration patterns. These sources of information have their problems, however. Make sure the area for which data are collected coincides with the area in which you are interested, and take seasonal variations into account.

Watch out for annexations, which can inflate growth and mask demographic change. In Tampa, Florida, for example, a 1985 test census showed a 2 percent population gain since 1980. On closer examination, however, city planners discovered much of the growth was due to annexation. If Tampa had not added new areas to its territory, its increase would have been just 1 percent.

Annexation can affect other statistics as well. When suburban neighborhoods are added to urban areas, for example, minorities shrink as a share of the total population. Both annexations and deannexations are common in incorporated areas. Don't confuse a change in geography with a change in demographics.

Data collection at the local level can be as simple as a telephone call. Private consultants can provide you with detailed local data, tailored to your needs. Or you can spend weeks collecting and sorting through data provided by dozens of public agencies. Which route you take depends on the number of local areas you need to analyze, your analytical skills, and the time and money you want to invest. The more involved you are in the data-collection process, however, the more you'll learn about the local market.

ALABAMA

State Data Centers

Alabama State Data Center for Business and Economic Research — **205-348-2953**
University of Alabama
Box 870221
Tuscaloosa, AL 35487-0221
● Annette Watters
The main branch of the state data center also provides state estimates, projections, and economic information.

State Data Center — **205-284-8778**
Alabama Department of Economic and Community Affairs
P.O. Box 2329
Montgomery, AL 36105-0939
● Gilford C. Gilder
Also provides state estimates and projections.

Alabama Public Library Service — **205-277-7330**
6030 Monticello Drive
Montgomery, AL 36130
● Hilda Dent

Economic Sources

Research & Statistics
State of Alabama Department of Industrial Relations
649 Monroe Street
Montgomery, AL 36130
● Douglas Dyer, Chief

Alabama Department of Economic & Community Affairs — **205-284-8778**
c/o State Capitol
Montgomery, AL 36130
● Gil Gilder

Local Information

The Birmingham News — **205-325-2134**
P.O. Box 2553
Birmingham, AL 35202
● Thomas M. Adams

ALASKA

State Data Centers

Alaska State Data Center **907-465-4500**
Research and Analysis
Alaska Department of Labor
P.O. Box 25504
Juneau, AK 99802-5504
● Kathryn Lizik
The main branch of the state data center also provides state estimates and projections.

Office of Management & Budget **907-465-3568**
Division of Policy
Pouch AD
Juneau, AK 99811
● Gregg Erickson

Department of Education **907-465-2927**
Alaska State Library
Pouch G
Juneau, AK 99811-0571
● Patience Frederiksen

Department of Community & Regional Affairs **907-465-4756**
Division of Municipal & Regional Assistance
P.O. Box BH
Juneau, AK 99811
● Paul Cunningham

State Projections

Institute for Social & Economic Research **907-786-7710**
University of Alaska
3211 Providence Drive
Anchorage, AK 99508
● Jack Kruse

ARIZONA

State Data Centers

Arizona Department of Economic Security — **602-542-5984**
1300 W. Washington
P.O. Box 6123-045Z
Phoenix, AZ 85005
● Betty Jeffries
The main branch of the state data center also provides state estimates and projections.

Center for Business Research — **602-965-3961**
College of Business Administration
Arizona State University
Tempe, AZ 85287
● Tom Rex
Also provides state and local economic information.

College of Business Administration — **602-523-3657**
Northern Arizona University
Box 15066
Flagstaff, AZ 86011
● Dr. Joseph Walka
Also provides state and local economic information.

Federal Documents Section — **602-621-4121**
Department of Library, Archives & Public Records
Capitol, Second Floor
1700 West Washington
Phoenix, AZ 85007
● Janet Fisher

Economic Sources

Division of Economic & Business Research — **602-621-2155**
University of Arizona
Tucson, AZ 85721
● Holly Penix

Local Information

Market Research Manager — **602-271-8870**
Phoenix Newspapers, Inc.
P.O. Box 1950
Phoenix, AZ 85001
● Ellen Baar Jacobs

ARKANSAS

State Data Centers

Arkansas State Data Center **501-569-8530**
University of Arkansas at Little Rock
2801 South University
Little Rock, AR 72204
● Sarah Breshears
The main branch of the state data center also provides state estimates and projections.

Arkansas State Library **501-682-2864**
1 Capitol Mall
Little Rock, AR 72201
● Mary Honeycutt

Research & Analysis Section **501-682-3159**
Employment Security Division
Arkansas Department of Labor
State Capitol Mall
P.O. Box 2981
Little Rock, AR 72203
● Coy Cozart

Economic Sources

Research & Public Service **501-569-8550**
University of Arkansas at Little Rock
2801 South University
Little Rock, AR 72204
● John Shelnutt

CALIFORNIA

State Data Centers

State Census Data Center 916-322-4651
State Department of Finance
915 L Street
Sacramento, CA 95814
● Linda Gage, Director
The main branch of the state data center also provides state estimates and projections.

State Data Program 415-642-6571
University of California, Berkeley
2538 Channing Way
Berkeley, CA 94720
● Ilona Einowski/Ann Gerken

Sacramento Area Council of Governments 916-441-5930
106 K Street, Suite 200
Sacramento, CA 95814
● Bob Faseier

Association of Bay Area Governments 415-464-7937
Metro Center
8th and Oak Streets
P.O. Box 2050
Oakland, CA 94604-2050
● Patricia Perry

Regional Research Institute of Southern California 213-385-1000
600 S. Commonwealth Street
Los Angeles, CA 90005
● Tim Douglas

San Diego Association of Governments 619-236-5353
Security Pacific Plaza
1200 3rd Avenue, Suite 524
San Diego, CA 92101
● Karen Lamphere

CALIFORNIA

(continued)

Economic Sources

Business Forecasting Project **213-825-1623**
Graduate School of Management
University of California
Los Angeles, CA 90024
● Larry J. Kimbell, Director

Local Information

The Press-Enterprise **714-782-7694**
P.O. Box 792
Riverside, CA 92502
● Madeleine Pruett

Los Angeles Times **213-237-5965**
Marketing Research Department
Los Angeles, CA 90053
● John Mount, Director of Mktg. Rsch.

Orange County Register **714-953-7963**
625 N. Grand Avenue
P.O. Box 11626
Santa Ana, CA 92711
● Robert Olinto

COLORADO

State Data Centers

Division of Local Government — **303-866-2156**
Department of Local Affairs
1313 Sherman Street, Room 521
Denver, CO 80203
- Reid T. Reynolds, State Demographer
- Rebecca Picaso, Staff Assistant

The main branch of the state data center also provides state estimates, projections, and economic information.

Division of Business Research — **303-492-8227**
Graduate School of Business & Administration
University of Colorado
Boulder, CO 80309
Also provides state and local economic information.

Documents Department — **303-491-1101**
The Libraries
Colorado State University
Fort Collins, CO 80523
- Karen Jacob

Natural Resources & Economics — **303-491-5706**
Department of Agriculture
Colorado State University
Fort Collins, CO 80523
- Sue Anderson

Economic Sources

Labor Market Information Branch — **303-894-2575**
Department of Labor and Employment
251 East 12th Avenue
Denver, CO 80203
- Kenneth Anderson

Research Manager — **303-892-5485**
Rocky Mountain News
P.O. Box 719
Denver, CO 80201
- Pam Michener

Local Information

The Denver Post — **303-820-1500**
1560 Broadway
Denver, CO 80202
- Ann Abernethy

CONNECTICUT

State Data Centers

Policy Devlopment & Planning Division **203-566-8285**
Office of Policy and Management
State of Connecticut
80 Washington Street
Hartford, CT 06106
● Bill Kraynak
The main branch of the state data center also provides state projections and economic information.

Government Documents **203-566-4971**
Connecticut State Library
231 Capital Avenue
Hartford, CT 06106
● Albert Palko

Processing Center **203-486-4440**
Institute for Social Inquiry
University of Connecticut, U-164
Storrs, CT 06268
● Marilyn Potter

Economic Sources

Research & Information **203-566-2120**
Employment Security Division
Connecticut Labor Department
200 Folly Brook Boulevard
Wethersfield, CT 06109
● Richard Vannuccini, Director

Local Information

The Day **203-442-2200, ext. 290**
P.O. Box 1231
New London, CT 06320
● Timothy W. Clements

The Hartford Courant **203-241-6273**
285 Broad Street
Hartford, CT 06115
● John J. Burnett

The New Haven Register **203-562-1121, ext. 4416**
40 Sargent Drive
New Haven, CT 06511
● Tracy K. Potter

DELAWARE

State Data Centers

Delaware Development Office **302-739-4271**
99 Kings Highway
P.O. Box 1401
Dover, DE 19903
● Judy McKinney-Cherry
The main branch of the state data center also provides state estimates, projections, and economic information.

College of Urban Affairs & Public Policy **302-451-8405**
University of Delaware
Graham Hall, Room 286
Academy Street
Newark, DE 19716
● Ed Ratledge
Also provides state estimates, projections, and vital statistics.

DISTRICT OF COLUMBIA

State Data Centers

Data Services Division **202-727-6533**
Mayor's Office of Planning
Presidential Building
Suite 500, 415 12th Street, NW
Washington, DC 20004
● Gan Ahuja
Also provides estimates, projections, and economic information.

Metropolitan Washington Council of Governments **202-223-6800**
1875 Eye Street, NW, Suite 200
Washington, DC 20006
● Robert Griffiths
● Jenean Johanningmeier
Also provides economic information.

FLORIDA

State Data Center

Executive Office of the Governor — **904-487-2814**
Office of Planning & Budget
The Capitol
Tallahassee, FL 32399-0001
● Steve Kimble

Center for the Study of Population — **904-644-1762**
Institute for Social Research
654 Bellamy Building
Florida State University
Tallahassee, FL 32306-4063
● Dr. Ike Eberstein

State Library of Florida — **904-487-2651**
R.A. Gray Building
Tallahassee, FL 32399-0250
● Evelyn Turkinton

Economic Sources

Bureau of Economic & Business Research — **904-392-0171**
221 Matherly Hall
University of Florida
Gainesville, FL 32611
● Stanley K. Smith, Program Director
Also provides state estimates and projections.

Department of Economics — **305-284-5540**
University of Miami
P.O. Box 248126
Coral Gables, FL 33124
● Phil Robins, Chairman

Computer Services Office — **904-488-4255**
Florida Department of Commerce
Room 404 Collins Building
Tallahassee, FL 32399
● Gail Cruce

Local Information

The Orlando Sentinel — **407-420-5790**
P.O. Box 2833
Orlando, FL 32802
● Jim Jackson

(continues next page)

FLORIDA

Local Information
(continued)

Florida Publishing Co. **904-359-4524**
P.O. Box 1949F
Jacksonville, FL 32231
● Wallace Parker

St. Petersburg Times **813-893-8451**
P.O. Box 1121
St. Petersburg, FL 33731
● Steve Kirchner

The Palm Beach Post **800-926-7678**
P.O. Box 24700
West Palm Beach, FL 33416-4700
● Suzanne S. Willcox

Miami Herald Publishing Co. **305-376-2791**
One Herald Plaza
Miami, FL 33132
● Jack N. O'Hearn, Jr.

Tampa Tribune **813-272-7766**
P.O. Box 191
Tampa, FL 33601
● Theodore Stasney

GEORGIA

State Data Centers

Operational Support & Development **404-656-0911**
Georgia Office of Planning & Budget
254 Washington Street, SW, Rm. 640
Atlanta, GA 30334
● Marty Sik
The main branch of the state data center also provides state estimates and projections.

Documents Librarian **404-651-2185**
Georgia State University
University Plaza
Atlanta, GA 30303
● Gayle Christian, Reference/Documents Librarian

Main Library **404-542-0664**
University of Georgia
Athens, GA 30602
● Susan C. Field

Georgia Department of Community Affairs **404-656-5526**
Office of Research and Information
100 Peachtree Street, NE #1200
Atlanta, GA 30303
● Paul W. Lycett

State Data Center Program **912-430-4799**
Albany State College
504 College Drive
Albany, GA 31705
● Juanita Miller

Data Services **404-542-0727**
University of Georgia Libraries
6th floor
Athens, GA 30602
● Hortense L. Bates

State Data Center Program **912-744-2667**
Mercer University Law Library
Mercer University
Macon, GA 31207
● Steve Thorpe

(continues next page)

GEORGIA

State Data Centers (continued)

Price Gilbert Memorial Library — **404-894-4519**
Georgia Institute of Technology
Atlanta, GA 30332
● Richard Leacy

Robert W. Woodruff Library for Advanced Studies — **404-727-6880**
Emory University
Atlanta, GA 30322
● Elizabeth McBride

Documents Librarian — **912-681-5117**
State Data Center Program
Georgia Southern College
Statesboro, GA 30458
● Lynn Walshak

Economic Sources

Georgia Department of Industry, Trade, & Tourism — **404-656-3573**
P.O. Box 1776
Atlanta, GA 30301
● George Rogers

Labor Information Systems — **404-656-3177**
Georgia Department of Labor
148 International Boulevard
Atlanta, GA 30303
● Joyce A. Morris/Milton Martin

Division of Research — **404-542-4085**
College of Business Administration
University of Georgia
Athens, GA 30602
● Albert Niemi, Jr.

Economic Forecasting Center — **404-651-3282**
Georgia State University
University Plaza
Atlanta, GA 30303
● Donald Ratajczak, Director

HAWAII

State Data Centers

State Department of Business & Economic Development — **808-586-2493**
P.O. Box 2359
Kamamalu Building, Rm. 602A
Honolulu, HI 96804
● Jan Nakamoto
Also provides state estimates, projections, and economic information.

Electronic Data Processing Division — **808-548-5190**
Department of Budget and Finance
Kalanimoku Building
1151 Punchbowl Street
Honolulu, HI 96813
● George Okamura

Economic Sources

Research & Statistics Office — **808-548-7639**
Department of Labor and Industrial Relations
P.O. Box 3680
Honolulu, HI 96811
● Frederick Pang, Chief

IDAHO

State Data Centers

Idaho Department of Commerce — **208-334-2470**
700 W. State Street
Boise, ID 83720
● Alan Porter

Institutional Research — **208-385-1613**
Room 319, Business Building
Boise State University
Boise, ID 83725
● Don Canning

The Idaho State Library — **208-334-2150**
325 West State Street
Boise, ID 83702
● Charles Bolles, State Librarian

Center for Business Research & Services — **208-236-2504**
Campus Box 8450
Idaho State University
Pocatello, ID 83209
● Dr. Paul Zelus

Economic Sources

Economic Analysis Bureau — **208-334-2906**
Division of Financial Management
Statehouse, Rm. 122
Boise, ID 83720
● Derek Santos, Economist
Also provides state estimates.

University Research Center — **208-385-1158**
Boise State University
1910 University Drive
Boise, ID 83725
● Dr. Chuck Skoro, Economist
Also provides state projections.

Research & Analysis — **208-334-6169**
Idaho Department of Employment
317 Main Street
Boise, ID 83735
● James C. Adams, Chief

IDAHO

Economic Sources
(continued)

Center for Business Development & Research — **208-885-6611**
College of Business & Economics
University of Idaho
Moscow, ID 83843
● Lawrence Merk, Director

ILLINOIS

State Data Centers

Illinois State Data Center Cooperative **217-782-1381**
Illinois Bureau of the Budget
605 Stratton Office Building
Springfield, IL 62706
● Suzanne Ebetsche

Community Research Services **309-438-5946**
Department of Sociology, Anthropology
& Social Work
Illinois State University
604 South Main Street
Normal, IL 61761-6901
● Dr. Roy Treadway

Center for Governmental Studies **815-753-1901, ext. 221**
Northern Illinois University
Social Science Research Building
DeKalb, IL 60115
● Ruth Anne Tobias

Regional Research & Development Service **618-692-3500**
Southern Illinois University at Edwardsville
Box 1456
Edwardsville, IL 62026-1456
● Charles Kofron

Chicago Area Geographic Information Study **312-996-6367**
Room 2102, Building BSB
P.O. Box 4348
University of Illinois at Chicago
Chicago, IL 60680
● Jim Bash

Economic Sources

Illinois Center for Health Statistics **217-785-1064**
Illinois Department of Public Health
535 West Jefferson St.
Springfield, IL 62761
● Mark Flotow, Demographer
Also provides state estimates

ILLINOIS

Economic Sources
(continued)

Office of Planning & Financial Analysis — **217-782-3500**
Illinois Bureau of the Budget
605 Stratton Office Building
Springfield, IL 62706
● Cheng H. Chiang
Also provides state projections.

Bureau of Economic & Business Research — **217-333-2330**
University of Illinois
1206 South Sixth Street
Champaign, IL 61820
● William R. Bryan, Director

Department of Commerce & Community Affairs — **217-782-1438**
Division of Research & Analysis
620 East Adams Street
Springfield, IL 62701
● Wallace Biermann

Local Information

The Pantagraph — **309-829-9411**
301 Washington Street
P.O. Box 2907
Bloomington, IL 61701
● Stephen W. Clark

INDIANA

State Data Centers

Indiana State Library 317-232-3733
Indiana State Data Center
140 North Senate Avenue
Indianapolis, IN 46204
● Roberta Eads

School of Business 812-855-5507
Indiana Business Research Center
Indiana University
Bloomington, IN 47405
● Dr. Morton J. Marcus, Director
Also provides state projections and economic information.

Division of Economic Analysis 317-232-8959
Indiana Department of Commerce
1 North Capitol, Suite 700
Indianapolis, IN 46204
● Charles A. Sim, Director

Indiana Business Research Center 317-274-2205
P.O. Box 647
801 West Michigan, B.S. 4013
Indianapolis, IN 46223
● Carol Rogers

IOWA

State Data Centers

State Library of Iowa **515-281-4350**
Historical Building
East 12th and Grand
Des Moines, IA 50319
● Beth Henning

Census Services **515-294-8337**
Iowa State University
320 East Hall
Ames, IA 50011
● Willis Goudy

Census Data Center **515-281-4730**
Department of Public Instruction
Grimes State Office Building
Des Moines, IA 50319
● Steve Boal

Center for Social & Behavioral Research **319-273-2105**
University of Northern Iowa
Cedar Falls, IA 50614
● Robert Kramer

Laboratory for Political Research **319-353-3103**
University of Iowa
345 Schaeffer Hall
Iowa City, IA 52242
● Jim Grifhorst

Small Business Development Center **515-271-2655**
College of Business
210 Aliber Hall
Drake University
Des Moines, IA 50311
● Carolyn Ramsay

Ballou Library **712-749-2127**
Buena Vista College
Storm Lake, IA 50588
● Dr. Barbara Palling

(continues next page)

IOWA

(continued)

Economic Sources

Labor Market Information Unit **515-242-5861**
Iowa Department of Employment Services
1000 East Grand Avenue
Des Moines, IA 50319
● Mike Blank

Department of Management **515-281-3322**
Iowa State Capitol
Des Moines, IA 50319
● Patrick D. Cavanaough

Cooperative Extension Service **515-294-6147**
560 Heady Hall
Iowa State University
Ames, IA 50011
● Daniel Otto

KANSAS

State Data Centers

State Library **913-296-3296**
State Capitol Bldg., Rm. 343-N
Topeka, KS 66612
● Marc Galbraith

Division of the Budget **913-296-2436**
State Capitol Building, Rm. 152-E
Topeka, KS 66612
● Dana Farrell
Also provides state estimates and projections.

Institute for Public Policy & Business Research **913-864-3123**
607 Blake Hall
University of Kansas
Lawrence, KS 66045-2960
● Thelma Helyar
Also provides state and local economic information.

Population & Resources Laboratory **913-532-5984**
Department of Sociology
Kansas State University
Manhattan, KS 66506
● Dr. Jan L. Flora

Center for Urban Studies **316-689-3737**
Box 61
Wichita State University
Wichita, KS 67208
● Mark Glaser

Economic Sources

Kansas Department of Commerce **913-296-3481**
400 S.W. 8th St. Suite 500
Topeka, KS 66603
● A. Edwin Riemann

Labor Market Information Services **913-296-5058**
Department of Human Resources
401 SW Topeka Boulevard
Topeka, KS 66603
● William H. Layes, Chief

KENTUCKY

State Data Centers

State Data Center of Kentucky — **502-588-7990**
Urban Research Institute
University of Louisville
Louisville, KY 40292
● Ron Crouch
Also provides estimates and projections

Office for Policy & Management — **502-564-7300**
State of Kentucky
Capitol Annex
Frankfort, KY 40601
● William Hintze

Department for Libraries & Archives — **502-875-7000**
State Library Services Div.
300 Coffeetree Rd.
P.O. Box 537
Frankfort, KY 40601
● Brenda Fuller

Economic Sources

Cabinet for Human Resources — **502-564-7976**
275 East Main Street, 2nd Floor East
Frankfort, KY 40601
● Ed Blackwell

Local Information

The Courier-Journal — **502-582-4351**
Analysis & Research Department
525 West Broadway
Louisville, KY 40202
● Mark R. Schneider

LOUISIANA

State Data Centers

Louisiana State Planning Office **504-342-7410**
P.O. Box 94095
Baton Rouge, LA 70804
● Karen Paterson
The main branch of the state data center also provides state projections and economic information.

Division of Business & Economic Research **504-286-6248**
University of New Orleans
New Orleans, LA 70122
● Vincent Maruggi
Also provides state projections and economic information.

Division of Business Research **318-257-3701**
Louisiana Tech University
P.O. Box 10318
Ruston, LA 71272
● Dr. Edward O'Boyle

Louisiana State Library **504-324-4918**
Reference Department
P.O. Box 131
Baton Rouge, LA 70821
● Blanche Cretini

Center for Life Cycle & Population Studies **504-388-5359**
Department of Sociology
Louisiana State University
Baton Rouge, LA 70803
● Dr. Alan C. Acock

Center for Business & Economic Research **318-342-2123**
Northeast Louisiana University
Monroe, LA 71209
● Dr. Jerry Wall

Economic Sources

Research & Statistics Dept. **504-342-3141x321**
Louisiana State Dept. of Labor
1001 North 23rd Street
P.O. Box 94094 - Capitol Station
Baton Rouge, LA 70804-9094
● Oliver Robinson, Director

MAINE

State Data Centers

Division of Economic Analysis and Research — **207-289-2271**
Maine Department of Labor
20 Union Street
Augusta, ME 04330
● Jean Martin
The main branch of the state data center also provides state and local economic information.

Maine State Library — **207-289-3561**
State House, Station 64
Augusta, ME 04333
● Gary Nichols

State Estimates

Division of Data, Research & Vital Statistics — **207-626-5445**
Department of Human Services
Statehouse
Augusta, ME 04333
● Dale E. Welch

Economic Sources

University of Maine — **207-581-1504**
201 Alumni Hall
Orono, ME 04469
● Dr. Gregory N. Brown,
Vice President for Research & Public Service

Local Information

Guy Gannett Publishing Co. — **207-780-9000**
P.O. Box 1460
Portland, ME 04104
● Robert W. Cuzner, Director, Marketing Research

MARYLAND

State Data Centers

Maryland Office of Planning **410-225-4450**
301 West Preston Street
Baltimore, MD 21201
● Robert Dadd
The main branch of the state data center also provides state projections and economic information.

Computer Science Center **301-454-6030**
University of Maryland
College Park, MD 20742
● John McNary

Government Reference Service **301-396-5468**
Pratt Library
400 Cathedral Street
Baltimore, MD 21201
● Wesley Wilson

State Estimates

Division of Statistics and Population Estimates **301-225-5950**
Department of Health & Mental Hygiene
201 West Preston Street
Baltimore, MD 21201
● Rose Marie Martin

Economic Sources

Maryland Department of Economic & Employment Development **301-333-5000**
Office of Labor Market Analysis and Information
1100 North Eutaw St., Rm. 601
Baltimore, MD 21201
● Pat Arnol

Local Information

The Baltimore Sun **301-332-6245**
501 N. Calvert St.
Baltimore, MD 21278
● John W. Cordes, Marketing & Research Manager

MASSACHUSETTS

State Data Centers

Massachusetts Institute for Social and Economic Research **413-545-3460**
State Data Center Program
University of Massachusetts
128 Thompson Hall
Amherst, MA 01003
● Dr. Steve Coelen
The main branch of the state data center also provides state estimates and projections.

Massachusetts Institute for Social and Economic Research **617-727-3237**
Box 219
State House, Room 50
Boston, MA 02133
● William Murray
Also provides state estimates, projections, and economic information.

Economic Sources

Massachusetts Institute for Social and Economic Research **413-549-4930**
Thompson Hall
University of Massachusetts
Amherst, MA 01003
● Steve Coelen

MICHIGAN

State Data Centers

Michigan Information Center **517-373-7910**
Michigan Department of Management and Budget
Office of Revenue & Tax Analysis
P.O. Box 30026
Lansing, MI 48909
● Eric Swanson
The main branch of the state data center also provides state projections and economic information.

MIMIC/Center for Urban Affairs **313-577-8359**
Wayne State University
5050 Cass Avenue
Detroit, MI 48202
● Dr. Mark Neithercut

Library of Michigan **517-373-1593**
Government Documents Service
P.O. Box 30007
Lansing, MI 48909
● F. Anne Diamond

Economic Sources

Business Research Office **517-373-4600**
Department of Commerce
P.O. Box 30225
Lansing, MI 48909
● Mark Murray

Local Information

The Detroit News **313-222-2223**
Research Department
615 W. Lafayette Blvd.
Detroit, MI 48226

MINNESOTA

State Data Centers

State Planning Agency 612-296-2557
State Demographic Unit
300 Centennial Office Building
658 Cedar Street
St. Paul, MN 55155
● David Birkholz

Minnesota Analysis and Planning System 612-624-1812
University of Minnesota-St. Paul
309 19th Avenue S.
St. Paul, MN 55455
● Phil Smith-Cunnien
Also provides state and local economic information.

Interagency Resource and Information Center 612-296-6684
Minnesota Department of Education
501 Capitol Square Building
St. Paul, MN 55101
● Patricia Tupper

Economic Sources

Agri-Statistician 612-296-2230
Box 7068
St. Paul, MN 55107
● Carroll Rock

Bureau of Business and Economic Research 218-726-7298
SBE Bldg., Rm. 150
University of Minnesota-Duluth
10 University Drive
Duluth, MN 55812
● Jerrold M. Peterson, Director

Research and Statistics 612-296-6545
Minnesota Department of Jobs and Training
390 N. Robert Street,
St. Paul, MN 55101
● Med Chottepanda

Local Information

St. Paul Pioneer Press-Dispatch 612-228-5305
345 Cedar Street
St. Paul, MN 55101
● Diane Moser, Research Director

MISSISSIPPI

State Data Centers

Center for Population Studies **601-232-7288**
The University of Mississippi
Bondurant Building, Rm. 3W
University, MS 38677
Dr. Max Williams, Director
● Rachel McNeely
The main branch of the state data center also provides state projections.

Governor's Office of Federal-State Programs **601-949-2219**
Department of Community Development
301 W. Pearl Street
Jackson, MS 39203-3096
● Glenn Duckworth

State Estimates

Mississippi Institutions of Higher Learning
Center for Policy Research & Planning
3825 Ridgewood Road
Jackson, MS 39211
● Edward Ranck **601-982-6516**
● Philip Pepper **601-982-6408**

State Projections

Information Services Library **601-982-6314**
3825 Ridgewood Road
Jackson, MS 39211

Economic Sources

Labor Market Information **601-961-7424**
Mississippi Employment Security Commission
P.O. Box 1699
Jackson, MS 39215-1699
● Raiford G. Crews, Chief

College of Business & Industry **601-325-3817**
Mississippi State University
P.O. Drawer 5288
Mississippi State, MS 39762
● J. William Rush

MISSOURI

State Data Centers

Missouri State Library — **314-751-1823**
2002 Missouri Blvd.
Jefferson City, MO 65102
● Kate Graf

Urban Information Center — **314-553-6035**
8001 Natural Bridge Road
University of Missouri
St. Louis, MO 63121
● Dr. John G. Blodgett, Manager

Missouri Office of Administration — **314-751-2345**
Capitol Bldg, Rm. 124, Box 809
Jefferson City, MO 65102
● Ryan Burson
Also provides state estimates, projections, and economic information.

Office of Social and Economic Data Analysis — **314-882-7396**
University of Missouri-Columbia
811 Clark Hall
Columbia, MO 65211
● Evelyn J. Cleveland

Economic Sources

B and PA Research Center — **314-882-4805**
University of Missouri
10 Professional Building
Columbia, MO 65211
● Edward Robb

MONTANA

State Data Centers

Census & Economic Information Center — **406-444-2896**
Montana Department of Commerce
1424 9th Ave.
Helena, MT 59620-0535
● Patricia Roberts
The main branch of the state data center also provides state projections and economic information.

Bureau of Business & Economic Research — **406-243-5113**
University of Montana
Missoula, MT 59812
● Jim Sylvester
Also provides state estimates and economic information.

Survey Research Center — **406-994-4481**
Wilson Hall, Room 1-108
Montana State University
Bozeman, MT 59717
● Lee Faulkner

Montana State Library — **406-444-3004**
Capitol Station
1515 E. 6th Avenue
Helena, MT 59620
● Darlene Staffeldt

Research & Analysis Bureau — **406-444-2430**
Employment Policy Division
Montana Department of Labor & Industry
P.O. Box 1728
Helena, MT 59624
● Cathy Shenkle

NEBRASKA

State Data Centers

Center for Applied Urban Research **402-595-2311**
The University of Nebraska-Omaha
Peter Kiewit Conference Center
1313 Farnam-on-the-Mall
Omaha, NE 68182
● Jerome Deichert

Policy Research Office **402-471-2414**
P.O. Box 94601
State Capitol, Rm. 1321
Lincoln, NE 68509
● Prem L. Bansal

Nebraska Library Commission **402-471-2045**
1420 P Street
Lincoln, NE 68508
● John L. Kopischke

Central Data Processing Division **402-471-2065**
Nebraska Department of Administrative Services
1306 State Capitol
Lincoln, NE 68509
● Skip Miller

State Estimates

Nebraska Natural Resources Commission **402-471-2081**
P.O. Box 94876
Lincoln, NE 68509-4876
● Mahendra Bansal

Economic Sources

Nebraska Department of Revenue **402-471-2971**
Research Division
P.O. Box 94818
Lincoln, NE 68509
● Gary B. Heinicke

Department of Economic Development **402-471-3783**
P.O. Box 94666
301 Centennial Mall South
Lincoln, NE 68509
● Stuart Miller, Director of Research

NEVADA

State Data Centers

Nevada State Library and Archives **702-687-5160**
Capitol Complex
401 North Carson
Carson City, NV 89710
- Betty McNeal
- Joan Kerschner

Department of Data Processing **702-885-5823**
Capitol Complex
Blasdel Building, Room 304
Carson City, NV 89710
- Bob Rigsby

State Estimates

Bureau of Business & Economic Research **702-784-6877**
College of Business Administration
University of Nevada-Reno
Reno, NV 89557
- Maud Naroll

Economic Sources

Employment Security Research **702-885-4550**
500 East Third St.
Carson City, NV 89713
- James Hanna, Chief

NEW HAMPSHIRE

State Data Centers

Office of State Planning **603-271-2155**
2 1/2 Beacon Street
Concord, NH 03301
● Thomas J. Duffy
The main branch of the state data center also provides state estimates, projections, and economic information.

State Library **603-271-2392**
20 Park Street
Concord, NH 03301
● Shirley Gray Adamovich

Office of Biometrics **603-862-1700**
COLSA UNH
James Hall, 2nd Floor
Durham, NH 03824
● Owen Durgin

Economic Sources

Economic Research Office **603-271-2591**
Department of Research &
Economic Development
State of New Hampshire
Concord, NH 03301
● Bill Herman

NEW JERSEY

State Data Centers

New Jersey State Data Center **609-984-2595**
Occupational & Demographic Research
Department of Labor
CN 388 –John Fitch Plaza–Room 200A
Trenton, NJ 08625-0388
● Connie O. Hughes
The main branch of the state data center also provides state and local economic information.

New Jersey State Library **609-292-6220**
185 West State Street
CN 520
Trenton, NJ 08625-0520
● Beverly Railsback

Princeton-Rutgers Census Data Project **609-452-6052**
Computer Center
Princeton University
87 Prospect Avenue
Princeton, NJ 08544
● Judith Rowe

Princeton-Rutgers Census Data Project **201-932-2483**
Center for Computer & Information Services
Rutgers University
CCIS-Hill Center, Busch Campus
P.O. Box 879
Piscataway, NJ 08854
● Gertrude Lewis

Department of Urban Planning and Policy Development **201-932-3822**
Rutgers University
Lucy Stone Hall, B Wing
New Brunswick, NJ 08903
● Dr. James Hughes, Chair and Graduate Director

State Estimates and Projections

Office of Demographic & Economic Analysis **609-292-0076**
292-0077
Department of Labor, CN 388
Trenton, NJ 08625
● Alfred Toizer

(continues next page)

NEW JERSEY

(continued)

Economic Sources

Center for Health Statistics **609-984-6702**
Dept. of Health, Rm. 405, CN-360
Trenton, NJ 08625
● Henry A. Watson

Department of Community Affairs **609-292-7898**
Division of Housing
South Broad & Front Streets, CN-802
Trenton, NJ 08625
● Lawrence W. Dolan

Local Information

The Press of Atlantic City **609-272-1100, ext. 306**
1000 W. Washington Ave.
Pleasantville, NJ 08232
Susan S. Plage, Research Director

Asbury Park Press **201-922-6000**
3601 Highway 66, Box 1550
Neptune, NJ 07754
● Cheryl Christiansen, Research Manager

NEW MEXICO

State Data Centers

Economic Development and Tourism Department — **505-827-0276**
1100 St. Francis Drive
Santa Fe, NM 87503
● John Beasley

Bureau of Business & Economic Research — **505-277-6626**
University of New Mexico
Albuquerque, NM 87131
● Juliana Boyle
Also provides state estimates, projections, and economic information.

Center for Business Research & Services — **505-646-4905**
Box 3CQ
New Mexico State University
Las Cruces, NM 88003
● Dr. Kathleen Brook
Also provides state and local economic information.

New Mexico State Library — **505-827-2033**
P.O. Box 1629
Santa Fe, NM 87503
● Norma McCallan

NEW YORK

State Data Centers

New York Department of Economic Development — **518-474-6005**
One Commerce Plaza, Rm. 905
Albany, NY 12245
● Robert Scardamalia
The main branch of the state data center also provides state estimates, projections, and economic information.

Law & Social Sciences Unit — **518-474-5128**
New York State Library
Cultural Education Center
Empire State Plaza
Albany, NY 12230
● Elaine Scheerer

Division of Equalization & Assessment — **518-474-6742**
16 Sheridan Avenue
Albany, NY 12210
● Wilfred B. Pauquette

Center for Governmental Research, Inc. — **716-325-6360**
37 South Washington Street
Rochester, NY 14608
● Melinda Whitbeck

Capital District Regional Planning Commission — **518-393-1715**
214 Canal Square
Schenectady, NY 12305
● Chanchin Chen

Nelson A. Rockefeller Institute of Government — **518-472-1300**
411 State St.
Albany, NY 12203

Central New York Regional Planning and Development Board — **315-422-8276**
90 Presidential Plaza, Suite 122
Syracuse, NY 13202
● Jan Lindenfall

NEW YORK

State Data Centers
(continued)

CUNY Data Service **212-354-0640**
Graduate School and University Center
City University of New York
33 West 42nd Street
New York, NY 10036
● Jonah Otelsberg

Center for the Social Sciences **212-280-3038**
Columbia University
814 International Affairs Building
420 West 118th Street
New York, NY 10027
● Walter Bourne

Cornell Institute for Social and Economic Research (CISER) **607-255-1358**
323 Uris Hall
Cornell University
Ithaca, NY 14853
● Ann S. Gray

Dutchess County Department of Planning **914-431-2480**
47 Cannon Street
Poughkeepsie, NY 12601
● Carolyn Purcell

New York Metropolitan Transportation Council **212-938-3352**
One World Trade Center, 82nd Fl. E.
New York, NY 10048
● Juliette Bergman

Niagara Frontier Economic Development **716-731-3271**
Technical Assistance Center
Niagara County Community College
3111 Saunders Settlement Road
Sanborn, NY 14132
● Bill Bordeau, Director

(continues next page)

NEW YORK

State Data Centers
(continued)

Southern Tier West Regional Planning & Development Board — **716-945-5301**
465 Broad St.
Salamanca, NY 14779
● Ron Southard

Center for Social and Demographic Analysis — **518-442-4905**
Social Science 376
State University of New York
Albany, NY 12222
● Richard Alba, Director

State University of New York at Buffalo — **716-636-3240**
Regional Economic Assistance Center
305 Jacobs
Buffalo, NY 14260
● Gail W. Parkinson

Economic Development and Technical Assistance Center — **518-564-2214**
State University of New York
Plattsburgh, NY 12901
● Gordon DeVries

Population Division Department of City Planning — **212-720-3434**
22 Reade Street
New York, NY 10007
● Evelyn Mann, Director
Also provides state and local economic information.

Economic Sources

Program in Urban & Regional Studies — **607-255-4331**
209 West Sibley Hall
Cornell University
Ithaca, NY 14853
● Barclay Jones, Director

NEW YORK

(continued)

Local Information

Newsday **516-454-2401**
Research Department
Long Island, NY 11747

Gannett Rochester Newspapers **716-258-2247**
55 Exchange Blvd.
Rochester, NY 14614-2001
● Cindi A. Spezio, Research Analyst

NORTH CAROLINA

State Data Centers

North Carolina Office of State Planning — **919-733-4131**
The Governor's Office
116 West Jones St.
Raleigh, NC 27603-8003
● Francine Stephenson
The main branch of the state data center also provides state estimates, projections, and economic information.

State Library — **919-966-3683**
North Carolina Department of Cultural Resources
109 East Jones Street
Raleigh, NC 27611
● Joel Sigmon

Institute for Research in Social Science — **919-966-3346**
University of North Carolina
Manning Hall 026A
Chapel Hill, NC 27514
● Diana McDuffie

Land Resources Information Service — **919-733-2090**
Division of Land Resources
P.O. Box 27687
Raleigh, NC 27611
● Karen Siderelis/Tim Johnson

Economic Sources

Tax Research Division — **919-733-4549**
North Carolina Department of Revenue
Raleigh, NC 27601
● S. N. Underwood, Director

Center for Business and Economic Research — **704-597-2185**
University of North Carolina
Highway 49, Friday Bldg., Rm. 232
Charlotte, NC 28223
● John Connaughton, Director

Local Information

The Charlotte Observer — **704-379-6342**
P.O. Box 32188
Charlotte, NC 28232
● John Koslick, Marketing Research Director

NORTH DAKOTA

State Data Centers

North Dakota State Census Data Center — **701-237-8621**
P.O. Box 5636
North Dakota State University
Fargo, ND 58105
● Richard Rathge
The main branch of the state data center also provides state estimates, projections, and economic information.

Office of Intergovernmental Assistance — **701-224-2094**
State Capitol, 14th Fl.
Bismarck, ND 58505
● Jim Boyd

Department of Geography — **701-777-4246**
University of North Dakota
Grand Forks, ND 58202
● Floyd Hickok

North Dakota State Library — **701-224-2490**
Liberty Memorial Building
Capitol Grounds
Bismarck, ND 58505
● Susan Pahlmeyer

Economic Sources

State Tax Commissioner — **701-224-2770**
State Capitol
600 E. Boulevard Avenue
Bismarck, ND 58505
● Kathryn L. Strombeck

Bureau of Business & Economic Research — **701-777-2637**
University of North Dakota
290 Gamble Hall, Box 8255
Grand Forks, ND 58202
● Bulent Uyar, Director

Research & Statistics — **701-224-2868**
Job Service North Dakota
1000 East Divide, Box 1537
Bismarck, ND 58502
● Tom Pederson, Chief

OHIO

State Data Center

Ohio Data Users Center **614-466-2115**
Ohio Department of Developmen **800-848-1300 x2115**
Box 1001
Columbus, OH 43266-0101
● Barry J. Bennett, Manager
Also provides state estimates, projections, and economic information.

Economic Sources

Labor Market Information Division **614-481-5783**
Ohio Bureau of Employment Services
P.O. Box 1618
Columbus, OH 43216
● James Hemmerly, Acting Director

Local Information

The Cincinnati Enquirer **513-369-1805**
617 Vine Street
Cincinnati,OH 45202
● Gerald T. Silvers, Research Director

The Columbus Dispatch **614-461-5281**
34 South Third Street
Columbus, OH 43215
● Doug Cavanaugh, Research Manager

OKLAHOMA

State Data Centers

Oklahoma State Data Center **405-841-5184**
Department of Commerce
6601 Broadway Extension
P.O. Box 26980
Oklahoma City, OK 73126
The main branch of the state data center also provides state projections and economic information.

Head of U.S. Documents **405-521-2502**
Oklahoma Department of Libraries
200 N.E. 18th Street
Oklahoma City, OK 73105
● Steve Beleu

Economic Sources

Office of Business & Economic Research **405-744-5125**
College of Business Administration
Oklahoma State University
Stillwater, OK 74078
● Dr. Robert C. Dauffenbach, Director

Center for Economic & Management Research **405-325-2931**
College of Business Administration
University of Oklahoma
307 W. Brooks St., Rm. 4
Norman, OK 73019
● Neil Dikeman, Jr.

Local Information

Oklahoma Publishing Co. **405-231-3577**
P.O. Box 25125
Oklahoma City, OK 73125
● Clydette Womack, Marketing Research Manager

OREGON

State Data Centers

Center for Population Research & Census — **503-725-3922**
Portland State University
P.O. Box 751
Portland, OR 97207
● Maria Wilson-Figueroa
Main branch also provides state estimates and projections.

Bureau of Governmental Research & Service — **503-686-5232**
University of Oregon
Hendricks Hall, Room 340, P.O. Box 3177
Eugene, OR 97403
● Karen Seidel

Oregon State Library — **503-378-4502**
State Library Building
Salem, OR 97310
● Craig Smith

Economic Sources

Economic Development Department — **503-378-3732**
595 Cottage Street, NE
Salem, OR 97310
● Lana Holman

Oregon Housing Agency — **503-378-5953**
1600 State
Salem, OR 97310-0161
● Mike Murphy

Executive Department — **503-378-3405**
State of Oregon
155 Cottage St., NE
Salem, OR 97310
● Paul Warner

OSU Extension Service — **503-737-2942**
Oregon State University
Corvallis, OR 97331
● Bruce Weber

Library — **503-373-1227**
Department of Economic Development
595 Cottage Street, NE
Salem, OR 97310
● Peter Tryon

PENNSYLVANIA

State Data Centers

Pennsylvania State Data Center **717-948-6336**
Institute of State & Regional Affairs
Pennsylvania State University at Harrisburg
The Capital College
Middletown, PA 17057
● Michael T. Behney
The main branch of the state data center also provides state estimates, projections, and economic information.

Department of Education **717-787-2327**
State Library of Pennsylvania
Forum Building
Harrisburg, PA 17120
● John Gerswindt

Office of Administration **717-787-1764**
Bureau of Management Services
903 Health and Welfare Bldg.
Harrisburg, PA 17120
● Ray Kasper

Economic Sources

Center for Regional Business Analysis **814-865-7669**
Pennsylvania State University
108 Business Administration Bldg. II
University Park, PA 16802
● Rodney A. Erickson, Director

Bureau of Research & Statistics **717-787-3265**
Pennsylvania Department of Labor & Industry
7th & Forster Sts.
Harrisburg, PA 17121
● Carl Thomas, Director

Local Information

The Morning Call **215-820-6729**
P.O. Box 1260
Allentown, PA 18105
● Linda C. Gibbard, Market Research Supervisor

PUERTO RICO

State Data Centers

Puerto Rico Planning Board **809-728-4430**
Minillas Government Center
North Bldg., Avenida De Diego
P.O. Box 41119
San Juan, PR 00940
● Lillian Torres Aguirre
The main branch of the state data center also provides estimates and projections.

Department of Education **809-724-1046**
Carnegie Library
Avenida Ponce de Leon, Parada 2
San Juan, PR 00901
● Carmen Martinez

General Library **809-834-4040**
University of Puerto Rico
Mayaguez Campus
Road #2
Mayaguez, PR 00708
● Grace Quinones-Seda, Director

RHODE ISLAND

State Data Centers

Rhode Island Dept. of Administration **401-277-6493**
Office of Municipal Affairs
1 Capitol Hill
Providence, RI 02903-5873
● Paul M. Egan
The main branch of the state data center also provides state estimates and projections.

Rhode Island Department of State Library Services **401-277-2726**
95 Davis Street
Providence, RI 02908
● Frank Iacona

Social Science Data Center **401-863-2550**
Department of Sociology
Brown University
P.O. Box 1916
Providence, RI 02912
● Lauralee Thompson

Rhode Island Department of Health **401-277-2550**
75 Davis Street, Room 409
Providence, RI 02908
● Jay Buechner

Economic Sources

Department of Employment Security **401-277-3704**
101 Friendship Street
Providence, RI 02903
● Robert Langlais

Department of Economic Development **401-277-2601**
7 Jackson Walkway
Providence, RI 02903
● Vincent Harrington

SOUTH CAROLINA

State Data Centers

Division of Research & Statistics **803-734-3780**
State Budget & Control Board
Rembert Dennis Bldg., Rm. 425
1000 Assembly St.
Columbia, SC 29201
● Mike Macfarlane
The main branch of the state data center also provides state estimates, projections, and economic information.

South Carolina State Library **803-734-8666**
P.O. Box 11469
Columbia, SC 29211
● Mary Bostick, Documents Librarian

Economic Sources

Division of Research **803-777-2510**
College of Business Administration
University of South Carolina
Columbia, SC 29208
● R. C. Martin, Director

SOUTH DAKOTA

State Data Centers

Business Research Bureau **605-677-5287**
School of Business
414 E. Clark
University of South Dakota
Vermillion, SD 57069
● DeVee Dykstra, Director
The main branch of the state data center also provides state projections and economic information.

Documents Department **605-773-3131**
South Dakota State Library
800 Governors Dr.
Pierre, SD 57501-2294
● Margaret Bezpaletz

Center for Health Policy & Statistics **605-773-3355**
State Department of Health
523 E. Capitol Avenue
Pierre, SD 57501
● Jan Smith
Also provides state estimates.

Labor Market Information Center **605-622-2314**
South Dakota Department of Labor
P.O. Box 4730
Aberdeen, SD 57402-4730
● Mary Susan Vickers, Director
Also provides state projections and economic information.

Census Data Center **605-688-4132**
Rural Sociology Department
South Dakota State University
Scobey Hall, 226
Brookings, SD 57007
● Dr. Jim Satterlee

Economic Sources

Economics Department **605-688-4141**
South Dakota State University
Brookings, SD 57007
● Ardelle Lundeen, Head

TENNESSEE

State Data Centers

Tennessee State Planning Office — **615-741-1676**
John Sevier State Office Building
500 Charlott Avenue, Suite 307
Nashville, TN 37219
● Charles Brown
The main branch of the state data center also provides state estimates and economic information.

Center for Business & Economic Research — **615-974-5441**
University of Tennessee
Room 100, Glocker Hall
Knoxville, TN 37996-4170
● Betty Vickers
Also provides state projections and economic information.

Economic Sources

Bureau of Business & Economic Research — **901-678-2281**
Memphis State University
Memphis, TN 38152
● John E. Gnuschke

Department of Economics & Finance — **615-898-2520**
Middle Tennessee State University
Murfreesboro, TN 37132
● Kiyosho Kawahito, Chairman

Department of Employment Security — **615-741-2284**
Research & Statistics Division
500 James Robertson Parkway
11th floor
Nashville, TN 37245
● Joe Cummings, Director

TEXAS

State Data Centers

Texas State Data Center — **512-472-5059**
Texas Department of Commerce
P.O. Box 12728 Capitol Station
Austin, TX 78711
● Susan Tully
Main branch also provides state estimates and projections.

Department of Rural Sociology — **409-845-5332 or 845-5115**
Texas A & M University
Special Services Building
College Station, TX 77843
● Dr. Steve Murdock, Head
Also provides state estimates.

Texas Natural Resources Information System — **512-463-8346**
P.O. Box 13087
Austin, TX 78711
● LaVerne Willis

Texas State Library & Archive Commission — **512-463-5455**
Box 12927, Capitol Station
Austin, TX 78711
● Bonnie Grobar

Economic Sources

Bureau of Business Research — **512-471-1616 or 471-5180**
University of Texas
P.O. Box 7459, University Station
Austin, TX 78713
● Rita Wright

Institute for Studies in Business — **512-691-4317**
College of Business
University of Texas at San Antonio
San Antonio, TX 78285
● Dr. Lynda Y. de la Vina, Director

Water Uses and Projections Section — **512-463-7940**
Texas Water Development Board
P.O. Box 13231, Capitol Station
Austin, TX 78711-3231

Economic Research & Analysis

Texas Employment Commission — **512-463-2616**
Tec Building
Austin, TX 78778
● Horace Goodson, Chief

UTAH

State Data Centers

Office of Planning and Budget **801-538-1036**
Rm. 116, State Capitol Bldg.
Salt Lake City, UT 84114
● Julie Johnsson
The main branch of the state data center also provides state estimates, projections, and economic information.

Bureau of Economic & Business Research **801-581-6333**
401 Garff Building
University of Utah
Salt Lake City, UT 84112
● Frank Hachman
Also provides state estimates, projections, and economic information.

Population Research Laboratory **801-750-1231**
Department of Sociology
Utah State University
Logan, UT 84322-0730
● Yun Kim

Utah Department of Employment Security **801-533-2372**
P.O. Box 11249
174 Social Science Hall
Salt Lake City, UT 84147
● Kenneth E. Jensen
Also provides state and local economic information.

VERMONT

State Data Centers

Policy Research & Coordination Staff 802-828-3326
Pavilion Office Building
109 State Street
Montpelier, VT 05602
Bernard Johnson/David Healy
The main branch of the state data center also provides state and local economic information.

Center for Rural Studies 802-656-3021
University of Vermont
25 Morrill Hall
Burlington, VT 05405-0106
Tom Arnold

Vermont Dept. of Libraries 802-828-3265
111 State Street
Montpelier, VT 05602
Patricia Klinck, State Librarian

Vermont Agency of Development & Community Affairs 802-828-3211
Pavilion Office Building
109 State Street
Montpelier, VT 05602
Jed Guertin

State Estimates

Div. of Public Health Statistics 802-863-7300
Vermont Department of Health
P.O. Box 70
Burlington, VT 05402

Economic Sources

Policy & Information 802-229-0311
Vermont Department of Employment & Training
P.O. Box 488
Montpelier, VT 05602
Robert Ware, Director

VIRGINIA

State Data Centers

VA Employment Commission **804-786-8308**
703 East Main Street
Richmond, VA 23219
● Dan Jones
The main branch of the state data center also provides state projections.

Center for Public Service **804-971-2661**
University of Virginia
2015 Ivy Road, 4th Fl.
Charlottesville, VA 22903
● Dr. Michael Spar
Also provides state estimates and economic information.

Virginia State Library **804-786-2175**
12th and Capitol Streets
Richmond, VA 23219-3491
● Jim Martinelli

Economic Sources

Bureau of Business Research **804-221-2933**
School of Business Administration
College of William & Mary
Williamsburg, VA 23185

Bureau of Research **804-683-3578**
School of Business and Public Administration
Old Dominion University
Norfolk, VA 23508-8507

Economic Information Services Division **804-786-7496**
Virginia Employment Commission
P.O. Box 1358
Richmond, VA 23211
● Dolores A. Esser

Department of Economics **804-367-1593**
Virginia Commonwealth University
1015 Floyd Avenue
Richmond, VA 23284
● Max Moszer

Local Information

The Virginian-Pilot & The Ledger-Star **804-446-2578**
150 W. Brambleton Avenue
Norfolk, VA 23510
● Nancy Lewis, Marketing Services Manager

VIRGIN ISLANDS

State Data Centers

University of the Virgin Islands **809-776-9200**
Caribbean Research Institute
Charlotte Amalie
St. Thomas, VI 00802
● Dr. Frank Mills

Department of Economic Development **809-774-8784**
P.O. Box 6400
Charlotte Amalie
St. Thomas, VI 00801
● Thomas Gordon

WASHINGTON

State Data Centers

Estimation & Forecasting Unit **206-586-2504**
Office of Financial Management
Insurance Bldg., MS AQ44
Olympia, WA 98504-0202
● Sharon Estee
The main branch of the state data center also provides state estimates and economic information.

Documents Section **206-753-4027**
Washington State Library, AJ-11
Olympia, WA 98504
● Ann Bregent

Social Research Center **509-335-1511**
Department of Rural Sociology
Room 133, Wilson Hall
Washington State University
Pullman, WA 99164
● Dr. Annabel Cook

Demographic Research Laboratory **206-676-3617**
Department of Sociology
Western Washington University
Bellingham, WA 98225
● Lucky M. Tedrow, Director

Puget Sound Council of Governments **206-464-7532**
215 1st Avenue South
Seattle, WA 98104
● Howard Feltmann

Technical Information Services **509-359-7894**
University Library
Eastern Washington University
Cheney, WA 99004
● Jay Rae

Department of Sociology **509-963-3131**
Central Washington University
Ellensburg, WA 98926
● David Kaufman

WASHINGTON

(continued)

Economic Sources

Extension Service **509-335-2852**
203C Hulbert Hall
Washington State University
Pullman, WA 99164-6230
- Gary Smith, Extension Economist

Department of Revenue
MS AX-02
Evergreen Plaza Building
Olympia, WA 98504
- Bret Bertolin

Local Information

Morning News Tribune **206-597-8563**
P.O. Box 11000
Tacoma, WA 98411
- Cathy J. Brewis, Director of Research & Promotion

WEST VIRGINIA

State Data Centers

West Virginia Development Office **304-558-4010**
Research & Strategic Planning Division
State Capitol Complex
Building 6, Room 553
Charleston, WV 25305
● Mary C. Harless
The main branch of the state data center also provides state estimates, projections, and economic information.

Reference Library **304-348-2045**
West Virginia State Library Commission
Science and Cultural Center
Capitol Complex
Charleston, WV 25305
● Karen Goff

Office of Health Services Research **304-293-2601**
Department of Community Health
West Virginia University
900 Chestnut Ridge Road
Morgantown, WV 26505
● Stephanie Pratt

State Estimates & Projections

Applied Research, Evaluation & Planning **304-293-4201**
Center for Extended & Continuing Education
17 Knapp Hall, P.O. Box 6031
West Virginia University
Morgantown, WV 26506-6031
● Sarah S. Etherton

Economic Sources

Bureau of Business Research **304-293-5837**
West Virginia University 293-5839
P.O. Box 6025
Morgantown, WV 26506-6025
● Tom S. Witt, Executive Director
Also a branch of the state data center.

State Department of Tax and Revenue **304-348-8730**
Research and Development Group
P.O. Box 2389
Charleston, WV 25328
● Alan L. Mierke
Also provides state projections.

WISCONSIN

State Data Centers

Demographic Services Center **608-266-1927**
Department of Administration
101 South Webster
P.O. Box 7868
Madison, WI 53707-7868
● Robert Naylor/Nadene Roenspies
The main branch of the state data center also provides state projections.

Department of Rural Sociology **608-262-1515**
1450 Linden Drive
University of Wisconsin
Madison, WI 53706
● Doris Slesinger/Robert Wilger

Economic Sources

Bureau of Labor Market Information **608-266-7034**
Department of Industry, Labor & Human Relations
P.O. Box 7944
Madison, WI 53707
● Hartley Jackson, Director

External Relations **608-262-1550**
School of Business
University of Wisconsin-Madison
1155 Observatory Drive
Madison, WI 53706
● William Strang, Associate Dean

Department of Industry, Labor & Human Relations **608-266-0230**
201 East Washington Avenue
P.O. Box 7944
Madison, WI 53707
● Gerald Snow

Bureau of Business and Economic Research **608-785-8500**
University of Wisconsin
La Crosse, WI 54601
● Bill Colclough

Local Information

Journal Sentinel, Inc. **414-224-2115**
333 West State Street
Milwaukee, WI 53201
● Sandra M. Wysocki, Research Manager

WYOMING

State Data Centers

Department of Administration & Information — **307-777-7504**
Division of Economic Analysis
Emerson Building
Cheyenne, WY 82002-0060
● Steve Furtney, Administrator
The main branch of the state data center also provides state and local economic information.

Survey Research Center — **307-766-5141**
University of Wyoming
P.O. Box 3925
Laramie, WY 82071
● G. Fred Doll
Also provides state and local economic information.

Economic Sources

Employment Security Commission — **307-237-3646**
ESC Building
100 West Midwest Avenue
P.O. Box 2760
Casper, WY 82602
● Bill Davis

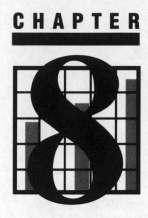

CHAPTER

8

International Sources

The emergence of a global economy means it's increasingly important to keep up with the rest of the world. These sources will help you do just that.

How to Use This Chapter

Sources for international demographic and consumer data run the gamut from government and political entities to private firms. Here are some that we have found most useful and comprehensive when seeking worldwide information. The subject index at the end of this book lists additional sources of international demographic and consumer information.

THE LISTINGS:

The United States of Europe

Europe is segmenting by lifestyle rather than national borders.

by Blayne Cutler

Winston Churchill had a dream. It was called the United States of Europe. When he spoke of that union in 1945, he hardly had the 1992 consumer in mind. But lately, business and government leaders have taken the British statesman's fantasy and given it a new twist.

In 1992, 356 million Western Europeans are expected to gel as they never have before. The European Economic Community—already an economic umbrella for 12 countries—has set 1992 as a target for the adoption of a pan-European society: a federal union of sorts with one market and one system of communications.

HOW WILL THIS NEW COUNTRY CLUB WORK?

Recent changes in the European Economic Community give an indication of future plans. Europe has lowered trade barriers between countries to save private industries money and time. Truckers, for example, can haul French wine into Germany cheaper and with far less paperwork than they could ten years ago. And advertisers no longer need to change the content of their copy to meet different national marketing requirements. But these changes are relatively cosmetic—they don't address the larger obstacles of money, language, and culture.

While "Eurocurrency" (the European currency unit—a weighted basket of national currencies) has begun to attack the money problem, "Eurospeak" has yet to solve the language problem. Will a generic "Euroculture" be too large a price for the consumer to pay?

"I don't think it will be a smooth road to 1992," says Bo Ekman, director of the Swedish Institute for Opinion Research and former vice president of Volvo. "It's a tedious process, but the important thing is that it's moving."

Rather than diluting their choices through the European mass merger, Ekman thinks consumers will have more options. Businesses will have to expand their offerings to attract more diverse buyers.

LIFESTYLE SEGMENTATION

The European population will divide along value and lifestyle lines rather than along nationalistic lines, according to Ekman. The next generation will adopt a dual set of values—a local attitude and an international attitude. "Problems like national security are international. They won't be solved by the nation-state. The nation-state is becoming less viable by the week," says Ekman.

In Sweden, this changing attitude takes the form of experimentation with foreign ideas and products. "People want to internationalize. They want to drink fine wine. Suddenly, every newspaper in Sweden has a wine expert. Wine tasting is spreading like wildfire."

A driving force for a new Europe may be its youth. Of the population of the ten European Economic Community nations in 1982 (Portugal and Spain became members in 1986), only 16 percent—44 million people—were aged 15 to 24. But "these youths are so experienced in travel and in understanding world problems through television that they are a different breed," says Ekman. Businesses will have to respond to this demanding generation.

Already Volvo is planning for the increased diversity. "The new Volvo 480 is a small, sportslike coupe. It is designed for the sophisticated European career woman. It doesn't have a very powerful engine. And it has sex appeal," according to Ekman. Volvo used to produce 200 to 300 variations of a model like this. For today's more diverse market, Volvo will produce 5,000 to 6,000 variations. "You will see this development in a number of markets like appliances and fashions," he says.

Ekman sees great economic and social benefit in a federated Europe. "The mood of Europe is much more optimistic. This will mean a more unified goods and services market. The industrial structure will change. Competitiveness will be more equal. The market will become richer."

CENTER FOR INTERNATIONAL RESEARCH

(U.S. Bureau of the Census)

Kevin Kinsella
Bureau of the Census
Washington, DC 20233
301-763-4014

Country/Subject Specialists:

Africa, Asia, Latin/North America, and Oceania, Frank Hobbs	**301-763-4221**
China, Judith Banister	**763-4012**
Europe, Godfrey Baldwin	**763-4022**
Soviet Union, Barry Kostinsky	**763-4022**
Demographic techniques, Eduardo Arriaga	**763-4086**
Health studies, Peter Way	**763-4086**
International database, Peter Johnson	**763-4811**
Women in development, Ellen Jamison	**763-4086**

You might not think of the U.S. Census Bureau as a source for international demographic data, but the Center for International Research tracks population developments around the world. Its **International Database** contains 107 tables with demographic and socioeconomic data for 206 countries.

Because most developed countries have advanced statistical systems of their own, the Census Bureau collects their data but rarely provides the same depth of analysis that it does for less-developed countries (LDCs). For LDCs, the analysts at the bureau not only compile data, but review, evaluate, and adjust the statistics to provide as complete and consistent a database as possible. Principal sources for the bureau's international statistics are population censuses, surveys, and vital registration systems supplied by the countries.

The bureau publishes only a portion of the vast amount of information it compiles, and the best way to get data for a specific country is to call the specialist assigned to that region of the world. The center does publish **World Population** every two to three years. This reference volume has demographic data for every country in the world, as well as regional summaries. Data include population estimates and projections to 2050, birth and death rates, and other benchmark demographic indicators such as life expectancy and proportion urban population.

Other reports look at various topics in a crossnational context. For example, a **Women of the World** series contains four regional reports and a summary chartbook on socioeconomic characteristics of women in LDCs. Two recent **International Population Reports** examine the aging of populations worldwide and future implications for societies at different levels of economic development. Staff papers present detailed investigations of specific subjects for individual countries and crossnationally. A publications list is available on request. Users can also buy machine-readable tapes of the entire or partial international database.

EAST-WEST CENTER

Alice Harris, Research Information Specialist
Population Institute
1777 East-West Road
Honolulu, HI 96848
808-944-7450

The East-West Center includes the Population Institute, which contains some of the world's best demographic resources on Asia, a market of growing importance. The institute publishes many research studies annually and its researchers make frequent trips to Asian countries and work closely with Asian experts.

Asian and Pacific Population Forum is a quarterly newsletter that reports on census, vital registration, and survey activities in Asia. **Asia-Pacific Population and Policy** is an occasional publication on population topics for the general reader. A recent issue discussed the growing population of young singles in many Asian countries. The institute also publishes books and working research papers.

The **Resource Materials** collection includes a documentation and demographic reference service, plus a compilation of current census and survey data from Asian and Pacific countries. The collection has over 25,000 volumes, tapes, and films. Census and survey data are available on computer tape through the Data Analysis Unit, which also develops demographic software and maintains a software library for demographic analysis for mainframe and microcomputers.

ESOMAR

(European Society for Opinion and Marketing Research)

Central Secretariat
J.J. Viottastraat 29
1071 JP Amsterdam
Netherlands

telephone
31-20-664.21.41

ESOMAR is a professional marketing society which originated in 1948 and now has more than 2,400 members worldwide. Members are required to adhere to the International Code of Marketing and Social Research Practice in order to ensure high quality, accurate, and objective research. It offers a variety of directories and other publications which are available to non-members (although members get discounts on many items).

The **ESOMAR Annual Directory** lists members working in marketing and in marketing, social, and opinion research in over 50 countries, as well as marketing and marketing research professional associations worldwide. It also publishes regular reports on the European market research industry. **Marketing and Research Today** is a quarterly journal reporting on techniques, applications, and issues facing the industry. **Newsbrief** is a bimonthly newsletter providing a forum for member communication.

Other ESOMAR efforts are aimed at unifying European market research. To that end, it has recently published the **Glossary of Marketing Research: English, Francais, Deutsch, Italiano, Espanol, Nederlands.** In anticipation of a single European market in 1993, a working party is producing a **Harmonisation of Demographic Classifications.**

ESOMAR also holds an Annual Marketing Research Congress and 8 to 10 seminars on subjects such as marketing financial services, research for the automotive industry, and the quality of media information. Copies of papers from seminars and congress proceedings are available for purchase.

EUROMONITOR

Susan Austin
87-88 Turnmill Street
London ECIM 5QU
England
telephone 071-251-8024

Many titles available in the U.S. through:
Gale Publications
Dept. 77748
Detroit, MI 48277
800-223-4153

Euromonitor Consultancy offers a full range of consumer survey research services, including qualitative and quantitative surveys. It also publishes a variety of statistical reference books that cover 16 Western European nations. One recent title is **European Advertising, Marketing, and Media Data.** Euromonitor also publishes the annual **International Marketing Data and Statistics, European Marketing Data and Statistics, Consumer Europe,** and **European Directory of Non-Official Statistical Sources,** all available in the U.S. through Gale Publications in Detroit.

THE EUROPEAN COMMUNITY

2100 M Street, NW
Suite 707
Washington, DC 20037
202-862-9500

Publications available from:
UNIPUB
4611-F Assembly Drive
Lanham, MD 20706
301-459-7666

The 12-nation European Community, headquartered in Belgium, is a major source of demographic data for its member countries—Belgium, Denmark, France, Germany, Greece, Ireland, Italy, Luxembourg, The Netherlands, Portugal, Spain, and the United Kingdom. The European Community's Statistical Office, located in Luxembourg, publishes the quarterly **Eurostat News,** which describes new publications. Each issue contains an order form for the publications listed, as well as a form for requests to be added to the mailing list for new information about a particular topic.

The organization's most important compendium of demographic data is its annual yearbook, **Demographic Statistics.** This contains data on age, sex, region, vital statistics, migration, and life expectancy, as well as demographic indicators such as age at first marriage. Data for the United States are often included for points of comparison.

Current demographic statistics for the Community's members are published in the monthly **Eurostatistics: Data for Short-Term Economic Analysis** and include aggregate data on population, labor force, and employment. Two other annual publications combine demographic and economic data. **Basic Statistics of the Community** has demographic data on population change and density, and household size. **Eurostat Review** gives a ten-year retrospective view on demographic topics such as births, marriage, and divorce. The European Community Statistical Office also publishes occasional reports of demographic interest.

INSTITUTE FOR RESOURCE DEVELOPMENT, INC.

(IRD)

Martin Vaessen, Vice President
8850 Stanford Boulevard
Columbia, MD 21045
301-290-2800

IRD conducts nationally representative surveys of the female population aged 15-49 in developing countries. A wide variety of data are available in **Country Reports** and from the databases maintained at IRD on such topics as education, fertility, family planning, infant and child mortality, and maternal and child health care. The results from 34 surveys are currently available, with 25 more planned for the next four years. Data are generally available for further analysis and policy use. Reports are distributed free of charge and datasets are provided at a cost of $200 each.

LATIN AMERICAN DEMOGRAPHIC CENTRE

(CELADE)

Reynaldo F. Bajraj
Director
Casilla 91
Santiago, Chile
011-56-2-485051

CELADE was established in 1957 by the United Nations; since 1975 it has been an independent entity of the Economic Commission for Latin America and the Caribbean (ECLAC) system. The Centre's objectives are to "assist the Latin American and Caribbean countries to increase their self-reliance and horizontal cooperation in the field of population, providing them at the same time with the backstopping, technical cooperation, information, and other services that can be furnished more efficiently and effectively from the regional level." To these ends, CELADE conducts applied research of specific interest to the countries in the region and produces a variety of publications. Topics include international migration flows and the status of women and the elderly.

CELADE also helps countries prepare and process population and housing censuses, including the development of specialized software such as REDATAM (retrieval of census data for small areas by microcomputers).

MACFARLANE & COMPANY

Ian MacFarlane
Suite 450, One Park Place
Atlanta, GA 30318
404-352-2290

This consulting firm offers directories of interest to the international researcher. **MARKETSEARCH, The International Directory of Published Market Research** covers multi-client study references worldwide and includes a mid-year supplement and hotline access (in London). The **International Directory of Market Research Organisations** lists information on over 1700 marketing research firms in 70 countries. The latter directory is also available in two regional volumes, one covering the European Community and the other covering the Far East.

THE ORGANIZATION FOR ECONOMIC COOPERATION AND DEVELOPMENT

(OECD)

2001 L Street, NW
Suite 700
Washington, DC
20036-4905
202-785-6323

Headquartered in Paris, the OECD has 24 member nations, including the U.S. The easiest way to follow the OECD's work is by subscribing to the bimonthly **OECD Observer.** In addition to reporting OECD activities, the Observer's annual supplement features a selection of current demographic statistics for each member country, from population totals and birth rates to such indicators of living standards as school enrollment and per capita consumption of energy. Many data series are available on disk as well as in printed reports.

The OECD surveys almost every country every year and produces the **Economic Survey** series. The reports contain current economic data and short-term forecasts, as well as per capita consumption, car ownership, consumer prices, school enrollment, presence of telephones and televisions, prevalence of doctors, and other socioeconomic indicators.

To keep up with OECD publications of demographic and economic relevance, get on the mailing list for leaflets announcing new publications in Employment and Social Affairs, or order the free monthly bulletin, **News from OECD,** and publications catalog.

POPULATION INDEX

Richard Hankinson
21 Prospect Avenue
Princeton, NJ 08544
609-258-4949

Population Index is an annotated bibliography to the world's population literature. Published as a quarterly journal, it provides 3,500 citations to the most important population studies published in all languages and countries. The cumulative Population Index ia also available online through POPLINE *(see page 165)*.

POPULATION REFERENCE BUREAU, INC.

(PRB)

1875 Connecticut Ave., NW
Suite 520
Washington, D.C. 20009
202/483-1100

Founded in 1929, the Population Reference Bureau (PRB) is the oldest private educational and research organization in the population field. Its work is based on the assumption that many of the world's most important problems and challenges—from famine in East Africa to migration patterns in the U.S.—have important demographic dimensions. The PRB's goal is to increase public awareness of the facts and implications of population trends. To that end, it supplies data with which individuals, groups, or governments can tackle these issues.

In its research and publications, the PRB casts one eye on demographic trends and their implications for the U.S., the other on what is happening globally. Two of its four annual **Population Bulletins** analyze American demographics, the other two focus on international trends. Two recent bulletins focused on "American Education: The Challenge of Change" and "The Graying of Japan."

The PRB puts out a wide variety of publications. Members receive the quarterly Population Bulletins, a monthly newsletter, **Population Today,** which summarizes new demographic research and reports on population policies, trends, and data-gathering around the world. Members also receive the annual **United States** and **World Population Data Sheets.** These poster-sized wall charts provide current population estimates and projections, vital statistics, GNP and other useful data-at-a-glance for all 50 U.S. states and all but the world's smallest nations. Annual membership ranges from $25 for students to $55 for libraries.

PRB members also receive discounts on other publications, such as the regularly updated **Population Handbook**—an introduction to the basics of demographic analysis which is published in American English, as well as in "international" English, Spanish, French, Arabic, and Thai editions. PRB's policy studies department produces a series of reports on the policy implications of U.S. population trends such as poverty, immigration, and internal migration. Recent titles from the **Population Trends and Public Policy** series include "U.S. Hispanics: Challenging Issues for the 1990s" and "Juggling Jobs and Babies: America's Child Care Challenge." Members also have access to the PRB's extensive library, online bibliographic retrieval service, and the research services of its professional demographers.

All publications are also available to non-members and a free publications catalog is available on request.

Decision Demographics is a for-profit subsidiary of PRB. It operates on a fee-for-service basis and provides personalized, in-depth data and analyses for corporate, government, or individual clients seeking professional interpretation of demographic trends.

STATISTICS CANADA

R.H. Coats Building
Tunney's Pasture, Ottawa
Ontario K1A OT6
Canada
publication sales office,
613-951-7277

Statistics Canada is the Canadian equivalent of the U.S. Census Bureau, and then some. In effect, it offers the products and services which in the U.S. are provided by several different federal agencies. Statistics Canada conducts a population census every five years—the last one was in 1991 and the next is in 1996. It also conducts numerous surveys in between, on subjects ranging from education to environment to expenditures.

Statistics Canada Daily is a daily listing of new numbers and publications coming out of all branches of Statistics Canada. **Infomat** is a weekly compendium of the *Daily* listings. Of particula interest to those looking for demographic and socioeconomic information, the **Canadian Social Trends Journal** is a quarterly publication on social, economic, and demographic changes affecting the lives of Canadians. **Perspectives on Labour and Income** is a quarterly publication covering a wide range of data following recent trends in labor market trends, and income patterns. All publications are available by calling the sales office listed above.

The following telephone listings will get you to the appropriate department at Statistics Canada.

General information numbers

Media information 613-951-4636
Statistical information 613-951-8116
Library 613-951-8219
National toll-free sales line 800-267-6677
(outside Canada) 613-951-7277

Key contacts

Advisory services 613-951-9285
Agriculture 4253
Business register 9021
Business survey methods 9185
Business survey redesign project 8096
Business survey transition 9740
Canadian Social Trends Journal 2557
Census operations 5895
Communications 2808
Content and planning 1991 census 0444

Statistics Canada
(continued)

Corporate assignments	613-951-9470
Data access and control services	9349
Demography	9589
Education, culture, and tourism	1506
Electronic data dissemination	1365
Environment and natural resources	8585
Geocartographies	9714
Geography	3889
Headquarters operations	5907
Health	1746
Health and activity limitation survey	4532
Household surveys	2889
Housing, family and social statistics	9301
Income and expenditure accounts	9152
Industrial organization and finance	9840
Industry	9820
Industry measures and analysis	3621
Informatics user services	8428
Input-output	8907
Integration and development	0262
International and financial economics	9055
International and professional relations	8917
International trade	9647
Justice (Candian Centre for Justice Statistics)	9023
Labour	1523
Labour and household surveys analysis	9456
Labour force survey	9448
Language studies	3763
Library services	8218
Main computer centre	6453
Operations automation	9196
Population studies	9752
Prices	9606
Publications	9880
Public institutions	8558
Regionalization planning	9994
Science, technology, and capital stock	9686
Services	2198
Small area and administrative data	9719
Small business and special surveys	5967
Social and economic studies	8216
Social survey methods	9811
Standards	8577
Survey operations	9421

System development	613-951-9933
Target group data bases project	2556
Time series research and analysis	9876
Transportation	1986

Regional Reference Centres

St. John's	709-772-4073
Halifax	902-426-5331
Montreal	514-283-5725
Ottawa	613-951-8116
Toronto	416-973-6586
Winnipeg	204-983-4020
Regina	306-780-5405
Calgary	403-292-6717
Edmonton	403-495-3027
Vancouver	604-666-3691

UNITED NATIONS

Public Inquiries Unit
Public Services Section
Department of
Public Information
United Nations
(Room GA-057)
New York, NY 10017
212-963-4475

Sales Section
Publishing Division
Department of
Conference Services
United Nations
(Room DC2-0870)
New York, NY 10017
212-963-8302

The UN Secretariat has two offices responsible for compiling, analyzing, estimating, and projecting demographic statistics for every country of the world—the Demographic and Social Statistics Branch (DSSB) and the Population Division. You can get free copies of several catalogs from the Sales Section of the Department of Conference Services, including the **United Nations Publications in Print, United Nations Periodicals,** and **Microfiche Price List.**

The UN system is relatively decentralized. While the Statistical Office is responsible for population and economic statistics, the International Labor Office produces labor force and consumer expenditure data, the World Health Organization produces health statistics, and the Educational, Scientific, and Cultural Organization publishes education statistics.

Demographic & Social Statistics Branch

Public Inquiries Office
Statistical Office
New York, NY 10017
212-754-7721

The DSSB publishes the **Demographic Yearbook,** an annual compilation of demographic and economic data based on a lengthy survey sent to each national statistical office. The *Yearbook* includes only a selection of the data that results, but each year a specific topic is featured in completeness, rotating among fertility, mortality, marriage and divorce, families and households, migration, and economic characteristics. Because statistical practices vary widely from country to country, the *Yearbook* is heavily annotated to allow readers to make valid comparisons.

For more up-to-date but less detailed data, the DSSB publishes the quarterly **Population and Vital Statistics Report.** The DSSB's parent Statistical Office also pulls together a **Compendium of Social Statistics.**

Population Division

Department of International Economic and Social Affairs
United Nations Secretariat
(Room DC2-1950)
New York, NY 10017
212-963-3179

Broadly speaking, the Population Division deals with the analysis of population trends and policies in relation to social and economic development. Its research work is published in a variety of formats to meet the needs of diverse audiences. They include estimates and projections of the population of the world, the more developed and less developed regions, eight major areas, 24 regions, and over 200 countries, territories, and areas. The projections are published biennially.

Other research work includes technical manuals on methodology of demographic analysis and projections; findings of expert group meetings, seminars, and workshops; special studies of major demographic phenomena and population policy issues. The Population Division publishes the semi-annual journal **Population Bulletin of the United Nations** and **Population Newsletter.** Detailed reports are published in the **Population Studies** series.

Population Fund (UNFPA)

Jyoti Shankar Singh, Chief
Information and External Relations Division
220 East 42nd Street
New York, NY 10017

A major part of the demographic research activity undertaken by the United Nations is funded by the UNFPA. Its mandate is to build up the capacity to respond to needs in population and family planning; to promote awareness of population problems in both developed and developing countries and possible strategies to deal with them; and to play a leading role in the United Nations system in promoting population programs, and to coordinate projects supported by the fund.

The UNFPA has an extensive array of publications. Write for a free catalog, **Publications and Audio-Visual Guide.** Free publications include the monthly newsletter, **Population.** The quarterly journal, **Populi,** covers a broad range of population issues and features special country reports.

THE WORLD BANK

Customer Service
World Bank Publications
1818 H Street, NW
Washington, DC 20433
202-473-2943

The World Bank is officially known as the International Bank for Reconstruction and Development. Since its focus is on economic data, it produces a narrow range of demographic statistics—primarily population estimates. However, these data are valuable because the bank maintains independence from reporting countries and is able to select the sources for the data it uses. Each year the Population and Human Resources Department provides demographic statistics for the bank's regular country economic reports, using information from the most reliable sources. When possible, recent census and survey data are used, but alternate sources include the United Nations, U.S. Census Bureau, and other international and government agencies.

The annual **World Bank Atlas** contains these population estimates, as well as a limited amount of the bank's economic data such as per capita GNP. The bank also publishes population projections for all countries in the annual **World Development Report.** Detailed projections are published in conjunction with Johns Hopkins University in **World Population Projections.**

Since economic development is related to population trends, the bank continually does research on demographic topics. Publicly available reports are listed in the annual **Index of Publications,** free from the Publications office. Recent titles include "Analysis of Household Expenditures" and "Private Business in Developing Countries: Improved Prospects."

The bank also offers descriptions of current research in the quarterly **World Bank Research News,** which is free to "institutions and individuals with a professional interest in development." The **World Bank Research Observer** is published twice a year and provides non-technical overviews of key issues in development economics research.

WORLD HEALTH ORGANIZATION (WHO)

Ms. C. Roch
Distribution and Sales
Avenue Appia
1211 Geneva 27
Switzerland
791-21-11

The WHO is the UN's health organization. It publishes **World Health Statistics Quarterly,** an English/French periodical which provides, among other things, international comparisons of health-related topics for more than 165 countries and territories. WHO also publishes **Demographic Trends in the European Region, Health and Social Implications.**

APPENDIX

&

For Further Reference

About the Articles

The following pieces originally appeared in American Demographics *magazine:*

"How to Manage Consumer Information," by Peter Francese, page 9, August 1985.

"How to Size Up Your Customers," by Marvin Nesbit and Arthur Weinstein, page 15, July 1986.

"Psychographic Glitter and Gold," by Bickley Townsend, page 20, November 1985.

"Back to the Source," by Joe Schwartz, page 24, January 1989.

"How to Evaluate Population Estimates," by William O'Hare, page 30, January 1988.

"How to Think Like a Demographer," by Thomas Exter, page 33, September 1987.

"How to Find Your Next Thousand Customers," by Thomas Exter, page 36, December 1988.

"What the 1990 Census Will Show," by Thomas Exter and Judith Waldrop, page 41, January 1990.

"The Census Means Business," by Joe Schwartz, page 55, July 1989.

"A Guide to the 1990 Census," by Joe Schwartz, page 61, April 1990.

"Who Owns Who, and What It Means to You," by Joe Schwartz, page 121, January 1990.

"How to Get to the Grass Roots," by Judith Waldrop, page 185, May 1989.

"The United States of Europe," by Blayne Cutler, page 253, June 1988.

About the Contributors

Blayne Cutler is a senior editor of *American Demographics* magazine.

Thomas Exter is research director of *American Demographics* magazine.

Peter Francese is president and founder of American Demographics, Inc.

Marvin Nesbit is director of the Small Business Development Center at Florida International University.

William O'Hare is director of policy studies at the Population Reference Bureau and a contributing editor of *American Demographics* magazine.

Joe Schwartz is a senior editor of *American Demographics* magazine.

Bickley Townsend is a vice president of The Roper Organization and a contributing editor of *American Demographics* magazine.

Judith Waldrop is research editor of *American Demographics* magazine.

Arthur Weinstein is regional manager and marketing analyst of the Small Business Development Center at Florida International University.

Useful Publications for Additional Information

The following items can be ordered directly from American Demographics, P.O. Box 68, Ithaca, NY 14851. Send in your order with payment, or call 1-800-828-1133 between 8 a.m. and 5 p.m. EST to charge to your Visa, MasterCard, or American Express account.

American Demographics Magazine
The "magazine of consumer trends" examines consumer trends, lifestyles, buying behavior and media preferences. Monthly, $58/year.

The Numbers News
A newsletter offering late-breaking demographic news, analysis of consumer trends, and listings of products and services from the private and public sectors. Monthly, $149/year.

1990-1991 Almanac of Consumer Markets
by Margaret Ambry, Ph.D., Editor of American Demographics Press
This reference volume presents demographic, socioeconomic, and consumer data for all age groups in the U.S. 407 pages, $59.95.

Marketing Tools Alert
A quarterly catalog of books, audiocassettes, and other products of use to marketers. Free.

Glossary

A

ADI Area of Dominant Influence, a television market, as defined by Arbitron, a firm which measures TV audiences. (See *television market.*)

affluent market Usually refers to households with incomes of $50,000 or more, although definitions vary from study to study.

audience measurement methods Methods to determine who is listening to radio and watching TV.

B

baby boom The large generation of Americans born between 1946 and 1964.

baby boomlet (echo boom) Children of the baby boom, born between 1977 and the present.

baby bust The generation born between 1965 and 1976, when birth rates dropped rapidly and remained low.

benchmark An area against which you compare an area you're studying. Some good benchmarks are reports on the United States as a whole, and reports for the state, metropolitan area, county, or city in which a site is located.

birth rate Number of births a year per 1,000 population.

— **general fertility rate** Number of births a year per 1,000 women aged 15 to 44.

— **total fertility rate** Expected number of live births per 1,000 women in their lifetime given current age-specific rates; an approximation of completed family size.

blocks Census administrative areas, generally equivalent to city blocks.

block groups Groups of blocks, averaging 1,000 to 1,200 population; the major advantage of using block groups over blocks in area analysis is that more data are available for block groups.

blue collar See *occupation.*

boundary The border around a market area that is being studied.

boundary files Geography—streets, railroads, blocks, and census tracts—that is described in a manner that is understandable to a computer.

C

CAPI Computer-assisted personal interviewing.

CATI Computer-assisted telephone interviewing.

CD-ROM Compact disk with read-only memory; technology used in desktop marketing.

CENSPAC A computer program developed by the Census Bureau to manipulate its computer files from the 1980 census.

census The official collection of information on the demographic, social, and economic situation of all people residing in a specified area at a certain time.

—**divisions** The nine census divisions are:
1. Pacific: Alaska, California, Hawaii, Oregon, Washington
2. Mountain: Arizona, Colorado, Idaho, Montana, Nevada, New Mexico, Utah, Wyoming,
3. West North Central: Iowa, Kansas, Minnesota, Missouri, Nebraska, North Dakota, South Dakota
4. East North Central: Illinois, Indiana, Michigan, Ohio, Wisconsin
5. West South Central: Arkansas, Louisiana, Oklahoma, Texas
6. East South Central: Alabama, Kentucky, Mississippi, Tennessee
7. South Atlantic: West Virginia, Delaware, Florida, Georgia, Maryland, North Carolina, South Carolina, Virginia, Washington, DC, West Virginia
8. Middle Atlantic: New Jersey, New York, Pennsylvania
9. New England: Connecticut, Maine, Massachusetts, New Hampshire, Vermont, Rhode Island

—**geography** The U.S. Census Bureau collects and publishes data for many government and statistical areas.

—**government areas** U.S., Puerto Rico, and outlying areas under U.S. sovereignty or jurisdiction; states, counties, and county equivalents; incorporated places and minor civil divisions; Congressional districts and election precincts; American Indian reservations and Alaska Native villages.

—**maps** The Census Bureau publishes two kinds of maps:
1. Outline maps that show the names and boundaries of the geographic areas for which data are produced
2. Statistical maps that display selected data by the use of color and shading.

—**products** Information from the census is available in printed reports, microfiche, computer tape, online, in diskettes, and on maps.

—**regions** The four census regions are
1. West: Washington, Oregon, Alaska, Hawaii, California, Idaho, Montana, Wyoming, Colorado, New Mexico, Arizona, Utah, and Nevada
2. Midwest: North Dakota, South Dakota, Nebraska, Kansas, Missouri, Iowa, Minnesota, Wisconsin, Illinois, Indiana, Ohio, and Michigan
3. South: Texas, Oklahoma, Arkansas, Louisiana, Mississippi, Alabama, Florida, Georgia, South Carolina, North Carolina, Virginia, Washington, DC, Maryland, West Virginia, Kentucky, Delaware, and Tennessee

4. Northeast: Pennsylvania, New Jersey, New York, Connecticut, Rhode Island, Massachusetts, Vermont, New Hampshire, and Maine.

—**statistical areas** Four census regions and nine census divisions, all of which are groupings of states; metropolitan areas; census county divisions in states where minor civil division boundaries are not satisfactory for statistical purposes; census designated places; urbanized areas; census tracts and subdivisions of counties averaging about 4,000 people; census blocks; enumeration districts; block groups.

—**tracts** Small, relatively permanent areas into which metropolitan and certain other areas are divided for the purpose of providing statistics for small areas. When census tracts are established, they are designed to be homogeneous with respect to population characteristics, economic status, and living conditions. Tracts generally have between 2,500 and 8,000 residents.

—**undercount** The number of Americans who did not answer the decennial census.

centroid Geographic points marking the approximate centers of populations of the 260,000 block groups and enumeration districts in the U.S.

choropleth maps Computer-generated maps that represent values with shading.

cluster A category assigned to a neighborhood based on the assumption that the households share certain demographic, social, and economic characteristics.

cluster analysis The process of categorizing neighborhoods by lumping together such characteristics as income, age, housing types, education, and occupation. Cluster analysis assumes that averages describe the households in a neighborhood.

cohort A group of people who experience the same significant demographic event (birth, marriage) during a specific short time period, usually a year, and who can thus be identified as a group in subsequent analysis.

cohort measures Analysis of the activity of a cohort over an extended time period.

concentric circle The shape of a geometric study area, sometimes referred to as a ring.

congressional districts The 435 congressional districts are defined by state legislatures for the purpose of electing persons to the U.S. House of Representatives.

Consolidated Metropolitan Statistical Area (CMSA) Two or more adjacent primary metropolitan statistical areas, such as Miami-Fort Lauderdale.

consumer expenditure What consumers spend on goods and services.

Consumer Expenditure Survey (CEX) Data gathered in an ongoing survey by the Bureau of Labor Statistics on the expenditures of consumer units.

Consumer Information System Consumers generate four types of information of importance to businesses: demographics, lifestyles, media preferences, and purchasing behavior. By linking this information together, companies can build a complete picture of the consumer to analyze products, define markets, target advertising, and plan marketing strategies.

Consumer Price Index (CPI) The CPI compares the current cost of purchasing a fixed set of goods and services with the cost of the same set at a specific base year. The resulting measures can be compared over time.

consumer unit All related members of a particular household; a person living alone or as a roomer, or sharing a household with others, who is financially independent; two or more persons living together who pool their incomes to make joint purchases, as defined by the Consumer Expenditure Survey.

Current Population Survey (CPS) The CPS is how the Census Bureau monitors changes between the decennial censuses. Each month, CPS interviewers ask people in about 60,000 households about their employment-related activities during the preceding week. The results provide marketers with up-to-date estimates of population size and characteristics.

D

database marketing A method whereby customer databases are enhanced with demographic and other information for the purpose of improving direct marketing efforts.

daytime population The population of an area during the daytime, which is usually far different from the residential population measured by the census. Businesses that are daytime-oriented—banks, auto repair shops, laundries, etc.—need to know where a given population is during the day in order to know where to locate or expand, and what products, services, and price levels to offer.

decennial census The census that is conducted by the U.S. Census Bureau every ten years in a year ending in a "0."

demography/demographics A social science concerned with the size, distribution, structure, and change of populations.

desktop demographic or **desktop marketing system** A personal computer system that combines multiple databases with software for use in market analysis and other tasks.

diary panel A survey in which the same respondents keep a diary of what they watch, listen to, or buy, etc., over a period of up to several weeks.

digitizing The process of assigning latitude and longitude coordinates for each twist and turn of a market area that is to be studied.

discretionary income See *income.*

disposable income See *income.*

divisions See *census divisions.*

DMA (Designated Marketing Area) A television market, as defined by Nielsen, a firm which measures TV audiences. (See *television market*.)

E

educational attainment Usually measured as years of school completed by the population aged 25 and older; as of the 1990 census, measured in degrees attained.

elderly Usually defined as the population aged 65 and older. (See *mature market*.)

emigration The process of leaving one country to live in another.

enumeration districts (EDs) Census enumeration areas, averaging around 500 inhabitants.

estimate An inference of the size of a population group or demographic characteristic based on a sample or another statistical method. Estimates are useful between the official counts produced by the decennial census.

ethnicity See *Hispanic*.

F

family A group of two or more persons, one of them the householder, related by birth, marriage, or adoption and residing together. Families can be headed by married couples or by women or men without a spouse present, and may or may not contain children under age 18.

fertility See *birth rate*.

focus group A qualitative market research method in which a topic is discussed by ten or fewer people led by a trained moderator.

forecast A projection which is believed likely to occur. *Forecasts* and *projections* are terms that are often used interchangeably.

G

geocoding (or geographic encoding) The process whereby addresses are segmented by county, MSA, postal route, etc., in order to compare them with information about the demographics and psychographics of those geographies. Geocoding is integral to demographically enhanced mailing lists and cluster analysis.

geodemographic segmentation system See *cluster analysis*.

geography The geographic characteristics of a study area:
- **postal areas** Zip codes
- **political areas** States, counties, cities
- **census areas** Metropolitan Statistical Areas, census tracts, block groups, enumeration districts
- **telephone areas** Area codes and three-digit prefix calling areas
- **media marketing areas** ADIs and DMAs.

geometric study area A market site in the shape of a concentric circle or polygon that is to be analyzed. Private data companies use the data available for standard political and census geography to approximate the data for a geometric study area.

GIS Geographic Information System.

group quarters population Residents of military barracks, college dormitories, prisons, long-term-care hospitals, boarding houses, nursing homes, and the like.

H

Hispanic person of Spanish origin; can be of any race.

household All the persons who occupy a housing unit.

householder In most cases, the person in whose name the home is owned or rented; formerly called head of household. In some cases, the individual who was surveyed or interviewed.

housing unit A house, apartment, group of rooms, or a single room occupied as separate living quarters.

I

immigration Movement into a country from another country.

income
- —**gross** The total amount of money people have before taxes and necessities are paid for.
- —**disposable** The income available to persons for spending or saving after taxes have been deducted.
- —**discretionary** The amount of money people have for spending after taxes and necessities are paid for.
- —**mean (or average)** This is derived by dividing the total income of a population by the population.
- —**median** The amount of income which divides the distribution into two equal groups, one with an income above the median and the other with an income below the median.
- —**money** Earnings, interest, dividends, royalties, net rental income, Social Security payments, and money from public assistance; i.e., all of the money people receive before they pay personal income taxes, Social Security taxes, and union dues.
- —**per capita** The average amount of income per person in a population, regardless of age or labor force status. It is derived by dividing the total income by the total population.
- —**personal** Money income plus certain noncash benefits.
- —**types of** As defined by the Census Bureau: wage or salary income; nonfarm self-employment income; farm self-employment income; interest, dividend, or net rental income; Social Security income; public assistance income; all other income, which includes unemployment compensation, veterans' payment, pensions, alimony, etc.

industry Sector of employment. The three major divisions are: agriculture, goods-producing (includes construction, manufacturing, and mining), and service-producing (includes services, wholesale and retail trade, transportation and public utilities, financial services/insurance/real estate, and public administration).

inmigration Movement of people into one part of a country from another part of the same country. Net migration is the balance between inmigration and outmigration for a given area.

L

labor force All civilians who are working or actively looking for work, plus members of the Armed Forces stationed in the U.S.

labor force participation rate The ratio of any segment of the population working or looking for work to the total population in that segment.

life expectancy The average number of remaining expected years of life at a given age, usually measured from birth.

long census form The decennial census questionnaire that was answered by a sample of the population. Data from the long form are not available for the smallest geographic areas because the Census Bureau has promised to protect the anonymity of individual respondents.

longitudinal survey A long-term survey based on repeated analysis of either the same sample (called a panel study) or new samples chosen at regular intervals.

M

mapping The process by which a computer generates thematic maps that combine geography with demographic information and a company's sales data or other proprietary information.

marital status Usually measured for the population aged 15 and older. The categories are: never-married (or single), married (includes separated and spouse absent for other reasons), divorced, and widowed.

mature market Usually defined as the population aged 50 and older or 55 and older.

Metropolitan Statistical Area (MSA) A free-standing metropolitan area surrounded by non-metropolitan counties and not closely associated with other metropolitan areas. Each MSA is grouped by population size: Those with a population of 1 million or more are in the "A" group; those with a population of 250,000 to 1 million are in the "B" group; those with a population of 100,000 to 250,000 are in "C" areas; and "D" areas are those with a population of less than 100,000.

microdata Census records of individual respondents stripped of their identifying information. Census microdata are available as public-use microdata samples (PUMS).

migration Movement of residence from one political area to another.

minor civil division A political and administrative subdivision of a county, generally a township.

mobility Geographic movement involving a change of residence.

modeling The formulation of mathematically expressed variables to simulate a business decision environment. For example, a model could be formulated using demographics, local business conditions, the competition, and a company's financial data to select new markets that have the same winning combination of factors that are present in currently successful markets.

mortality Death.

N

natality See *birth rate*.

nonfamily household A household comprised of a person living alone or with nonrelatives, as defined by the Census Bureau.

nonmetropolitan Places outside of Metropolitan Statistical Areas.

O

occupation Type of job. Major categories are white-collar (includes professional specialty, managerial and executive, technical, sales, and administrative support) and blue-collar (includes precision production/craft/repair and operator/fabricator/laborer), service (sometimes called pink-collar), and farming/forestry/fishing.

outmigration Movement out of a given area to another part of the same country. Net migration is the balance between inmigration and outmigration for a given area.

P

panel survey A survey in which the same respondents are interviewed several times over an extended period; also called longitudinal analysis.

polygon The shape of a geometric study area.

population The number of people who are in a certain area on a certain date.

- **— density** A measure that is computed by dividing the total population of a geographic unit by its land area measured in square miles or square kilometers.
- **— estimate** A calculation of the current population between decennial censuses, arrived at by a variety of methods.
- **— growth rate** The total increase or decrease in a population during a given period divided by the average population in that period.

population pyramid The graphic representation of a population's age-sex composition. It is a bar graph with the population divided into ages or age groups, represented from the youngest at the bottom to the oldest at the top, with males on the left and females on the right.

poverty thresholds The income cutoffs used by the Census Bureau to determine the poverty status of families and unrelated individuals, based on family size. The poverty thresholds are revised annually to allow for changes in the cost of living as reflected in the Consumer Price Index.

Primary Metropolitan Statistical Area (PMSA) A metropolitan area that is adjacent to another.

projection An estimate, based on assumptions about future trends in births, deaths, and migration, of a demographic characteristic such as population or number of households.

psychographics Lifestyle and attitude research.

Q

qualitative research Research characterized by the absence of empirical measurements and an interest in subjective evaluations; e.g., focus groups.

quantitative research Research conducted for the purpose of obtaining empirical evaluations of attitudes, behavior, or performance. Most quantitative research is based on information supplied by a relatively small group (sample) that is representative of a larger population.

R

race White, black, Asian or Pacific Islander, and native American.

random sampling A sample in which each unit has an equal and independent chance of selection.

rate The number of occurrences of an event, such as births, divided by a base population.

ratio A measure that expresses the relative size of two numbers.

region See *census region.*

regional marketing Marketing aimed at local rather than national markets.

rural population As defined by the 1980 census, those areas not classified as urban. (See *urban population.*)

rustbelt States in the Great Lakes region whose economies suffered during the late 1970s, causing many of their residents to move to other states; e.g., the Sunbelt.

S

sampling The method of selecting a specified portion, called a sample, from a population, from which information concerning the whole can be inferred.

sampling error The estimated inaccuracy of the results of a study when a population sample is used to explain behavior of the total population.

scanner data Purchase and other data collected through the use of scanner devices, usually in food stores.

separate living quarters Those in which the occupants live and eat separately from other persons in the building and have direct access from the outside of the building or through a common hall.

sex ratio The number of males per 100 females in a population.

short census form The decennial census questionnaire that all Americans answered, or were supposed to answer.

single-parent family A family household headed by a man or woman with no spouse present and with children under age 18.

single-source data Integrated data on demographic characteristics, media use and purchase behavior collected from the same individuals.

site evaluation Determining, through an analysis of a given area's demographic and economic characteristics, whether it offers a good market for a product or service.

snowbirds People who are temporary residents of an area; e.g., retirees who spend the winter in Florida.

social indicator A numerical measure of the quality of life.

state data center An organization within a state, generally a planning agency, university, or library, to which the Census Bureau furnishes products, training in data access and use, technical assistance, and consultation. The data center in turn disseminates the products to the public and provides assistance with their use in the state.

Summary Tape Files (STFs) Census computer tapes, organized according to subject and geography, containing a broad range of population and housing data from the short and long decennial census forms.

sunbelt As defined by the Census Bureau, it is the Census Regions South and West. According to American Demographics magazine and many marketers, it is the 13 states that are entirely below the 37th parallel, plus one county in Nevada and nine counties in California that are also below the belt, and, of course, Hawaii.

T

telephone sample A group of randomly- or otherwise-selected people who are surveyed by telephone.

television market This term is best defined by an example: Pike County, Pennsylvania, is located 100 miles from Philadelphia and 100 miles from New York City. Pike County falls into the New York television market because the largest share of viewing in Pike County is tuned to New York stations. The two firms which measure TV audiences, Arbitron and NPD/Nielsen, have slightly different definitions of television markets, based on sampling, etc. Arbitron's TV markets are called Areas of Dominant Influence (ADIs), while Nielsen's are Designated Market Areas, or DMAs.

temporary population Tourists, commuters, "snowbirds," and other temporary residents of an area.

thematic maps Computer-generated maps that combine geography with demographic data and company information on sales, etc.

TIGER Topologically Integrated Geographic and Encoding Reference file, developed for use in the 1990 census; a complete boundary file of the U.S.

time use survey A survey of how people use their time, taken by asking people to record what they do and how they do it in a diary over several days or weeks.

trade area The geographical area from which the customers of a business are drawn; it can be as small as a section of a city or as large as the entire country.

U

urban population As defined by the 1980 census, all persons living in urbanized areas and in places of 2,500 or more inhabitants outside urbanized areas.

urbanized areas A central city or cities and the surrounding closely settled territory or "urban fringe."

V

variance The statistical measure of how similar a population is in a characteristic being studied.

vernacular regions Self-identified places, defined by those who live in them, ranging in size from city neighborhoods to groups of states.

W

white collar See *occupation.*

Y

youth market Usually defined as the population aged 18 to 24; sometimes includes younger teenagers. Also called *young adults.*

Z

zip code demographics The demographic characteristics of a population living in a particular zip code.

Source Name Index

Subject Index

About the Author

Diane Crispell is associate editor of *The Numbers News,* an award-winning newsletter about the data industry, and associate national editor of *American Demographics* magazine. She also writes a column for *The Wall Street Journal* on demographic trends. She and her husband live in Burdett, New York.